WHITE TEACHERS, BLACK STUDENTS

WHITE TEACHERS, BLACK STUDENTS

In the Spirit of Yes to African American Student Achievement

Mack T. Hines III

ROWMAN & LITTLEFIELD
Lanham • Boulder • New York • London

Published by Rowman & Littlefield
A wholly owned subsidiary of
The Rowman & Littlefield Publishing Group, Inc.
4501 Forbes Boulevard, Suite 200, Lanham, Maryland 20706
www.rowman.com

Unit A, Whitacre Mews, 26-34 Stannary Street, London SE11 4AB

British Library Cataloguing in Publication Information Available

Library of Congress Cataloging-in-Publication Data

ISBN 978-1-4758-3164-1 (cloth : alk. paper)
ISBN 978-1-4758-3165-8 (paperback : alk. paper)
ISBN 978-1-4758-3166-5 (electronic)

Printed in the United States of America

To Mack and Gladys for giving me life
and
To Kathryn, Tye, and Grayson for being my life

Contents

Acknowledgments

This book is a reflection of all of the people, places, and things that facilitated the organization of my thoughts into an official viewpoint on White teachers and Black students. I want to give a special thanks to Lasonja, Labridget, Yolanda, Annissa, and John (my glam squad) for influencing my expression of thoughts in this book.

I express gratitude to Rowman & Littlefield's Tom Koerner and Carlie Wall for their support in the development of this book. I give a special thank you to Suzanne Canavan. You pushed me to turn rejection into self-reflection, which turned into an opportunity for me to write this book.

I also acknowledge the purpose of doing this book, which was for Black culture, Black People, and Black children.

Introduction

What Do We Do with Our Black Kids?

A few years ago, I received an e-mail from a school leader who requested my help in addressing the education of the Black children in her school district. The e-mail consisted of the following subject line: Help with Black Kids. Intrigued, I opened the e-mail to find the following commentary (textbox I.1):

Dear Dr. Hines,

My name is Dr. Bethany Henson, and I am the Assistant Superintendent of Elementary Education of Liberty School District. I attended your "Reaching Black Students" session and was duly impressed with what you had to say. I am writing to see if you are available to offer services to my school district.

Our elementary schools are majority White-teacher staffed, with a 23% African American, 76% White, and 87% Economically Disadvantaged population. We are having a variety of issues with our African American students (academics, discipline, etc.). So much so that the main thing that keeps coming up in our principals meetings is "What do we do with our Black kids?"

Sincerely,
BH

After consulting with numerous school districts, I have learned that the implied question within this and similar lines of questioning is "Can White teachers teach Black children?" My response to these inquiries is this book, *White Teachers, Black Students: In the Spirit of Yes to African American Student Achievement*. More than a fixed response to inquiries for help, *White Teachers, Black Students* is a comprehensive approach to developing White teachers' effectiveness with African American students. I lay out this approach across a framework of chapters, rationales, and aspirations regarding these two racial groups.

Chapters

This book is organized into six chapters. The first chapter, "The White Racial Framework of Cultural Formality," analyzes the role of Whiteness in framing the original dynamic of American racial relations—White people and Black people. Specifically, I explore the ways in which history, heritage, and identity have allowed Whiteness to have long-term effects on the lives of Black people.

In chapter 2, "The Dominant White Teaching Frame," I provide an interventionist account of the White racial framework's impact on White teachers' orientations toward effecting change with Black students. Specifically, you will see how race, identity, and culture influence White teachers' response to interventions conducive to Black student achievement. My overall focus in this chapter is to highlight professional development as the cultural litmus test in gauging White teachers' growth into effective instructors of African American children.

With chapter 3 "Decentering Whiteness via Awakening to Whiteness," I shift the book's focus to White racial decision making. Specifically, I outline an approach for guiding White teacher development into conscious and conscientious White people and White teachers. I center this delineation on two perspectives. First, the purpose of consciousness is to help White teachers realize that they are indeed White racialized beings. In addition, their positions as White people do impact their roles as White teachers.

Second, conscientiousness is needed to add a layer of morality to Whiteness. It is not enough for White teachers to realize the meanings of being White. The awareness must be transitioned into a moral compass for understanding the cultural perspectives of non-White people. The overarching point is that Whiteness is not the only form of cultural significance in society. As such, this decentered view of Whiteness must factor into White teachers' lives as White people and White teachers.

I use chapters 4, 5, and 6 to articulate a "Culturally Relevant Passport to Black Student Achievement." Here, I describe how White teachers should translate Black cultural knowledge into a framework—not formula—for achieving success with African American students. Chapter 4 looks at this success in terms of relationship building with African American students. The central focus of chapter 5 is using race and culture to address Black children during disciplinary moments. The art of teaching Black children is explained in chapter 6. These chapters are contextualized through principles, approaches, samples, and strategies pertaining to cultural responsiveness.

I conclude the book with a call for the "The Will to Change." Here, I reiterate my belief in White teachers' ability to teach Black students. I also argue that this belief hinges on these teachers' willingness to revise certain aspects of their approaches to working with these students.

Rationales

The rationale for this book is the need to understand the relevance of race to White teachers' work with Black children. In essence, African American students represent 17 percent of the student population in American public schools (Jackson, 2007). Along those same lines, a large percentage of African American students are enrolled in urban schools. In addition to urban locales, African American students constitute an overall 27 percent of the public school populations in the southern states.

There are African American students who are excelling in some of these school systems (Camera, 2015; Cook, 2015). However, one of the most enduring and compelling statistic in education is the continuing underachievement of African American students. Decades of statistical research continue to show that African American students experience difficulties with successfully negotiating achievement in school (Camera, 2015; Cook, 2015).

Statistical analyses have shown that African American children are least likely to reach grade-level proficiency on standardized measures in mathematics, reading, and science. African American students are least likely to become proficient readers by third grade. This trend continues with indications that African American high school students have the lowest SAT scores among racial groups. Along those same lines, African American students are least likely to either enroll or be placed in gifted or talented classes, as well as Advanced Placement (AP) and Honors courses. When Black students do take Advanced Placement classes, they achieve much lower scores on AP tests than students from other races, especially White students (Camera, 2015).

Conversely, African American students are nearly three times more likely to be held back as White students (Camera, 2015). African American students are most likely to NOT earn a high school diploma or college degree. In addition, whereas African American students comprise 15 percent of school populations, they constitute the largest population of students to receive special education services.

From a behavioral standpoint, Black students are more likely to account for many of the disciplinary issues in schools. In fact, a recent snapshot from the U.S. Department of Education's Office for Civil Rights (2014) revealed the following school discipline statistics:

1. Whereas Black children represent 18 percent of preschool enrollment, they make up 42 percent of the children with at least one out-of-school suspension. Black children also

account for 48 percent of preschool children receiving multiple out-of-school suspensions.

2. Black students are suspended and expelled at a rate three times greater than White students. On average, 5 percent of White students are suspended, compared to 16 percent of Black students.

3. While Black students represent 16 percent of student enrollment, they account for 32 percent of in-school suspensions and 42 percent of out-of-school suspensions.

4. With regard to the criminal justice system, Black students represent 27 percent of students referred to law enforcement and 31 percent of students subjected to a school-related arrest.

In addition, even Black students with disabilities experience a high frequency of out-of-school suspensions (Losen, Hodson, Ee, & Martinez, 2013). Along those same lines, the study *Disproportionately Disciplined: Black Students Discipline Rates in the South* revealed that 55 percent of all suspensions administered to Black students occurred in the southern part of the country (Smith & Harper, 2015). These disciplinary issues have culminated into a school-to-prison pipeline that mostly encompasses African American male students (Fenning & Rose, 2007; Reese, 2014).

These statistics are a part of the same dynamic that shows high Black student enrollment in "Dropout Factories"—schools with minority seniors who make up 60 percent or less of the students enrolled in the school as freshmen (Cook, 2015; DePaoli, Fox, Ingram, Maushard, Bridgeland, & Balfanz, 2015). Overall, the data may offer some understanding on why many Black students sometimes struggle to see the overall relevance of school.

Many scholars have suggested that these disparities can best be resolved through strategies such as addressing poverty and single-parent-family structures (Dobbie & Fryer, 2009; Holzman, 2013). Others have called for an increase in Black parental involvement in schools (Cousins & Mickelson, 2011). The driving force behind many of these suggestions is change. Better stated, the idea is that changes must be made within Black families and communities to create Black children who are ready to succeed in school.

To agree with this notion is to believe that Black under-achievement is the result of deficits inherent in Black children. In addition, Black children could achieve success by entering schools as ready-made matches for teaching and learning criteria within predesigned curricula. To avoid this pathology, I am suggesting that we look inside our school systems. To be specific, this book is a call for studying the dynamic of Black students' interactions with White teachers (Landsman & Lewis, 2006).

The reason is twofold. First, education has played a significant role in the upward mobility of African Americans, starting with Black children (Foster, 1998; Orfield, 1969; Woodson, 1933). Along those same lines, Black Star Project director Philip Jackson (1996) states, "Those who control the education of the children control the future of that race." Because of the predominant White teaching force in education, the advancement of Black children in today's education system is controlled by White teachers (Kunjufu, 2002), hence the reason to exclusively focus this book on White teachers.

In other words, this book is created only for White teachers—all White teachers. The impetus for this design is the vitality of racism as a distinct feature among White people. To see this view as a generalization may make White teachers—and other White readers—not even want to continue on with this book. If that moment occurs, bypass this temptation at all costs. Repeat: please bypass that temptation at all costs. Then carefully review the view in its actual form—a characterization.

Said plainly, all White people are socialized into Whiteness, a system that generates problematic White-framed behaviors throughout society. Rooted in America's White-Black racial history, these patterns are unavoidably reflected in interactions between White teachers and Black students. For example, there is well-established research that shows the disproportionate existence of

- cultural incongruence among White teachers and African American students (Kunjufu, 2002);

- White teachers' misunderstanding of African American students (Ferguson, 2001);
- low White teacher expectations for African American students (Egalite, Kisida, & Winters, 2015; Gershenson, 2015).

In addition, African American students are three times more likely than White students to be suspended when taught by White teachers (Owen, Wettach, & Hoffman, 2015).

A traditional research based response to difficulties between White teachers and Black students is "Why do White teachers continue to struggle to teach Black students in K–12 schools?" (Egalite, Kisida, & Winters, 2015; Gershenson, 2015). Another suggestion has been to advocate for the entry of more Black teachers into classrooms. Although reasonable suggestions, the perspectives do not explain why race factors into the dynamic of White teachers' interactions with Black students.

Throughout this book, I use broad strokes to conduct this analysis. Some parts of my development of this vision consist of theory and facts. Other parts are constructed around professional observations and opinions. Both aspects are filled with specific patterns of recurring behavior among White teachers.

The objective here is not to turn this inquiry into an individualized scientific fact-finding mission. That is, I am not aiming to see if and how race determines the individual and personal aspirations, dreams, of White teachers. The goal is to offer a well-researched body of evidence about the impact of race on White teachers' approaches to African American students. The other side of this offering is well-thought-out suggestions for making those approaches result in high Black student achievement.

Aspirations

I am hoping that with an open mind and an open heart, readers will see and feel the passion and optimism that serve as the motivation for this book. In case not, let me be clear—my motivation for this book is that I am a Black man with the God-given passion to strengthen the connection between White teachers and Black students. To understand my passion, consider the following experiences: I have worked in and with numerous schools and school districts on African American student achievement. The basis of my work has been "What do we do with our Black kids?"—a thought process that is consistently expressed in the majority of White school districts.

As a result, I spent the first five years of my consulting career inside a double consciousness. On the one hand, I was inspired to look for specific ways to increase White teachers' awareness of how to best work with African American students. The more I worked in these settings, the more I realized that I was to neither look nor think along the lines of "What is it that must be understood about White teachers to facilitate their success with African American students?" The cost for this approach was that I kept an eye on White teacher–Black student relationships without batting an eye toward Whiteness.

As a result, supporting White teachers was often defined as providing a rigid set of formulaic strategies that would "fix" their problems with African American students. A key part of the fixing was identifying specific ways of addressing the backgrounds of African American students. The irony of this focus was a lack of consideration of White teachers' backgrounds to establish common ground with African American students. As a result, these White teachers continued to work in classrooms without working the classrooms to the benefit of Black children. In other words, White teachers' approaches to teaching African American children lacked the critical racial analysis of the relationship between Whiteness and teaching.

In a few school districts, I experienced the precious—but rare—occasions of engaging White teachers through Whiteness. The result of this work (as will be seen in subsequent chapters) was White teachers who committed to reflecting on themselves as White people. From this epiphany emerged the following results:

1. White teachers saw enough in Black children to see that they deserved a quality education.

2. White teachers thought enough of Black children to realize that they could affirm the students with meaningful relationships, discipline, and instruction.
3. White teachers stood firm enough to leave Black students no room for underachievement.

These successes did not occur because of the transformation of White teachers into new and improved White teachers. Instead, these outcomes happened because these particular White teachers had enough of accepting the status quo as the rationale for Black student failure. They were also willing to do more than enough to make race and diversity a part of how they connected to African American students.

Because of these experiences, I feel a spirit of yes regarding White teachers and Black children. That is, yes, White teachers can teach Black children. Yes, White teachers can reach Black children. Yes, White teachers can make a positive impact in the lives of Black children. Yes, White teachers can help prepare Black children for achieving successful futures.

Central to this affirmation is the belief that every Black child deserves to experience success in schools and the classroom. If every African American child is to achieve this success, the experiences will be likely shaped by White teachers. As such, I encourage White teachers to take the first step of seeing the full potential of their ability to impact African American children. The second step begins on page 1 of chapter 1 of this book.

1

The White Racial Framework of Cultural Formality

As mentioned previously, the purpose of this book is to enhance White teachers' effectiveness with African American students. The initial step toward this goal is a review of race relations between White people and Black people. The term *review* does not mean that readers will receive an exhaustive overview of the history of race relations in America. But it is not wise to delve into White teachers and Black students without context. The chosen context is a historical analysis of White oppression of Black people.

This oppression is termed the "White Racial Framework of Cultural Formality." The White racial framework is the array of oppressive and discriminatory structures that have made America a White racist country (Feagin, 2013). Through this centuries-old framework, White people have created and benefited from pro-White systems of policies, practices, and procedures.

Another outcome of the framework is a two-dimensional view of Whiteness. One, White people are largely viewed as the symbol of superiority for all racial groups. Two, White superiority is rationalized through the promotion of Whites as the only standard of humanity in society (Frankenberg, 1993, 1997, 2001; Jensen, 2005; Roediger, 2003). Another way of reading this viewpoint is through the visual display below.

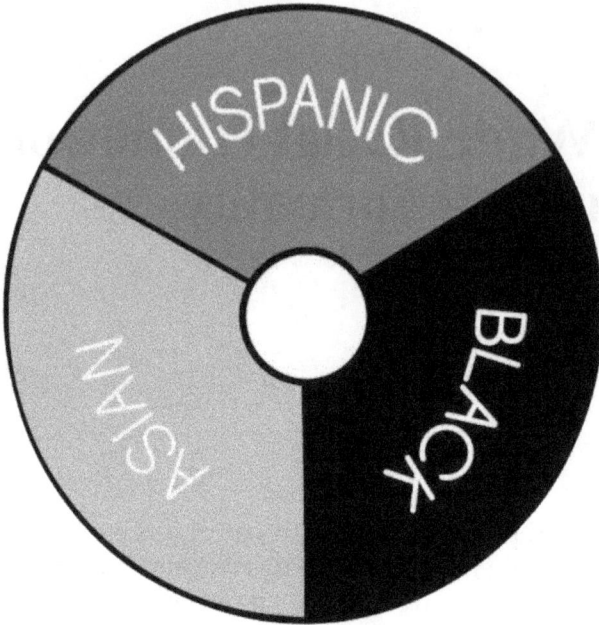

Figure 1.1.   Whiteness.

Figure 1.1 shows Asians, Blacks, Hispanics, and Whites—the four major racial groups in America. Yet Whites are not in racial terms. The reason? In reality, Whiteness is seen and treated with a great degree of normality and neutrality. The reason is that Whiteness is ingrained in American culture to the point of being neither named nor framed in racial terms. Yet, as indicated by its centered position, Whiteness is the central part of all racial realities in this country.

For example, consider the following unmentioned but unmistakable ideology that undergirds race in this country:

1. Society should operate as normal as possible.
2. White people are considered to be the closest thing to normal as possible.
3. The normalcy of a normal society must be measured against the values, attitudes, and practices of White people.

A very significant reality of the White racial framework is the continued racial marginalization of non-White people (Feagin, 2013). Since the beginning of time, the main target of White racial oppression has been Black people. To that end, consider the descriptions of how color coding and color blindness have framed much of the White framing of the Black racial group.

The White Racial Color-Coded Frame

Whites have a long-standing use of race to marginalize Black people. Two historical examples of this race marginalization are slavery and Jim Crow discrimination. Listed below is a brief—but important—description of how these eras emphasized color in relation to White oppression of color as a method of labeling African American people.

The Color Code Era of Slavery: Blacks as a Fraction of a People

The year is 1787, and America is 11 years removed from the control of England. On September 17, 55 White men gathered in Philadelphia to write the United States Constitution (Feagin, 2013; Lively, 1992). Starting with the phrase "We the People," this document advocated for the equality of all people.

But this mantra did not include the enslaved African American racial group. Their status as slaves was a key feature of many articles within the U.S. Constitution. A significant slavery-oriented article was the three-fifths clause (Degruy, 2005; Feagin, 2013). According to Article 1, Section 2, Clause 3, slaves would count as only three-fifths of White persons. The three-fifths clause did not convey that African American slaves were not human—but not as human as White people.

In addition, if slaves were viewed as fully human (100 percent), they would then have the same rights as White people. Slavery would then be rightfully considered an inhumane practice, thereby making it harder to justify the enslavement of human beings. This perspective was the subject of great debate during the framing of the Constitution (Feagin, 2013). Northern delegates wanted to abolish slavery, because there was no need for slave labor in Northern states. Southern delegates, however, wanted to maintain slavery. The reason is that the South wanted slaves to perform labor.

Drawing from this motive, Southern delegates refused to support the ratification of the constitution without the inclusion of provisions for slavery (Feagin, 2013; Lively, 1992). The inclusion of the three-fifths clause was especially important to Southern delegates for the purpose of representation. Specifically, slaves were mostly located in Southern states, creating a higher population in the South than the North.

Without the three-fifths clause, there would be an equal number of accounted for people in both Northern states and Southern states. With the three-fifths clause, there would be more accounted for people in Southern states than Northern states. The increased citizenry in Southern states increased Southern political representation in Congress.

For example, consider the impact of the three-fifths clause on the difference in Southern delegate representation in the 3rd United States congressional session. Because of the three-fifths clause, 47 Southern U.S. House of Representatives members were seated for the 3rd United States congressional session (1793–1795). Without the three-fifths clause, only 33 Southern delegates would have been eligible to participate in this congressional session. Until the Civil War, the three-fifths clause increased Southern delegate representation and disproportionate Southern power toward maintaining slavery.

A significant impact of this disproportionality was the congressional passage of the following pro-slavery laws and policies (Feagin, 2013):

- the Fugitive Slave Acts of 1793 and 1850,
- the U.S. Electoral College system,
- the United States Senate, and
- the U.S. Supreme Court.

Jim Crow Legislation: Blacks as a Separate and Segregated Entity

By 1863, Abraham Lincoln's Emancipation Proclamation reversed much of the pro-slavery policies across the country. But African Americans continued to face obstacles to enjoying full-fledged freedom (Bennett, 2000; Blackmon, 2005; Franklin & Higginbotham, 2010). Examples of setbacks included but were not limited to:

- Black codes—statutes used by Southern state legislatures to maintain the control of African Americans (Blackmon, 2005; Franklin & Higginbotham, 2010).
- Dismissal of Legal Decisions—a Northern-controlled congress passed legislation that granted African Americans full access to this country. However, Blacks were still routinely denied these privileges by citizens and officials from Southern states.

White resistance to Black freedom eventually led to the Jim Crow era of White racial framing. The Jim Crow Laws were the body of Southern statutes that enforced racial segregation between Whites and African Americans (Blackmon, 2005; Kennedy, 1990). A significant example of this statute was the 1896 *Plessy vs. Ferguson* court case (Hoffer, 2012), which upheld the "separate but equal" constitutionality of racially segregated public places. This decision further normalized racial segregation in virtually every aspect of public life.

To understand the segregated impact of Jim Crow, consider the role of the U.S. G.I. Bill. In his book, *When Affirmative Action Was White: An Untold History of Racial Inequality in Twentieth-Century America*, Ira Kaztnelson (2006) purports that the G.I. Bill was supposed to be available to all veterans. But Black veterans were denied the use of the G.I. Bill. These veterans were denied business loans and admission to Whites-only colleges and universities. They were also excluded from job-training programs for careers in promising new fields like radio and electrical work, commercial photography, and mechanics.

One of the most significant areas of discriminatory exclusion was in housing (Katznelson, 2006). Home loans and ownership opportunities were provided to a disproportionately higher number of White veterans than African American veterans (Katznelson, 2006). White servicemen were able to routinely use low-interest mortgage provisions to move from public housing to suburban home ownership. This trend continued throughout the late 1940s and the 1950s and 1960s, the golden age of the "American Dream."

Thus, through government assistance, Whites were able to achieve home ownership and home equity (Katznelson, 2006). The home equity created White privileges that ranged from living in thriving residential communities to financing children's college enrollments. In addition, many White children were bequeathed homes and other forms of valuable property from their parents.

Without home ownership, Black families struggled to move beyond the "American Nightmare" of economic stagnation (Katznelson, 2006). Evidence to this effect could be seen in the many African American families relegated to living in slums, public housing, and other impoverished living arrangements. The outcomes offer a plausible explanation of why White families are more likely than Black families to achieve home ownership (Jones, 2015).

Overall, these historical patterns of racial discrimination continue to perpetuate widespread racial disparities between Blacks and Whites (Avery & Rendall, 2002; Massey, 2001; Pager & Shepherd, 2009). Racial disparities in health, education, the criminal justice system, income, and wealth consistently show advantages toward White people. Over time, these disparities cause White people to develop specific attitudes and behaviors that reinforce the belief that the differences should continue to favor the White racial group.

The White Racial Color-Blind Frame

Since the elimination of Jim Crow segregation, Whites now claim color blindness in response to racial matters. From a rhetorical standpoint, color blindness is the notion that race no longer matters in this country (Bonilla-Silva, 2009; Feagin, 2013; Wise, 2010a). As such, all people are treated equal and given the same opportunities for upward mobility. But in *Two-Faced Racism: Whites in the Backstage and Frontstage*, Leslie Picca and Joe Feagin (2007) argue that Whites do in fact see race. Moreover, Whites' orientations to discussing race are dependent on the setting.

The authors assert that there are two settings that shape Whites' discussions about race—the back stage and the front stage. The private backstage setting is a Whites-only gathering to share disturbing racist views about other racial groups, usually Blacks. It is in this same race space that Whites are able to "perform, practice, learn, reinforce, and maintain racist views of and inclinations toward people of color" (pp. 27–28).

Critical to these demonstrations are the roles of the demonstrators within these backstage settings. Most backstage settings consist of protagonists, cheerleaders, bystanders, and mild dissenters. The protagonists give an aggressively racist account of other races, especially Blacks. The cheerleaders make commentary that encourages the protagonists to continue disparaging other racial groups. The bystanders are silent, meaning they neither condone nor challenge the racist discussions. The mild dissenters express minor disapproval of the actions of the protagonists.

The public racially diverse front stage setting is where Whites are faced with being politically correct regarding other races, especially Blacks (Picca & Feagin, 2007). As such, Whites approach front stage settings with a more nuanced and sophisticated approach to talking about race.

Overall, both stage settings foster White-framed talk and views that "play a central role in generating and maintaining the overt and covert racial discrimination that is still commonplace in major institutions of this society" (Picca & Feagin, 2007, pp. 27–28). They also set the stage for Whites to display racist views without penalty. In my opinion, these results are resultant of Whites' tendency to operate in a state of virtue and virtualization.

From a virtual standpoint, White people are White—but not really White. The reason is that many Whites view race as being only skin deep. In this vein, there is a virtual distance between white pigmentation and White socialization. The distance is far and subjective enough for Whiteness to be only skin deep. As a result, Whites feel they are unaffected by historical patterns of racial disparities that emanate from race-based advantages. In addition, they are not products of the historical legacy and lineage of how racism benefits White people.

Due to White dominance in America, this ideology allows Whites to oscillate between being "White Individuals" and "Individualized Whites." With the "White Individuals" identity, Whites rally together when they feel that Whiteness is underappreciated or under attack. Examples such as "Take back America" come to mind regarding this identity. The "Individual Whites" identity is used when Whites resist being seen as a part of the White racial group. Here, these Whites insist on using the privileges of Whiteness without being seen as either White or privileged. Both identities are interchangeably used by Whites to uphold Whiteness.

Another upheld belief is that being White is a virtue (DiAngelo, 2012; Feagin, 2013). Unlike patience, however, Whiteness doesn't wear thin. Instead, Whiteness is viewed as the highest order of morality, with Whites being above reproach on matters of race. To be specific, White people often see themselves as being more rational, patient, innocent, just, and principled than other racial groups, especially Black people. A consequence of this "good White person" syndrome is White people's inability to see the racial impact they cause on other racial groups.

For example, research shows that despite claiming color blindness, Whites still hold and express extremely negative views about Blacks (DiAngelo, 2012; Feagin, 2013). Specifically, the depiction of Black lives within Whites' minds is that of lacking virtue. Despite this deeply held dimension of racial framing, Whites object to being labeled as racist for their actions and views. Deeply embedded in this rejection is the following deductive reasoning:

1. White people are good people.
2. Good people do not commit racism.

3. Therefore, White people do not commit acts that are racist in nature.

Through this logic, Whites respond to allegations of racism with statements such as:

1. "I didn't mean anything by what I said."
2. "I was just joking."
3. "I didn't know that my actions were harmful in this way."

As an example, consider a racial incident that happened at a high school in Arizona (textbox 1.1).

Textbox 1.1

Friday, January 22, 2016, was "Senior Picture Day," a day in which seniors gather to take a class photo. In addition to the class photo, students are also allowed to take separate group pictures with shirts that spell out specific phrases.

In a semi-backstage setting, six White girls assembled in Black T-shirts with gold letters and spelled out N I ** E R. The photo placed the girls in the front stage when it was posted on Snapchat, going viral on Twitter and Facebook by that Friday afternoon. The photo immediately sparked local and national outrage, with many people denouncing the image. In addition to the national outcry, many parents of other students from the high school and other local citizens called for the girls to be expelled or suspended.

The girls received five-day suspensions, causing further outrage by the lack of expulsions for the students. By the following week, a petition with more than 40,000 signatures demanded consequences for the girls and a resignation from the school's principal. On the following Monday, the girl who wore the "R" part of the racial slur accompanied civil rights groups to a civil rights rally regarding the incident.

> The "R" girl immediately apologized for her actions. She then denied that she was a racist. To be exact, she said, "I have come here to say that I am incredibly, incredibly sorry." She continued, "I have love for everyone in my heart. I am not a racist and I'm asking everyone for forgiveness." She later explained to the news media that the photo was meant as a joke to be shared with the Black boyfriend of one of the other girls.

In the minds of many Whites, the apology will serve as virtuous atonement for teen angst. Outside of Whiteness, the mea culpa is seen as a direct reflection of White racial socialization. For years, we have been socialized to believe that actions speak louder than words. In following the White racial frame, we are to judge individuals by their actions instead of their words.

But in the case of six White individuals, we are to forget both the actions and a word. We are to overlook the use of a word that has historically spelled out danger, death, and destruction for millions of Black people. The words that are supposed to take precedence over everything else are "I am not a racist."

The phrase "I'm not a racist" is not an authentic acknowledgment of wrongdoing. Instead, the phrase is more of a White-framed expectation to focus on intent instead of impact. As mentioned, the photo was meant to be a joke among friends—namely, White girls and a Black boy. But Black people don't see jokes when thinking of photographic depictions of *nigger*. In their recollection of *nigger*, they see graphic images of Blacks hanging from trees (Allen, Als, Lewis, & Litwick, 2000; Dray, 2003; Wood, 2011). Their minds are fixated on high-pressured water hoses that tore the skin off of Black bodies (Cunningham, 2012). In their purview are pictures of German Shepherds making incisive tears into Black flesh (McWhorter, 2001). Their perspective is also pierced with the sounds of the bombs blowing up houses, churches, and the Blacks inside them to pieces (Grooms, 2002). Yet, the "R" girl still feels that her use of *nigger* was not racist in nature. Thus per the White racial frame, neither she nor the impact of her actions should be viewed as racist.

Overall, these perspectives suggest that color blindness does matter as a significant form of racial framing. To better understand this perspective, consider the significant differences in racial standings for White people and Black people.

White Racial Standing

As it stands, Whites believe they have very objective views about race and racism (DiAngelo, 2010, 2011, 2012b). On the one hand, race is a sociocultural construct that is rooted in socialization. In general, socialization is the internalization of culture to become socially developed human beings (Grusec & Hasting, 2014). There are two ways in which we internalize culture: (1) through group membership and (2) through the messages received about ourselves from society. Because of internalizing both patterns of socialization, we are trained to live a certain way with a certain position.

Such trainings are composed of the ongoing acquisition of specific values, attitudes, beliefs, and behaviors by significant others and through various interactions with society. The resulting nurturance shapes the specific ways in which we perceive and respond to our surroundings in various situations. This nurturance almost always produces enculturation, which is the socialization of human beings into a particular culture.

Despite this information, Whites believe that race is not a function of socialization. For most Whites, Whiteness is shaped by universalism and individualism (DiAngelo, 2012; Kendall, 2006). Universalism is the White racial belief that we are all human beings and race holds the same relevance to the values, attitudes, and behaviors of all people. As such, we all experience race in the same way as just human beings. Individualism is the White racial belief that we are all individuals and race has no significant relevance to the values, attitudes, and behaviors of people. As such, race does not have any bearing or impact on

our individual lives. We all only experience race in very incon-
sequential and individualized ways.

The impact of this belief is Whites' insistence on being seen
outside of race (DiAngelo, 2012). In this regard, White people
insist that they are unaffected by how the continuous positive
messages of Whiteness are reinforced in every aspect of society.
Individualism allows them to remain oblivious to the connection between their feelings as members of White culture and the
positive omnipresent visions of Whiteness in communities (res-
taurants, malls), media (movies, television shows), and schools
(textbooks and teachers).

Yet Whites still grossly misinterpret these and other glaring
advantages of being White (DiAngelo, 2012). In many instances,
the advantages for White people are not critiqued to examine
how White racial membership creates certain opportunities for
Whites. Instead, these advantages are often attributed solely to
hard work, independence, perseverance, and other characteristics related to individualism. The underlying premise is denial
of the evidence that shows that access to the opportunity for
success continually favors White people. Consequently, a White
person is more likely than a person of color to say, "As long as I
don't agree that my achievements have anything to do with race,
I can continue to disagree with the idea that I have ever received
race-based advantages."

Now compare these patterns of color-blind thought with a
few definitions of racism. The term *racism* is currently defined as
a system of advantage that is based on race (Rothenberg, 2013).
It is a system involving cultural messages and institutional
policies and practices as well as the beliefs and actions of individuals. Another definition of the term *racism* is prejudice plus
power. When racial prejudice is combined with social power,
there is a reduction in social, cultural, and economic resources
for non-White people.

Dr. Beverly Daniel Tatum (2003) relates to this perspective
with the following analysis of racism:

> In my view, reserving the term racist only for behaviors com-
> mitted by Whites in the context of a White-dominated society

is a way of acknowledging the ever-present power differential afforded Whites by the culture and institutions that make up the system of advantage and continue to reinforce notions of White superiority. (p. 10)

These definitions convey that racism is not just a series of isolated and individual acts of meanness. Racism is a system of power to use prejudice in ways to gear practices and policies to a specific group of people, specifically White people. However, the definition of *racism* takes on a very different connotation with White people. Noted African American filmmaker Omowale Akintunde (1999) makes the following observation:

Racism is a systemic, societal, institutional, omnipresent, and epistemologically embedded phenomenon that pervades every vestige of our reality. For most Whites, however, racism is like murder: the concept exists but someone has to commit it in order for it to happen. (p. 4)

This description means that most White people are unable to think about racism in complex and diverse ways. They are unable to assess or address the macro dimensions of racism that maintain White control over American laws and policies. Whites are only able to imagine racism as being a small microcosm of certain aspects of society.

Black Racial Standing

Blacks have a double consciousness that defines their standing on racial matters. *Double consciousness* is a term that was created by Dr. William Edward Burghardt "W. E. B." Du Bois (1903), one of the most important civil rights activists in American (both Black and White) history. In his turn-of-the-century treatise, *The Souls of Black Folk*, Dr. Du Bois used double consciousness to describe the Black experience in America. He argued that Blacks faced the daunting task of living in two distinct worlds—White America and Black America. The White America is a world that has historically disrespected and devalued Blacks. Yet, Blacks must still negotiate this world by looking at themselves through the eyes of White people.

Due to their long-standing status as Blacks in America, Blacks mustn't see race to realize its presence in life. The reason is that Blacks have a very in-depth understanding of race and racism. Such understanding can be attributed to centuries of experiences with enduring race-related stress. As a result, many Blacks have acquired the racial intelligence to sense and detect what feels and sounds like racism.

However, in his book *Faces at the Bottom of the Well: The Permanence of Racism*, Derrick Bell (1993) presents a diametrically different standing of Blacks in White-framed institutions. According to Bell, Blacks are viewed as having virtually no legitimate standing on racial matters. He summarizes this belief with the following standpoints about racism:

1. **Racial Rule 1**: No matter what their experience or expertise, Black people's views about race are deemed "special pleading" and thus not entitled to serious consideration.
2. **Racial Rule 2**: Blacks are depicted as being incapable of demonstrating racial objectivity. This deep-seated belief fuels a continuing effort to keep Black people off juries in cases involving race.
3. **Racial Rule 3**: White people respect Blacks who publicly criticize other Blacks for speaking or acting in ways that upset Whites. These Blacks are granted "enhanced standing" even when they have no special expertise or experience in the subject that brought on the condemnation.
4. **Racial Rule 4**: When Black people express ideas that upset White people, White people will actively recruit other Blacks to refute the belief. Blacks who accept the invitation are affirmed in White spaces. Blacks who decline the invitation experience severe repercussions from White people.

To further illustrate the differences between White and Black racial standings, consider the family dynamic. A family is a group of people united by intimate relationships. A significant aspect of the connection is family members' immediate, unconditional willingness to defend the virtue of each other. In the same vein, White people in America view each other as immediate family. Due to skin color, Blacks have distant relativity to the cultural family dynamic that is deeply ingrained in America. That's why Blacks, for the most part, have been kept at a relative distance (think: distant relatives) from America's highest levels of humane consideration.

Yet, despite its history of inveterate racism, the United States is still viewed by Whites as being a country of great virtue. It is for this reason that Whites defend America's continual oppression of non-Whites, especially Black people. A current and extremely relevant case in point is law enforcement. In 2015, Mapping Police Violence (2015) provided the following race-related statistics on police murders:

1. Police killed at least 101 unarmed Black people, which was more than any other race.
2. Nearly 1 in 3 Black people killed by police in 2015 were identified as unarmed, though the actual number is likely higher due to underreporting.
3. Despite being only 13 percent of the U.S. population, Black people represented 39 percent of unarmed people killed by police.
4. Unarmed Black people were killed at six times the rate of unarmed White people.
5. Only 7 of the 101 murders of unarmed Black people resulted in officer(s) being charged with a crime.

To put faces to these statistics, consider Walter Scott, Tony Robinson, and Freddie Gray—to name a few. But these names do not begin to tell the story of the larger narrative of police brutality toward Blacks. Consider Trayvon Martin, Tamir Rice, John Crawford III, Jerome Reid—to name a few more.

These numbers are racial in nature. The reason is not just because of the exclusivity of Blackness in describing the victims. The other logic is that White communities do not experience these situations. The main reason is that White people would not tolerate this type of treatment from any American institution.

Granted, police brutality could possibly reach White America. But the crisis would be quickly resolved. Why? No White community would tolerate this type of treatment for the sake of public safety in this country. These communities would use their racial capital to make policy-making Whites question the Americanness of this behavior toward White people.

However, the same racial power has never been a part of Black communities. This is why "No officer charged" remains the judicial response to police-related killings of unarmed Black people. Contrary to coincidence, these killings are neither random happenings nor isolated incidents of racial discord and misunderstanding. Historically speaking, these outcomes are very much an outgrowth of the underlying centuries-old White supremacist ideology of law enforcement.

Consider this perspective: the origin of policing was based on the need to maintain White dominance to enforce Black oppression (Love, 2017). This rationale allowed White slave patrols to freely "police" Southern slave systems. This logic also facilitated the Klu Klux Klan's infiltration of police departments to enforce "law and order" on Black people.

Despite its history, law enforcement is still one of the most powerful representations of what it means to be an American. The reason is that law and order and America are considered to be exclusively synonymous with White culture. Consequently, law enforcement remains intact in a rarefied air of unquestioned virtue by White people.

A major outcome of such esteem is for White people to evaluate the behaviors of Blacks, while lecturing on the "right" way to interact with the police. As a result, officers who kill an unarmed Black person can almost always cover themselves under the White-framed versions of rationale, patience, innocence, justice, calmness, principle, and peace. These descriptors are seldom, if ever, used to describe the Black victims (think: initially alive Black people) on the other end of the gun barrel. Words such as *corrupt, angry, impulsive, irrational, violent,* and *unethical* are usually reserved for this group. In the end, all that remains is the onus of the dead Black bodies to unjustify the brutality of police.

From a White-framed virtual standpoint, many officers report that they felt threatened by the African American suspect. There is a huge difference between virtually feeling threatened and actually being threatened. However, these differences are synonymous when presented as officers' reasons for inflicting harm on unarmed African Americans.

On the other hand, African Americans often cite specific racialized actions that comprise police brutality. Yet, in White-framed organizations such as law enforcement, they are viewed as lacking significant racial standing. The end result is for racial justice to be relegated to a state of virtualization. In other words, there is now a huge difference in being virtually abusive and actually abusive of powers held by abusive police officers.

A comprehension of these examples requires a view of America as still a system of White spaces. White spaces are public yet segregated racial spaces that are largely controlled and legitimatized by White people. These environments insulate Whites from race-based stress and racial inconvenience.

These spaces are based on the premise that White people are the ultimate exemplars of virtue. This message is reinforced through the centrality of White people in textbooks, media, heroes, leaders, neighborhoods, and other representations of America. Thus, by virtue of skin color and social standing, White people are considered to be the most valuable members in society.

As a result, White people and Black people internalize and experience society in very different ways. To explain, specific meaning is assigned to White racial membership and Black racial membership. As illustrated in earlier parts of this chapter, White people are considered to be positive representations of what it means to be an American. Blacks are continually viewed as negative representations of society. Over time, these meanings create predictable patterns of positive life outcomes for White people and negative life outcomes for Black people.

Frame Linkage

The color-coded and color-blind aspects of the White racial framework are connected across three orientations—White supremacy, White privilege, and White fragility. The sections below describe how each orientation operates as a cultural formality in this country.

White Supremacy

White supremacy is the conferred belief that Whites are superior and should therefore dominate other races, especially Blacks, in society (Bonilla-Silva, 2001; Gillborn, 2006). What makes the superiority significant is the world White people inhabit. White people are born atop a racial hierarchy that suggests that Whites are better than non-White people. This belief is reinforced because Whites interact with a society marked by White dominance, identification, and centeredness (Johnson, 2005).

In *Power, Privilege, and Difference*, Allan Johnson (2005) explains White dominance as the disproportionate occupation of positions of power by White people. In addition, when a person of color occupies a position of power, that will be noted as an exception to the rule (as when President Barack Obama is routinely identified as a Black President and not just "the President").

White identification means that White people are exclusively viewed as the standard for human beings in general (Johnson, 2005). On the other hand, people of color, for example, are routinely identified as "non-White," a term that doesn't tell us who they are, but who they are *not*. As explained by Johnson,

> When a category of people is named the standard for human beings in general, the path of least resistance is to see them as superior, there being no other reason to make them the standard. Several things follow from this, including seeing the way they do things as simply "human" or "normal," and giving more credibility to their views than to the views of "others," in this case people of color.

As a result, White people are often unaware of themselves *as* White. Strangely enough, Whites have no problem with conjuring the consciousness to discern when situations are structured in accordance to the needs of non-White people.

White centeredness is where we see the ubiquity of White culture throughout society (Johnson 2005, DiAngelo, 2015). The centrality of this representation can be seen on multiple levels, for example, White centeredness in textbooks, media and advertising, government, professions (doctors, lawyers, teachers, etc.), religion, and living spaces (DiAngelo, 2015).

The downside to this socialization is White racial confusion about race. In general, White people have a limited understanding about the significance of race and racism (DiAngelo, 2011, 2012, 2015; Feagin, 2013). The reason is that Whites haven't received critical insight on why and how race factors into their own lives.

But because of their internalized sense of superiority, Whites still feel that they are qualified to explain the mechanics of race. As a result, Whites frequently dismiss informed non-White perspectives on racial matters (DiAngelo, 2011, 2012, 2015; Feagin, 2013). This dismissal is upheld by the assertion of Whites' emotion-laden racial views as true examples of racial objectivity.

White Privilege

One of the most significant aspects of Whiteness is White privilege. Over the years, many researchers have provided definitions for this term. A few descriptions of White privilege are as follows:

1. White privilege has been defined as unearned advantages of being White in a racially stratified society, and has been characterized as an expression of institutional power that is largely unacknowledged by most White individuals (Neville, Worthington, & Spanierman, 2001).
2. White privilege refers to any advantage, opportunity, benefit, head start, or general protection from negative societal mistreatment, which persons deemed White will

typically enjoy, but which others will generally not enjoy (Wise, 2002).

Note the recurring themes of advantage throughout these definitions. Noted anti-racist activist Peggy McIntosh (2000) defines *privilege* as any advantage that is unearned, exclusive, and socially conferred. The advantage is not based on whether or not something has been done by a person. The advantage is resultant of having membership in a particular group.

In my opinion, the ultimate advantages of White privilege are position and freedom. Unlike other racial groups, White people are prominently featured in positions of value, influence, and being.

Position of Value

In his classic comedy special *Chewed Up*, comedian Louis CK says:

> I'm not saying that White people are better. I'm saying that be-
> ing White is clearly better. Who could even argue? Here's how
> great it is. I could get in a time machine and go to any time,
> and it would be awesome when I get there! That is exclusively
> a White privilege. Black people can't mess with time machines!
> A Black guy in a time machine is like, "Hey, anything before
> 1980, no thank you I don't want to go." But I can go to any
> time. The year 2. I don't even know what was happening then,
> but I know when I get there, "Welcome! We have a table right
> here for you, sir." Thank you. If you're White and you don't
> admit that it's great, you're an asshole!

The essence of Louis's routine is captured in the first and last sentence. White people are not better than people of other skin colors. But due to their skin color, they are viewed and treated with more value than non-White people. The operative word here is *value*. Valuing is society's continual categorization of Whites as credible, desirable, and redeemable people.

One well-documented example of credibility, desirability, and redeemability is the world of employment. In most work environments, Whites are mostly likely to have opportunities to demonstrate their abilities without restriction. Not only are Whites consistently identified as candidates for advancement, they are also given support for upward movement. When they make mistakes, the mishaps are seldom attributed to their character or ability. In most cases, a perceived lack of resources or understanding is used to justify the situation. This allows Whites to view failure as a learning experience instead of a onetime chance for achievement.

Position of Influence

The fate of people of color is still largely influenced by White people (Kendall, 2006). The main reason is that White people are consistently in the position to make decisions that affect but not include the perspectives of non-White others (Kendall, 2006). As a result, Whites' assessments are often perceived as being of higher value than the perspectives, opinions, and behaviors of others. So often, these assessments can be seen in both informal evaluations (i.e., comments) and formal evaluations (i.e., written recommendations) on whether or not the person is a good fit. Taken together, the assessments determine the reputation, opportunity, and future of people of color.

White people are consistently in the position to consider if and how they will listen to the perspectives of other people (Kendall, 2006). The *if* is significant because of denoting White people's power to validate non-White thoughts, ideas, and actions. An informal power sample is seen in Whites' tendencies to be offended when their views are challenged by non-White people. The *how* explains White people's position to be the sole interpreter of the true meaning of thoughts shared by other people.

These powers can be explained by two factors. First, Whites are more likely to control and dominate conversations that lead to major decisions in an organization. Second, when people of color make suggestions, their advice is often validated only when endorsed by a White person.

Position of Being

A key element of White skin privilege is to consistently be seen as the norm in racial situations (Frankenberg, 1993, 2001). The reason is that Whites live in a society that constantly reinforces Whiteness as the standard of society (DiAngelo, 2012, 2014). As a result, White people are seldom, if ever, required to define themselves in racialized ways.

Put another way, Whites are not consistently subjected to continuous attention to being White. In most cases, Whiteness is a simply ignored, taken-for-granted part of the racial identities of White people. As a result, Whites are usually in the position to make two decisions about their race. They can choose to recognize the White racial identity at their convenience. Conversely, Whites can outright ignore Whiteness and demand that they be recognized as individuals. The prevalence of the latter option is seen in White people's anger in being seen as White instead of non-racial human beings.

A full understanding of the inherent advantages within these positions requires a discussion about freedom and liberty. *Freedom* is the ability to consistently make decisions without major control. This designation is also seen in life experiences that consist of few or no major limitations or restrictions. On the other hand, *liberty* means to have choices that are confined to certain restrictions and controls. In addition, a liberty-led life can always be subjected to minor and major boundaries and parameters.

The different descriptions of liberty and freedom may be confusing to most readers. The reason is that we have been taught that the two terms are synonymous. This is especially the case when thinking about this country's history with declaring "Liberty and Justice" for all people.

But that framing of liberty is actually a reference to the American freedoms created by and for White people. For centuries, White people have been the only racial group with the freedom to enjoy the fullness of their humanity without justification to, consideration of, or stipulation from other racial groups. The term *justification* is used to convey that White people rarely, if ever, justify when, where, why, or how they should be White.

From a consideration standpoint, Whites are not generally required to consider the perspectives of other racial groups. I equate stipulation with assimilation. Some White people may need to become attuned to situations involving other racial groups. But they do not assimilate into the cultures of other racial groups. Other racial groups are required to assimilate into the ways of White people.

White Fragility

White fragility is White people's continual denial and defense of the significance of race (DiAngelo, 2011, 2012). From a denial perspective, White people continue to deny that race has important bearings on life in America. Defensiveness is seen in two distinct ways. In one example, White people continually defend the racial systems that oppress people of color. As the other example, White people minimize or explain away race, especially White privilege. The underlying fragileness is that White people seek to avoid the racial stress that arises from being challenged about their racial worldviews.

Noted anti-racist Robin DiAngelo (2011, 2012) argues that White people become extremely stressed when they are presented with ideas that challenge the following race-based expectations:

- Objectivity—White people's views are always non-racial in nature.
- Openness—It is inappropriate to openly discuss race.
- Protection—White people should be emotionally protected by non-White people during discussions about race.
- Divulgence—Non-White people should provide White people with their experiences about and answers to questions regarding race.
- Solidarity—White people should hold and share the same racial perspectives as other White people.
- Innocence—White people's intent and actions should be viewed as harmless in nature.

- Individualism—Racial group membership has no impact on the behavior of people, especially White people.
- Meritocracy—Equal access to opportunities and resources exists for all racial groups.
- Authority—White people represent legitimate leadership and authority.

The more these viewpoints are disrupted, the more White people experience racial disequilibrium.

This imbalance reminds me of rap group Public Enemy's *Fear of a Black Planet* album. On the one hand, the album was "as much a musical assault on America's racism as it was a call to blacks to effectively react to it" (Reaves, 2008). The other element of this musical piece was White fears of Black people. As Greg Sandow (1990) noted in his article "*Fear of a Black Planet* Review," that "it's hard to dispute the lyrics' assertion that many Whites *are* afraid of blacks." The album cover reinforced this belief with a picture of Earth being taken over by a black planet.

The irony of this Black artistic imitation of White lives is this: Whites hold this belief dear to their hearts. Whites really do believe that they have been eclipsed by Black values, attitudes, and actions. They feel that most forms of Black expression put Whites in a position of being public enemy number one in America.

Whites maintain this fear-based delusion with false equivalencies. This concept purports that no difference exists between centuries of White-on-Black oppression and current moments of temporary White racial discomfort. In other words, Whites and Blacks experience the same kinds and levels of racism. Remember that at no time in America's history have Whites experienced the debilitating effects of systemic or institutional racism. But they still assert one-to-one White-Black race comparisons as accurate and fair depictions of their lives in this country.

Conclusion

The point of this chapter was to provide a historical framework of how Whiteness has framed the lives of African American people. For centuries, Whites have devoted vast amounts of energy and power to frame the lives of Blacks. To be exact, Blacks have lived under various iterations of White oppression for their entire American existence. They also have the longest history of racial exploitation and marginalization at the hands of White people.

Central to this oppression are three factors. First, no moment in time has ever existed where race did not factor into the treatment of Black people (Muhammad, 2011). Second, Blacks have always been considered to be less than human. Third, Blacks have never been deemed worthy of full inclusion in America's cultural landscape.

This ideology was imbedded in America's founding documents (U.S. Constitution, Bill of Rights) and current institutions (economic, judicial, and legislative). From a social standpoint, this frame is still the reference point for how Whites construct attitudes about and actions toward African American people. For example, every time Blacks have made progress toward equality in America, the White racial frame has fueled White pushback against those gains.

Nowadays, this frame of reference and frame of mind are continually disguised as laws, policies, and procedures that benefit all Americans. But what still lurks behind this veneer are historical, race-based systems of power that maintain the dominance of White people. To this day, this system's oppression of Blacks is maintained in supremacist, privileged, and fragile ways. Thus, Whiteness begets Whiteness as a racially framed formality. In the next chapter, this framework is revisited through analyzing the impact of Whiteness on White teachers' interactions with Black children.

2

The Dominant
White Teaching Frame

The first chapter of this book provided a historical analysis of the impact of Whiteness on the asymmetrical relationship between White people and Black people. It also looked at the ways in which Whiteness facilitates White people's racialized mannerisms and actions within White-framed systems and institutions. In this chapter, we move toward a micro-level analysis of Whiteness with a specific group of White people—White teachers.

Having served in various consultant capacities to increase White teachers' effectiveness with Black students, these experiences have provided me with an in-depth understanding of why White teachers are such an integral part of teaching, learning, and schools. The word that best describes the importance of White teachers is not percentages—but culture. A common definition of *culture* is the system of values, attitudes, and beliefs that create shared patterns of similar behaviors for a group of people. The cultural impact of White teachers is the dominant White teaching frame.

The dominant White teaching frame holds that Whiteness is the frame upon which White teachers make sense of their teaching practices. Because of the historical legacy of Whiteness, this frame shapes White teachers' regard for themselves in relation to Black children. The three specific areas of regard are White supremacy, White fragility, and White privilege.

This chapter provides an explanation of how these areas directly impact White teachers' racial framing of African American students. First, it draws from chapter 1 to recap the definitions of White supremacy, White fragility, and White privilege. Then it narrates accounts of the impact of supremacy, fragility, and privilege on White teachers' views, attitudes, and responses to Black students. Also highlighted are the ways in which each regard is infused with the virtuousness and virtualization of Whiteness.

White Supremacy

White supremacy is the belief that White people are superior to and should therefore dominate non-White people (Bonilla-Silva, 2001; Gillborn, 2005, 2006).

White Teacher Supremacy Regard for African American Students

White supremacy is a significant part of White teachers' regard for African American students. To illustrate the significance, this chapter will provide two accounts of the relationship between supremacy, White teachers, and Black students. The first account is from Karen, a White seventh-grade teacher. The second account is given by Fatima, a Black fourth-grade teacher. Both accounts are representative of the many reflections of teachers who have shared personal stories about Black children.

Karen's Account

It's Friday and the last day of professional development week. I am having lunch with Jill, Dawn, and Jessica, the other three teachers on my grade-level team. Our principal makes the announcement we have been waiting for all week. We can now come to the office to get our class rosters. This is a period of trepidation because we are all praying that we don't have too many Black children. The four of us rush to the office to get our rosters. Everyone initially walks towards my car to privately discuss the rosters. Wrong move! I steer everyone towards Jill's car, because I know what's about to happen. Once we were safely inside Jill's jeep, here's what happened (textbox 2.1):

The Discussion

Textbox 2.1.

Jill: I hope this is not bad.

Jessica: Praise the Lord—I don't have too many Black students.

Dawn: You lucky bitch, Jessica! Look at all these names on my roster—Janequa, Rashaq, Rashonay . . .

Jessica: For the love of God, I can't figure out what would possess these Black parents to curse their kids with these names! This baffles me to no end!

Dawn: Unfair to say the least.

Karen: It's just . . .

Jill: Stupid! That's what it is!

(We all laugh.)

Jessica: These people don't get that you name your kids with real American names and not some concoction of half-ass, thrown together consonants and vowels.

I know it sounds bad, and the girls would kill me if they knew that I felt sad about this discussion. They would also be taken aback to know that their meanness is why I didn't want them in my car. But these girls are good people. They are not racist by any stretch of the imagination. And after teaching with them for the past two years, I can honestly say they really do have a heart for kids, Blacks included.

Analysis

In Karen's account, she provides compelling insight of White supremacy at play among her colleagues' views of their African American students. Initially, the discussion focused on their anger at having Black students in their classes. The teachers then began to make supremacist evaluations of the names of African American students. Their issues with Black-sounding names show a superior regard for White-sounding names. This is the same type of supremacist thought that denies job interviews (Bertrand & Mullainathan, 2004) while conjuring fear of the size of people with Black-sounding names (Holbrook, Fessler, & Navarrete, 2016).

Equally significant to names is the selection of the car for a backstage discussion (Picca & Feagin, 2007). The teachers' lounge is usually the place for negative teacher discussions of African American students. The teachers' use of a car for the discussion shows a strong need for an extremely private place to discuss African American students.

Once inside the car, Jill, Jessica, and Dawn assume the roles of protagonists. Drawing from Whiteness, they express an aggressive, White-framed dislike for Black children and Black cultural expressions. Karen is virtually a dissenter, not a mild dissenter. The reason is that Karen opposes the discussion, but not in a truly oppositional way. To be clear, Karen did object to having the discussion in her car. But it's also true that she sat in the car that hosted the White-framed supremacist discussion of African American students. Thus, Karen's opposition was virtually about justice—justice that comes from not wanting to feel White guilt.

An additional reason for Karen's attitude is that Whiteness is a virtue. Karen espouses White virtue by highlighting the good heart and character of her peers. Jill, Jessica, and Dawn's discussion was extremely racist in nature. However, Karen refuses to acknowledge their behavior in racial or racist terms. Instead, she maintains the virtue of Whiteness by categorizing her friends as being good people with a heart for children. Karen's response is akin to the larger pattern of Whites' tendencies to play down or overlook other Whites' racist views and behavior.

Fatima's Account

I am a fourth-grade teacher who serves on a grade-level team with three White teachers, Sally, Jackie, and Eve. We are all self-contained teachers. We recently had a grade-level discussion about the performance of Haley and Jaquan. Both students are from low-income backgrounds, as is most of our population. The difference is that Haley is White and Jaquan is Black. Here's what happened when we had a "discussion" about these students (textbox 2.2):

The Discussion

Textbox 2.2

Sally: Okay, we are here to discuss Haley's and Jaquan's issues with math. First, I will pass out the copies of both students' math folders.

(Copies of both students' math folders are distributed to teachers.)

Sally: Let's look at Haley first.

Fatima: Okay.

Sally: Where is she not doing well in math?

Fatima: Her benchmarks show that she is struggling with interpreting place value, comparing and ordering whole numbers, and representing place value.

Jackie: Well, I think that we should contact the curriculum coordinator to get some additional math materials to support Haley.

Eve: I'm Haley's math teacher and I see it differently. I think that she doesn't work fast enough with the activities I give to the class.

Sally: So you're saying with Haley, it's time and not necessarily ability?

Eve: Oh, yes! I believe that Haley can do the job, I really do. I will just work with her on moving a little faster with math activities.

Jackie: Good! With standardized testing around the corner, she's going to need to speed up to demonstrate mastery of these skills.

Sally: Okay. Next up—Jaquan Douglas. And it looks like Jaquan is having trouble in quite a few areas.

Fatima: No. He is having problems in the same areas as Haley. Like Haley, Jaquan is struggling with place value. He is also having issues with representing decimals, and relating decimals.

Eve: So it seems that decimals are the issue for Jaquan.

Jackie: I am his teacher and I think one of the reasons for this is that Jaquan is just low. I don't know how he's going to pass standardized testing.

Fatima: He's no lower than Haley, it seems.

Jackie: I just don't know what I'm going to do.

Fatima: What do you mean you don't know what you're going to do? You do what you do with all students— teach.

Jackie: If only it were that simple with Jaquan.

Sally: I don't mean to sound negative or racist, but I had his brother two years ago and it was hard to get him to do well in math, too.

Eve: Well, maybe the family is just not made of good math students.

(Denise, the White Curriculum Instruction Leader, enters the meeting.)

Denise: Hi, everyone. Who's struggling at this point on your grade level?

Jackie: Jaquan Douglas.

Fatima: and Haley Pearson.

Denise: Well, you know that his mom has been up here a few times because of discipline issues.

Jackie: Yeah, she even came up here in rollers—I just can't imagine.

Fatima: What does her appearance have to do with anything?

Eve: Oh, I don't know.

Fatima: Then why make that comment?

Sally: I do know that when I had his brother, I found out his mom is a single parent and she was caught stealing out of Walgreens.

(The room becomes awkwardly silent.)

Fatima: Hold up—wait a minute! Why is everybody all of sudden quiet? I look at your silence as accepting the idea that failure for Jaquan is normal and that he can't achieve.

Denise: No, No. That's not . . .

Fatima: Yes, it is, and I, as an African American teacher, am not going to sit here a minute longer without saying this is wrong and racist. Now when we were discussing Haley, everyone was trying to find explanations and solutions for helping her. But when we get to Jaquan, y'all are going negative with excuses and issues about his home life. That's not right!

(The meeting ends on a note of awkward silence and tension.)

Analysis

Fatima provides a powerful White supremacist account of White teachers' views of a Black student. Both Haley and Jaquan have the same backgrounds but are of different races. However, neither Haley's race nor class was an issue in explaining her academic difficulties in math. Evidence to this effect can be seen in the ways in which Jackie, Eve, and Sally were not concerned with Haley's academic difficulties. The reason is that these teachers still believe in Haley's intelligence and ability. In addition, her math teacher Eve is also willing to help her achieve success in math.

The discussion about Jaquan is quite different. At the very beginning of the discussion, doubt is expressed by Jackie, his teacher. Jackie asserts that Jaquan's low math scores are indicative of his overall ability as a math student. She goes a step further and declares that she is unsure of his ability to pass standardized testing.

Thus, unlike Haley, Jaquan is not seen as being capable of overcoming difficulties in math. The underlying supremacist logic occurs with the teachers' linking of Jaquan's ability to his background. Consider Sally's injection of her previous experiences with teaching Jaquan's brother. She explains that his brother struggled in mathematics. Eve's conclusion of the low ability of the brothers reflects the White supremacist tendency to equate Blackness with intellectual inferiority (Feagin, 2013).

This historical framing of Blacks is also inclusive of Jaquan's mother. Evidence to this effect can be seen in negative characterizations of Jaquan's mother's appearance and past behavior. All of the descriptions depict a front stage use of coded language to discuss Black children in the presence of a Black teacher (Giroux, 1997; Ladson-Billings, 1998; Picca & Feagin, 2007).

However, Fatima was still quite aware of her peers' White racial framing of a Black male student. She responds to the supremacy in two significant ways. First, Fatima argues that her peers' discussion of Jaquan perpetuates racial discrimination. Second, Fatima called for moving the discussion from assumptions about Jaquan's background to accommodations of his academic ability. Denise responded to Fatima's challenge with White virtue, reinforcing the White-framed minimization of race.

These two examples highlight how White supremacy shapes White teachers' views of African American students. A commonality between both cases is the White framing of Black bodies with deficit thinking. Generally speaking, deficit thinking is defined as blaming students, their families, and the environment for school failure (Valencia, 2010). The idea accented in this view is that some students bring cultural deficits to school. As a result, the deficit is regarded as a sign of student inferiority. In this context, something is wrong with the student, not the internal structure of the school. Richard Valencia best sums up this concept in his book *Dismantling Contemporary Deficit Thinking: Educational Thought and Practice* (2010) by writing:

> The deficit thinking model, at its core, is an endogenous theory—positing that the student who fails in school does so because of his/her internal deficits or deficiencies. Such deficits manifest, adherents allege, in limited intellectual abilities, linguistic shortcomings, lack of motivation to learn, and immoral behavior. (p. 6–7)

Racially speaking, Valencia's description is an accurate depiction of how many African American children are viewed by White teachers. Over and over, White teachers use deficit thinking to explain the underperformance of African American children in schools. This pathology is rooted in the belief that poor Blacks possess fundamentally flawed values that hinder their achievement. This belief system is undergirded by the following myths about low-income people and Black people:

Racial and Income-Based Myths and Realities

Myths and Realities: Percentages

1. Myth: People who receive government benefits are freeloaders.
   Reality: Many Americans pay for the benefits given to them. In fact, 39 percent of Americans receive benefits they paid for through payroll tax deductions from their own paychecks (Foster & Hawk, 2013; Mettler & Sides, 2012).
2. Myth: Majority of poor people are Black.

Reality: Blacks make up 22 percent of the poor. They receive 14 percent of government benefits, which equates to 12 percent of their population share. Whites make up 42 percent of the poor. They receive 69 percent of government benefits, which is 64 percent of their population share. Overall, more White Americans live in poverty than any other racial group. As recent as 2010, 31.6 million White Americans lived in poverty (Moore, 2014).

3. Myth: Black people abuse the welfare system.
Reality: In the early 1970s, 46 percent of welfare recipients were Black. By the end of the 20th century, only 39 percent of the welfare recipients were Blacks. During that same time, 38 percent of the recipients of welfare were White. Other statistics show that 35.7 percent of Supplemental Nutrition Assistance Program recipients and 43 percent of Medicaid recipients—two of the largest public benefit programs—are White (Statistics Brain Research Institute, 2015).

Myths and Realities: Parenting

1. Myth: Single moms are the problem.
Reality: Research shows that only 9 percent of low-income moms have been single throughout the first five years of their children's lives. In addition, 35 percent of single mothers were in a marriage or relationship with their children's father for the entire time (Bruening, 2014; Trail & Karney, 2012).

2. Myth: Absentee fathers are the problem.
Reality: The majority of fathers play an active role in their children's lives. Sixty percent of low-income fathers see at least one of their children daily. Another 16 percent of low-income fathers see their children every week (Jones & Mosher, 2013).

3. Myth: Black men are generally absentee fathers.
Reality: The Centers for Disease Control and Prevention's research on family life shows that most Black fathers are just as actively involved in their children's lives as Black mothers. Additional findings show that Black dads are

more involved with their kids on a daily basis than dads from other racial groups. Along those same lines, noncustodial Black fathers are more likely than noncustodial White or Hispanic fathers to be involved in their children's lives on a daily basis (Coles, 2010; Coles & Green, 2009). Sixty-seven percent of noncustodial Black fathers see their children at least once a month. Even when Black fathers don't live with their children, they still provide them with emotional support, discipline, and guidance. Finally, Black fathers are more likely than White fathers to emphasize the need to provide financial assistance for their children.

Myths and Realities: Work Ethic

1. Myth: Poor people are lazy.
   Reality: Research shows that in 2004, 60 percent of families on food stamps consisted of non-disabled adults with jobs. By 2013, that number rose sharply to 96 percent (Mettler & Sides, 2012; Rosenbaum, 2013).
2. Myth: Blacks are poor because they are lazy.
   Reality: The U.S. Census Bureau statistics show that 68.1 percent of Black men and 62.3 percent of Black women are in the civilian labor force. These figures are comparable to the 73 percent of White men and 59.9 percent of White women in the workforce. In addition, while the majority of poor people in America are Black, the majority of Black people are NOT poor. Of the 41.7 million Blacks in America, 8.1 million Blacks have incomes below the poverty line (Moore, 2014).

Responses from White Teachers

In numerous workshops, I have used this and similar research to counter prevalent myths about poor people and Black people. But White teachers insist on attributing Black underachievement to socioeconomic status. They believe that low-income Black children, as well as Black children in general, bring a "Culture of Poverty" to schools. Consider the written response to a survey question that I often administer to White teachers during a professional development workshop on race and Black children. The posed question was "How has race influenced your interaction with your African American students?" The answer below reflects a representative sample of almost all of the survey responses.

> *As a White middle-class woman, I don't see color—just see kids. I worry about these African American students so much. I just don't know what to do or how to react to the poverty lifestyles that they bring to our school. We love our kids at this school—we really do. But what I want to really know from you is how do we stop our African American students from bringing their culture of poverty to school?*

Here we see a White teacher using class to accent a supremacist view of African American students. The teacher sees low-income Black students as deficits. At the same time, the teacher draws from the White virtue perspective to assert her love for Black children.

Overall, this and other similar responses from White teachers reflect the depth of the White racial frame in the minds of White people. The power of this frame lies in its ability to trump truth and objectivity. Lacking this objectivity regarding race, Whites often respond to race-related information with emotion-laden beliefs instead of objective analyses and rational reasoning (Feagin, 2013). As with this case, they refuse to seriously and carefully listen to Black-framed perspectives on issues and experiences about Black people.

This dynamic is also seen when observing teachers' direct interactions with Black children. For example, after conducting a conference presentation on African American student success, a principal asked me to conduct a day of teacher observations at her school. Upon arriving at the school, the principal provided a list of teachers who experienced difficulties with Black children. She then requested that I make my first visit to Ms. Roe's classroom.

Upon entering Ms. Roe's classroom, I observed the following: a well-dressed, White female teacher standing in front of a room full of students of African descent. Ms. Roe starts the class by informing students to place math homework on their desks. She then says, "We must all work better together to improve our understanding of fractions." Ms. Roe continues, "That means that I hope that you all had your parents help you with this assignment."

This level of optimism contradicts the next set of events in the classroom. The reason is that Ms. Roe is very distant from the students. In addition, she talks to the students as if they are a bother to teach. At students' request, Ms. Roe gives additional time to review the math homework. But when students ask for help on specific problems, she begrudgingly assists them.

Toward the end of the observation, the teacher comes and stands next to me. With a sigh, she says, "I really love these kids." She continues, "But I just can't get them to really get into gear with my teaching."

Enter deficit thinking. The teacher then states, "I know that my African American kids are smart. But they are also economically disadvantaged. And so they just don't care about school. And their parents—I can't get a working number let alone a Black parent to actually attend family conference night to talk to me. And we wonder why Black kids are in this achievement gap?"

I pressed the teacher to explain why she thinks that neither her African American students nor their parents care about education. Her retort was "I assume that because of their low-income background, these parents are probably busy fending for themselves and their children."

This observation is a clear disconnect between thoughts, actions, and words. In her own words, Ms. Roe claims she loves the kids and—in this case—Black kids. Yet, her thoughts and actions are highly framed within a supremacist orientation of Whiteness. A White framing can be seen in the tone used to talk to her African American students. The White frame is seen in her rationale for the low achievement of her Black students.

As mentioned, Ms. Roe tells the students that "we must all work better together to improve our understanding of fractions." In my opinion, the "we" is actually the "they" of Black parents and Black children. This explains why Ms. Roe tells me that her students would do better on tests if Black parents—not her—were more involved with their children. Keep in mind that she was unable to provide any factual reasons to support her views of her students' parents. Because of White virtualization, Ms. Roe speaks of her unfounded assumptions as if they were truthful conclusions.

Over the years, I have encountered the same type of deficit thinking during professional development workshops. At the beginning of these workshops, I explain that African American students are a unique group of students who require teachers to understand them in culturally specific ways. I then ask, "Can anyone tell me what makes African American students unique?" In almost all of the sessions, different responses were received from African American teachers and White teachers. African American teachers respond with statements such as "Very Expressive," "Wants to Be Treated Fair," "Spiritual Background," and "Need for Movement." The responses make sense because of the shared background between African American teachers and African American students.

White teachers, on the other hand, provide responses that promote the idea that African American students are at a deficit because of the perceived negative aspects of their background experiences. Listed below are the three most common White teachers' responses about the cultural uniqueness of African American students:

1. "These kids come from parents who don't value education."
   There is a pervasive belief that African American parents don't care about education. You often hear White teachers make this statement when they are unable to reach African American parents by phone and don't see African American parents at school functions. They also make this assumption when African American parents do not assist their children with completing homework or any other school-related assignment.
2. "These kids live in single-parent homes."

White teachers feel that single-parent homes represent a dangerous living environment for African American children. These teachers criticize African American parents for being the only parent in the home.

3. "These kids don't have positive role models."
White teachers often perceive that when African American students—particularly males—lack a father in the home, they are lacking positive male role models. They tend to totally disregard the mother as a key role model in the lives of African American children.

The basis of these deficit beliefs is a sequential application of virtuousness and virtualization toward Black children. From a virtual standpoint, some White teachers have never been poor. Other White teachers have experienced poverty. But neither group has ever been Black and poor. Yet both groups believe that being poor and White is a universal experience. Using this White-framed view of class and race as a guide, both groups of White teachers assume a self-proclaimed expertise on "Black Mind-sets of Poverty." This expertise is used to frame Black children who do and do NOT live in low-income environments.

The virtuous link to these actions is heroism, which reinforces the status of Whites as good and helpful people (DiAngelo, 2012). As with most acts of White heroism, White teachers first develop sympathetic views of Black children, especially those who do not have money, both parents, and life experiences. In many instances, you see the sympathy give way to the tendency to compare the missed items to their superior views of what it means to have money, family, and life experiences.

Drawing from this supremacist orientation, White teachers then begin to believe that their main role is not to teach and reach Black students. Instead, their role is to save Black children from what they perceive to be horrible lives. Thus, these White teachers see their work with Black children as a form of charity instead of the actual paid profession of teaching.

To further understand the depth of this ideology, let's go back to the professional development sessions. White teachers are asked to explain why their characteristics make African

American students culturally unique. In a recent professional development session, a White teacher responded by stating:

> Dr. Hines, it makes them unique in the sense that they don't have a lot. So a lot of times, I wish that I could take these students home with me to give them a glimpse of a different home life.

In another session, a White teacher similarly responded:

> I wish that I could adopt one of these kids so that I could give them better life experiences, which would enable them to better understand what I am teaching.

As another representative example, consider another White teacher's commentary from another session:

> I just wish that I could keep one of my African American students so that he could have at least one consistent positive role model in his life.

In response to these answers, I investigate teachers' evidence to support these assertions. To put structure to strategy, I ask for raised hands to determine the number of teachers who have ongoing discussions with Black parents that do not focus just on academic or behavioral difficulties. Also investigated is the number of teachers who have or do make home visits to Black homes and communities. Research suggests that these actions are most likely to increase teachers' understandings of Black children (Delpit, 2006; Irvine, 2002).

What is often found is that of a mixed-race faculty, more than half of Black teachers usually have continuous discussions with Black children and parents. Just under a half of Black teachers have or do make visits to the homes of Black children. However, very few White teachers have ever visited the homes of Black children. In addition, I found that 2 out of 10 White teachers take the time to engage Black parents in ongoing discussions that go beyond school performance. In other words, White teachers lack authentic evidence to draw accurate conclusions about the cultural backgrounds of Black children. Yet, they still use White-framed assumptions to make sense of their unfounded conclusions about Black children.

The underlying factor of this and other examples from this section is the White supremacist theme of "More Like Us." In her autobiographical account *Waking Up White and Finding Myself in the Story of Race*, Debby Irving (2014) devotes an entire chapter to this theme. Drawing from an anti-racist White perspective, she writes:

> About a year into my waking up White journey, I realized I'd been unknowingly caught in a similar dynamic in the racial arena. During all the years I'd tried to help and fix people of color part of my subconscious expectation had been that people outside my culture should assimilate to my ways, see and do things the way I'd been taught was right and normal. Unlike in my marriage, however, Bruce and I felt free to tell each other how frustrated we were, in cross-racial relationships such freedom of expression does not exist. Because throughout history speaking up has cost people of color jobs, homes, and even lives, too often they chose to stay silent. There's a long and painful American history of people of color, when in the presence of White people, conforming to survive. (p. 191)

Though written from an anti-racist perspective, the author acknowledges that she is a product of the power of White supremacy. She further notes that because of her lifelong internalization of White supremacy, she only saw people of color as outsiders—meaning they were outside of the normalcy of Whiteness. This same supremacist lens that defined Irving's life is the same supremacist lens of cultural other that frames White teachers' characterization of Black children.

To fully understand this logic, let's take *cultural* and *other* apart and conduct a deeper examination of these lenses. Noted educator Gloria Ladson-Billings (2006) discusses culture in her powerful article "It's Not the Culture of Poverty, It's the Poverty of Culture: The Problem with Teacher Education." She writes:

> Of course "culture" is only the answer if the students in question are not White, not English-speaking, and not native-born

U.S. citizens. In a discussion with students who were completing their fourth field experience in our program, I listened as they described their students' misbehavior in terms of culture. "The Black kids just talk so loud and don't listen," said one teacher education student. I asked her why she thought they spoke so loudly. "I don't know; I just guess it's cultural." I then asked if she thought they were talking loudly because they were Black or because they were kids. She paused a moment and then said, "I guess I've never thought about that." This is an interesting response since so much of this student's teacher preparation includes a focus on development. Why don't more of our students say things like, "Since my students are eight years old I expect that they will behave in this particular way"? (p. 106)

The answer to Ladson-Billings questions is the term *other*. Kai Erikson (1966) provides an excellent analysis of how *other* is defined in the context of the collective American identity. Erikson writes, "One of the surest ways to confirm an identity, for a community as well as for individuals, is to find some way of measuring what one is *not*" (p. 124).

Thus, deficit thinking is used by White teachers to confirm African American students' identities as the "other." In essence, because Black students are not White, they are the "other." Because most Black students are perceived as not having access to money, and thereby class, they are the "other." As a result, African American students' cultural background and values are not viewed as being assets to their schooling experiences.

This framing adds a plausible explanation for White teachers' deficit tendencies to see themselves as "good White people" who work for the noble cause of "saving Black children" from chaos, stress, and other negative life situations. The next step is White teachers' excessive time and energy on talking about why low-performing African American students fail to display middle-class values. The underlying main point—and perhaps mind-set—of this discussion is that African American students are not acting like White teachers or their White student peers.

White Fragility

White fragility is defined as White people's stressful responses to recognizing or discussing race (DiAngelo, 2011, 2012).

White Teacher Fragility Regard for African American Students

White fragility is a mediating factor in the relationship between White teachers and Black children. One significant display of White fragility is color blindness, which is the avoidance of race. Many theorists and researchers have discussed White teachers' tendencies to use a color-blind approach to avoid discussions and issues related to race and racism in school settings (Kailin, 1999; McIntyre, 1997; Sleeter, 2001, 2013).

With regard to African American students, the trigger point for this type of fragility is as follows: it is racist to see race as having any relevance to teaching African American students.

Consider the emergence of White fragility during an icebreaker activity used during professional development workshops about African American student success. At the beginning of the workshops, a handout is provided that consists of the following reflection:

Please choose and expand on the title that best fits you.

1. Race Does Matter and Race Should Matter
2. Race Does Matter, But Race Should Not Matter
3. Race Doesn't Matter, But Race Should Matter
4. Race Doesn't Matter and Race Should Not Matter

Black teachers and Hispanic teachers provide descriptions related to titles A, B, C, and D. But the majority of White teachers' reflections reach the same conclusion: Race Doesn't Matter and Race Should Not Matter. The following anonymous White teacher responses (AWTR) are representative samples of descriptions given throughout my career. As you read these responses, be aware that the majority of these teachers are between the ages of 25 and 55 and have an average of 10 years of teaching experience:

- I treat everyone the same—no matter what color or race. I don't see color/race (AWTR-1).
- Race shouldn't matter in order to have a place in life whether it's a job, friendship, the way you are treated, or looked at (AWTR-2).
- Because I feel . . . rules should be equitable as well as consequences regardless of race. We're all God's children (AWTR-3).
- We all deserve to be treated the same way and have the same opportunities regardless of race, gender, and so forth (AWTR-4).
- Everyone should be given an opportunity to learn no matter what their ethnicity. It's when we start allowing ethnicity to matter that things mess up (AWTR-5).
- Our race should not reflect how we are treated and viewed as a person. Everyone has the ability to be gifted at something. We are special individuals (AWTR-6).
- It's your character not your color that counts. It's all about how you carry yourself with me. I couldn't give two flips about how you look racially (AWTR-7).
- The person should matter. Color shouldn't drive the decisions you make about or toward others. We just shouldn't make judgments based on race (AWTR-8).
- Race does not define what a person is capable of doing. We all want the same things in life—love, happiness, etc. (AWTR-9).
- Everybody has a need for respect, love, and guidance. This should not change due to race (AWTR-10).
- We should all be treated with respect. It does not matter the color of skin. We are all valued (AWTR-11).
- Race should not matter because we should look at the individual as a person with specific needs and goals. We all need different things in order to be successful (AWTR-12).
- Seeing race is not a good thing because God made everybody the same on the outside and underneath (AWTR-13).

- Everybody should be treated the same and should be treated equal—why is that so hard to understand? (AWTR-14).
- Race should not matter, and we should not depend on the color of skin. It causes so much more conflict when people think it does matter (AWTR-15).

Regardless of where the workshops are conducted, similar answers are received from White teachers. The teachers refuse to acknowledge the role of race as an influential factor in the development of African American students. Instead, they remain steadfast to the belief that race does and should not matter. Listed below are some additional statements pertaining to White teachers' beliefs about the irrelevance of Black children's race (DiAngelo, 2012).

- "You know, I have never thought about it because I don't see race. I just see students."
- "I don't think about my African American students as a color. I just think about them as individuals."
- "Until I met you, I never gave a second thought to the fact that I have Black students. I just don't see it that way."
- "Kids are kids."
- "Why do we need to bring race into the picture? Black kids are individuals like everybody else."
- "I don't need to understand race to teach Black students. I just need to teach my Black students as students."

As another example, White teachers minimize race by indicating that they treat all of their students in the same way. Some sample statements regarding this belief are as follows:

- "I don't care what color my Black kids are—all of my kids are the same."
- "I don't see color. I just see kids. And I treat them all the same."
- "I have 24 students and I don't care what color they are. They know that they will get the same exact treatment from me."

When working with a seventh-grade team on how to use race and culture to develop culturally responsive approaches to addressing the off-task behavior of African American male students, we explored the concept of using directness in an Afrocentric way. Pamela, a White teacher, yelled, "Enough!" I immediately stopped my presentation and stated, "Excuse me—what's wrong?" Pam responded:

> I've had enough of this talk about race and Black students. Why can't we all just understand that Black students are the same as White students, Hispanic students, and other racial students? It's just a shame that as White teachers, we have to be told that we should see and treat Black students, as well as any other students, different because of race. Kids are kids, which means that we've got to treat them as kids! And the only way to do this, Dr. Hines, is by seeing and treating them all the same.

Sensing frustration with this teacher's lack of understanding, the group dismissed for a 15-minute break. When we reconvened for the rest of the presentation, I resumed my talk by saying, "Pam, I want to let you know that I hear what you are saying with regard to treating all students the same." I then continued by saying, "But the truth of the matter is that students are not the same. They bring unique racial and cultural differences to the classroom." I closed this part of the discussion by stating, "So it is extremely important for you to look at cultural differences through the lens of African American culture in this case—and not your own worldview."

As I made this statement, I noticed that the remainder of the group of teachers—all of whom were White—nodded in agreement with me. Pamela continued to participate in the session. But her body language showed that she still did not agree with me.

Overall, these examples highlight White teachers' fragility to being challenged on their color-blind ideology toward race. The impetus for the patterned, stressful responses is twofold. First, there's a "should not matter" sentiment that suggests that skin color should have no bearing on a person's life. Also in existence is a "does not matter" suggestion to turn a "blind eye" to skin color. As complements to each other, both matters create the White-framed tendency to equate racial awareness with racial discrimination (DiAngelo, 2012; Sleeter, 2001).

It would seem that the fragility of "does not matter" and "should not matter" would make race irrelevant in all ways to White teachers. But as Black feminist Audre Lorde (1983) reminds us: "For the master's tools will never dismantle the master's house. They may allow us to temporarily beat him at his own game, but they will never enable us to bring about genuine change"(p. 101). Lorde's remarks reflected her criticism of White women who claimed to be concerned about all women but actually represented the interests of White women.

Lorde's (1983) critique is relatable to White teacher fragility and color blindness. It appears that the fragility of color blindness is triggered by White teachers' discomfort with acknowledging race. But with regard to Black children, the fragility is triggered by not being able to acknowledge race at their volition. In other words, White teachers are stressed only when unable to acknowledge race in ways that benefit them.

As such, White teachers are strategically conscious in their awareness of how they relate to African American students. The categories of consciousness are forced consciousness and semi-consciousness. The following section describes these categories.

Forced Consciousness

Forced-conscious White Teachers are teachers who have been forced into the fragile position of acknowledging race as a factor in their interactions with African American students. Through these experiences, these teachers reluctantly realize that their Whiteness and the Blackness of African American students make race a relevant factor in cross-racial teacher-student relationships.

For example, at a district-wide roundtable discussion on relationship building with African American parents, toward the end of the discussion, a White teacher stood up and fragilely stated, "I don't like talking about race or really see the importance of race—I really don't." She continued, "But I've been made to realize that as a White person dealing with some of my Black students and Black parents, I know that they may see me as a race." The teacher further said, "I don't like it, but I had to defend myself and then go out and show them that they could indeed trust me."

Similarly, during a recent professional development at a racially diverse high school, a teacher approached me and said, "There's a part of me that disagrees with everything being said about working with our Black students." She then continued, "But I have had some experiences that have made me realize just how important it is to recognize race when I deal with my Black students."

After I probed the teacher for more information, she shared the following story:

> You know, I had this African American girl one time and I had a really good relationship with her parents. So the year is moving along really well, and I realized that she may have some learning problems that I didn't want or know how to really help her with in some situations. So I went to the special education coordinator and told her, "Hey, I have a Black girl that needs to be tested for learning disabilities." I then called the girl's parents and told them I think that their child has some learning problems beyond my reach. But as soon as I told them that I contacted the special education coordinator to test the student, the mom hit the roof. She began to yell at me and said that I had no right to make a recommendation without talking to her. I tried to explain to both parents that as a teacher, I was with their child every day and I had some insight that should count for something. The parent then said, "You only made that recommendation because she's Black." She then slammed down the phone in my face.
>
> Needless to say, I was floored, stunned, and speechless. It was like, "After all I have done, how could you say that to me?" Race is not important at all and was never a factor in my recommendation. So the next day, I get called into my office by the principal and am reprimanded for the whole situation. So after that, I never saw the African American student the same. I also learned another important lesson: I need to be very aware of race, especially when I deal with my Black parents. They may very easily make any and everything about race.

Similar stories have been shared from numerous forced-conscious White teachers. Embedded in the stories are the palpable anger, distrust, and disillusion at being forced to acknowledge race. Because of seeing the situations as stressful experiences, these teachers often feel the need to guard themselves when interacting with Black students and families.

Semiconsciousness

Semiconscious White teachers apply a selective approach toward recognizing Whiteness as a part of their interactions with African American students. With great caution, these teachers move in and out of consciousness to handle Black-White interactions without being seen as a racist. In other words, race can be used to handle situations related to Black students—as long as the procedures do not have the potential to brand them as racist White teachers. This type of consciousness is used in the following situations:

Situation 1: Instructional Proceedings That Could Put White Teachers in Jeopardy of Being Seen as Racist. A few years ago, I was conducting classroom observations in a middle school during Black History Month. Ms. Winslow, a White eighth-grade teacher, asked me to provide her with feedback on her Black history lesson. I agreed and observed the lesson.

When I entered the classroom, I noticed that the lesson objective was for students to describe the slave auction in their own words. Ms. Winslow started the lesson with a short overview of the objective. Students then watched a short video about sequential events of the slave trade. Afterward, students then participated in a slave trade simulation. A mixture of students from all races was selected for the role of slave traders. However, Black students were not placed in the role of slaves. Only White students and Hispanic students were selected to be slaves.

After the lesson, the students went to lunch and I met with Ms. Winslow. I praised her for the introduction and powerful video. I then asked Ms. Winslow to explain why no Black student was placed in the role of a slave. Ms. Winslow's initial response was "Well, Dr. Hines, race doesn't matter." She continued by stating, "All kids need to know about slavery."

I responded by acknowledging Ms. Winslow's perspective. But I still explained that only Black students' background is inclusive of slavery. Therefore, at least one Black student should have been a part of the group of slaves.

At this point, Ms. Winslow confessed that her initial plan was to divide the class into an even mixture of slaves and slave owners. However, she feared accusations of racism if she put Black students in the role of slaves. Specifically, Ms. Winslow believed that she risked angering Black parents by involving their children in a slave auction.

Notice the politically fragile way in which Ms. Winslow moves in and out of consciousness regarding race. On the one hand, Ms. Winslow understood that race can be a critical factor in delivering instruction to students. Yet, she lacked the comfort and understanding with applying a culturally responsive approach to using race as a teaching tool with Black students. She mainly seemed unsure of Black parents' possible feelings about the lesson, which could impact her racial standing as a White teacher. Because of these concerns, Ms. Winslow made the fragile decision to frame the lesson with little to no authentic relevance to her Black students.

If I could redo this experience, I would make two suggestions to Ms. Winslow. My first suggestion would be for Ms. Winslow to inform parents that she would be discussing slavery with students. My second suggestion would be to do a preparatory lesson on slavery. The lesson would focus on activities such as exploring life in Africa before slavery. Here students would explore the language and cultural values of Africans before their bondage in American slavery. I would also inform Ms. Winslow to strengthen the lesson with the use of the following books:

- Haskins, J., & Benson, K. (1998). *African Beginnings*. New York, NY: Lothrop, Lee & Sheppard.
- Thompson, C. (1998). *African Civilizations: The Asante Kingdom*. New York, NY: Franklin Watts.

These steps could increase Ms. Watson's comfort with including Black students as slaves in the slave auction. Equally significant, Ms. Watson would be able to design a lesson that gives Black students an authentic view about slavery.

Situation 2: White Teachers Specifically Request Black Teachers to Handle Behavioral Situations with African American Students. Oftentimes I am asked by principals and superintendents to work in schools that have high numbers of discipline referrals for African American students. Upon arriving at the schools, my first objective is to identify teachers' level of cultural responsiveness to African American students. I usually find that most African American teachers do not have behavioral problems with African American children.

Within those same environments, I observe two groups of White teachers who have high behavioral issues with African American students. The first group has issues because of a lack of understanding on how to relate to and redirect African American students. The second group has the same problems as the first group of teachers. The only difference is that these teachers neither write referrals nor commit to applying culturally responsive approaches to addressing disciplinary situations with African American students. Instead, these teachers take the semiconscious approach of recruiting Black teachers to resolve the issues with Black students. Let me give you an example of this scenario played out in an elementary school.

At the beginning of the school year, Jennifer, a White second-grade teacher, had discipline issues with a Black male student, Rashad. The section below provides an account of his first four discipline referrals (figure 2.1).

These referrals are included as a visualization of the racial issue at play in this situation. In essence, all four referrals show that Rashad was cited for defiance. As the number of referrals increased, there was a change in Jennifer's perceptions of Rashad's defiance. His behavior progressed from defiance to defiance and disrespect. By the time Rashad committed his last two offenses of defiance, his behavior was defined as disrespect.

This example points to the deeper racialized framing of African American students' behavior in schools. Research continues

Discipline Referral Number One
Name: Rashad Williams   Date: August 28, 2013   Time: 9:03 a.m.   Category: Defiance
Nature of Offense: Refusal to complete work that was from yesterday and this morning and not completed during APR. Refused to sit appropriately. *Written By: J. Moss

Discipline Referral Number Two
Name: Rashad Williams Date: September 5, 2013 Time: 12:03 p.m. Category: Defiance, Disrespect
Nature of Offense: Rashad became upset when I told him that he had to wait to use the restroom and refused to participate in math groups. *Written By: J. Moss
Discipline Referral Number Three
Name: Rashad Williams   Date: September 16, 2013   Time: 2:14 p.m.   Category: Disrespect
Nature of Offense: Rashad has been clipped down all morning for doing the opposite of what is asked of him. His refusal is a daily occurrence. *Written By: J. Moss
Discipline Referral Number Four
Name: Rashad Williams   Date: September 24, 2013   Time: 11:03 a.m.   Category: Disrespect
Nature of Offense: Rashad received this referral for refusing to stop talking in the hallway during restroom break. *Written By: J. Moss

Figure 2.1. Discipline referrals.

to show that Black children are no more behaviorally challenged than students from other racial groups (Skiba, Michael, Nardo, & Peterson, 2002; Skiba, Horner, Chung, Rausch, May, & Tobin, 2011; Skiba & Williams, 2014). In other words, Black children do not have a monopoly on disciplinary issues in schools.

The difference is in the category of referrals. Among students from different racial groups, Black children are most likely to receive discipline referrals for behaviors requiring subjective judgment. In addition, disrespect, disruption, and defiance are the most common subjective perceptions of the behavior of Black students. Other researchers agree that these perceptions are teacher based and the beginning point of the majority of disciplinary moments and issues for Black students in the classroom (Fields, 2004; Monroe 2005, 2009; Noguera, 2003; Vavrus & Cole, 2002; Webb-Johnson, 2002).

These disciplinary moments continue to shape Jennifer's response to Rashad's behavior. One day, after experiencing issues with Rashad, Jennifer asks Carrie, her African American team teacher, to speak to him. Carrie obliges the request and admonishes Rashad about his behavior. She then sends Rashad back to Jennifer's classroom.

Rashad has no more disciplinary issues for the remainder of that day. However, Jennifer still experiences discipline issues with Rashad. Her new response is to send Rashad to Carrie's classroom. Within a matter of weeks, a Rashad misbehavior—Rashad-to-Carrie approach is used to maintain order in Jennifer's classroom.

In response, Carrie requests a meeting with me to talk about the situation. During the meeting, she discusses her frustrations with Jennifer's lack of involvement in addressing Rashad's behavioral issues. As a teacher, Carrie feels that it's not her role to address another teacher's disciplinary issues with students. The section below provides Carrie's commentary regarding this sentiment.

> *I am so tired of handling Jennifer's discipline problem with Rashad. She should be talking to me about what I am actually doing instead of just sending him over to me because we're both Black. We get paid the same thing to do the same job—but I feel like I have to expend extra energy on a situation that should be handled by the child's teacher.*

Carrie then adds a somewhat modified version of double consciousness to the discussion with the following statement:

> *Every day, I walk into this building saying, "I'm not handling Jennifer's discipline issues." But I always do it. Because I look at it like this—I feel that if I don't handle it, he's gonna end up going to the dogs. I mean she's just gonna send him to the office—which is still bad because another Black boy not in the classroom. And as a Black person, I feel like I can't just let one of my own go out like that—especially when I know that this child can be something in life. But if I keep handling the problem, she'll continue to think that it's not her issue—just a Black issue that must be addressed by a Black teacher.*

Here we see racial identity as the impetus for one Black person's compassion for another Black person. That both Black people operate in a White-dominated environment also increases the saliency of race in this equation. Notwithstanding, Carrie still feels the quandary of reconciling her identity as a Black person with her identity as a teacher.

In an attempt to address the struggle, a meeting was set up between Jennifer and Carrie. Jennifer was asked to explain how she attempts to address Rashad's behavior. Jennifer explains that she tells Rashad that she loves and wants what's best for him. Carrie then makes the following interjection, "It's time for you to go further than that, Jennifer." She continues, "You've got to make him feel your love by being direct with him when he starts to act a fool." Then it is suggested that Jennifer talk with Carrie about specific ways of demonstrating culturally responsive classroom management strategies with Black children. This request leads to the following exchange:

Jennifer: I just don't think that it's about race.

Me: What?

Jennifer: It's the behavior—not the race.

Carrie: Well, why do you keep sending him to me?

Jennifer: Well, we're on the same team, you have great classroom management . . .

Carrie (interrupting): And you know that I am Black.

Jennifer: Yes. But that's not the main reason that I ask for your help.

Me: So if she was White, would you send this student to her?

Jennifer: Yes. Probably.

Carrie: Okay. So we have two other White teachers on our team and they don't have problems with their Black students. So from here on out, send Rashad to those teachers.

Jennifer: I just think that it would be better if we worked together on this student.

Carrie: No, I think that you should call it what it is—you do not know how to handle Rashad and feel that I, a Black teacher, should be able to do your job for you.

This discussion provides an in-depth look at the White fragility within the responses from Jennifer. Drawing from White fragility, Jennifer insists on minimizing race as a factor in her decision to send Rashad to Carrie. Yet when advised to send Rashad to another White teacher, Jennifer still insisted that he be disciplined by Carrie.

Countless numbers of African American teachers have experienced this situation with at least one White teacher during their careers. For these teachers, the issue is frustrating because of White teachers' refusal to acknowledge race as a factor in their request for assistance with challenging African American students.

White Privilege

White privilege is defined as unearned advantages that are bestowed upon Whites by virtue of skin color (Dyer, 1997; Kendall, 2006; Neville, Worthington, & Spanierman, 2001; Sue, 2003; Tatum, 2003; Wise, 2002, 2010b).

White Teacher Privilege Regard for African American Students

The power of White teacher privilege is about standing. In effect, my work on African American students is built upon the following tenet:

> Seeing race is central to teacher effectiveness with Black children. The reason is that race is a central part of the socialization of Black people, including Black children. Thus, by understanding the racial socialization within Black culture, teachers will better understand how to ensure that they are inclusive of the cultural backgrounds of Black students.

This ideology violates White teachers' standing as privileged White people. Remember that Whites are privileged by their lack of requirement to justify, consider, or be stipulated by other racial groups. An emphasis on racial differences requires White teachers to justify the use of only a White-framed approach to teach African American students. White teachers are also in the unfamiliar position of considering an approach to Black student success that is not centered on Whiteness. In this context, racial awareness is a stipulation for White teachers to be effective with Black students.

As beneficiaries of the master's tools (Lorde, 1983), White teachers are always in a privileged position to dismantle these expectations. White teachers use three specific approaches that generate and are generated by racial privilege. The sections below provide an overview of these approaches.

The Privilege to Demand

In conducting over 2,000 workshops and trainings about African American students, I am always met with the demand for safety from White teachers. To be specific, White teachers insist on feeling safe before even considering ideas for teaching African American students. But when peeling back the refrain of "need for safety," what White teachers really want is comfort and convenience. That is, White teachers expect to be shielded from racial stress related to discussing Black children.

The reason is that, as White people, White teachers are almost always in racially comfortable spaces (DiAngelo, 2011, 2012). The downside of these environments is that White teachers are seldom required to develop tolerance and stamina for race. The resulting demand for avoiding racial stress contributes to their framing of racial matters with arrogance and simplicity.

Over and over, White teachers insist on a threefold component of comfort to discuss Black children. The parameters are as follows:

1. There is a limit to presenting straightforward views on the relevance of race to Black children.
2. There is a limit to the number of emotional responses or strong opinions that can be given on race and Black children.

3. There is a limit on requiring self-reflection on how race impacts teachers' views and responses to Black children.

In other words, White teachers' racial comfort is contingent upon the extent to which Black children are not the central focus of workshops about Black children. The culturally framed corollary to these stipulations is "Just Tell Me What to Do." A derivative of White racial comfort, this refrain represents White teachers' insistence on receiving unlimited strategies for addressing issues with Black students. Moreover, the strategies should work in the same exact way for every Black student.

This was initially viewed as an exclusive interest in doing what's best for Black children. Over the years, for many White teachers, the call for specific strategies is not a sign of genuine concern. These requests sometimes stem from the need to control Black students.

A response to "Just Tell Me What to Do" is to explain that the strategies alone do not guarantee success. That is, quickstep approaches will not effectively engage Black children in responding to expectations for behavior and instruction. The intent of this reply is to guide White teachers toward seeing the complexity required to teach Black students. That way, White teachers may be more likely to see that internalization and understanding—not memorization and quick fixes—are the most effective foundations for responding to Black students.

In some cases, these illustrations and explanations have prompted White teachers to take an in-depth approach to developing long-term approaches to working with Black students. All too often, however, my response does not move White teachers beyond their demands for specific methods to deal with Black children. As a result, White teachers seldom realize the need to understand the in-depth, complex process pertaining to teaching Black students.

The Privilege to Decide

In most cases, White teachers make two specific determinations about the need to understand the racial and cultural uniqueness of Black children. The decisions are between-group universalism and within-group individualism (DiAngelo, 2010). Between group universalism is a defensive move used during discussions on cultural differences between Black students and White students. Here, White teachers assert that all children are the same. In doing so, White teachers are attempting to diminish the unique cultural similarities that are among children from specific racial groups.

The within-group individualism approach is used when fostering discussions on the characteristics that create cultural uniqueness among Black children. Like players in a game of racial chess, White teachers move cultural uniqueness into a presenter framing of Black children as a monolithic group. In earlier years, this claim would be refuted, thereby moving the discussion away from the cultural significance of Black children.

Nowadays, the response to this racial distortion with research-based evidence regarding Black children as individuals from a shared history of cultural like-mindedness (Boykin, 1986, 1995; Boykin & Bailey, 2000; Hale, 2001; Hale-Benson, 1986; Kunjufu, 2005, 2007). More insight on this cultural framework will be offered in later chapters. But for now, let's focus on White teachers' continuous response of viewing Black children as non-racialized individuals who lack any significant racial commonalties.

Both individualism and universalism are outgrowths of a half-century-old, White-framed world of reasoning. Consistent with White culture, White teachers are socialized to see themselves as just "human" and "individuals" (DiAngelo, 2011, 2012; Frankenberg, 1993, 1997, 2001). As a result, White teachers are trained to believe that they don't have race—just unique identities. The privilege to this perspective is that only White individuals are able to navigate society in non-racialized ways. In other words, White people are seldom burdened with the cumbersome task of carrying their race.

When added to the dominant White teaching frame, this navigation system becomes the following: children from different racial groups are the same—same values, same attitudes, same traditions and same beliefs. In the same racialized vein, children from the same racial groups are extremely different—different values, different attitudes, different traditions, different beliefs. This belief system limits White teachers' effectiveness with knowing how to adjust for the between-group and within-group racial differences that impact African American children.

An example of this self-induced dilemma follows:

A few years ago, I was invited to work in an elementary school that wanted me to "tell them what to do with Black students." It seems that many of the teachers were unable to address discipline problems with Black students.

As is my customary practice, I spent the end of the school year conducting classroom observations of teachers' practices with Black children. I also talked with teachers to gather their views about Black children. I then talked with Black students to gain insight on their experiences within the school.

One of the most glaring issues within the schools was between White teachers and Black girls. I noticed that for the most part, White teachers often phrased their requests of Black students in an optional format. Instead of saying, "Sit down, Jackie," these teachers would use phrases such as "Jackie, what are our rules for entering class?" Another example is "Don't you want to sit down at this time, Jackie?" Given my exposure to Black research on discipline, I knew that this approach to discipline would be problematic for some of the Black children (Delpit, 2006; Hale-Benson, 1986; Irvine, 2002; Monroe & Obidah, 2004). The reason is that, by using a White-framed communication style, teachers were couching commands in the form of questions. They then expected the communication to yield obedience from Black children, many of whom are accustomed to direct communication for fulfilling expectations.

Using this information as a guide, I conducted a series of summer professional development trainings on classroom management strategies for African American students. I anchored the trainings on two premises: First, teachers must be able to build cultural connections with Black children to increase the likelihood of the children meeting expectations. Second, in addition to traditional classroom directives, teachers must use culturally responsive language to express expectations to Black children. Both points are well researched and will be further discussed in later chapters.

I was delighted to find that teachers understanding the critical relevance of relationships in helping Black children see expectations as being driven by love and support (Foster, 1998; Irvine, 2002; Kunjufu, 2005, 2007). However, the same response was not given to the role of language in providing discipline for Black children. Many of the White teachers interpreted the role of direct communication as being too harsh for elementary-aged Black children. I re-explained the premise about direct communication. However, many teachers still had apprehensions about this approach.

One such teacher was Meredith, a White fourth-grade teacher. Meredith argued that all children were the same (between-group universalism). She then indicated that it was racist to ever use a different tone with Black children. Again, I explained the cultural framework for how to use direct styles of communication to elicit appropriate behavior with Black children. I also reassured Meredith that this approach should be used in conjunction with her other approaches for redirecting the behavior of Black students. Instead of seeing the addition as cultural support, Meredith argued that the suggestions would have a racist impact on her classroom. Her final words to me were "No way in hell will I ever do what you are asking us to do."

In September of the following school year, I conducted a check-in phone conference with the school's principal, John. John explained that most teachers were able to apply either or both the relational and communicative frameworks toward reducing disciplinary issues with Black children. He and I then set some school-wide goals to guide my follow-up visits to the school.

John then informed me that Meredith had an experience that caused her to finally embrace the purpose of the summer workshops. It seems that after observing two White females engaging in off-task behavior, Meredith addressed the students with approaches from the workshop. Using a very firm, no-nonsense tone of voice, Meredith stated, "Girls, move back to your directions now" (Obidah & Teel, 2001; Weinstein, Curran, & Tomlinson-Clarke, 2003; Weinstein, Tomlinson-Clarke, & Curran, 2004). The girls complied with the directive.

However, when asked about her school day, one girl informed her mother that she was being yelled at by her teacher (Meredith). The mother requested a conference with Meredith and John. During the conference, the mother asked Meredith if she indeed yelled at her daughter. Meredith explained that she did not yell at her daughter. The mother relaxed and thanked Meredith and the principal for the conference.

Toward the end of the conference, Meredith said, "I can see how your daughter would interpret my directive as yelling." She continued, "Because I spoke to her in a new way I was taught to communicate to Black children." According to the principal, the mother's countenance changed from relaxation to rage. In a very firm, no-nonsense tone of voice, the mother said, "Do you think my daughter is Black?" Dumbfounded, Meredith was unable to respond to the question.

She continued, "Let me answer—hell no and don't you talk to her in that way!" The mother then exited the conference. Later that day, the girl was transferred out of Meredith's classroom. The mother also left the following irony at the school: a White person needed another White person to explain the danger of overlooking the relevance of race.

The Privilege to Dismiss

Unless the discussions are based on social class, White teachers dismiss meaningful dialogue about Black children with either silence or violence (DiAngelo, 2012; DiAngelo & Sensoy, 2014). In the following section, a description is provided of both methods of dismissal.

Silence

One of the most agonizing aspects of this work on Black student success is White silence—a deafening silence, to be exact (DiAngelo, 2012). *White silence* is defined as White teachers' refusal to add to discussions on teacher effectiveness with Black children. Commonly cited reasons for White teacher silence are "I don't feel safe," "I don't want to be attacked," "I don't want to be judged," "I don't want to be misunderstood," and "I don't want to offend." Whether it be an all-White or a mixed-race teacher audience, these statements are rarely developed from a place of reflection and growth. The statements are used by White teachers to maintain the White privileges of racial solidarity and protection.

In essence, much of White teachers' silencing behaviors are connected to the larger framework of Whiteness. As indicated in chapter one, Whiteness draws power from being unmarked and unnamed (DiAngelo, 2012; Frankenberg, 1993, 2001; Levine-Rasky, 2000; Roediger, 2003). As a result, Whiteness operates as an unchallenged, unconscious commonalty among White people. When pushed to recognize Whiteness, Whites refuse to discuss or even recognize their socialization within this dominant, hegemonic worldview. The emerging White silence thwarts racial discussions, distancing Whites from White racial introspection and change.

Witnessing the impact of this racial maneuvering on the dynamics of mixed-race discussions about Black children, over and over, Black teachers end up carrying the weight of the discussions on Black children. This allows White teachers to position teacher effectiveness with Black students as a Black issue.

As a consequence, some Black teachers will not discuss their views on Black students with White teachers. As one Black teacher explained, "I love our babies, but I am not about to put myself out there so Black words will be the only words analyzed in this room." This double consciousness has caused other Black teachers to abstain gradually from discussing Black children with White teachers.

Another important perspective to this equation is the silencing of White teachers who do want to learn effective ways of teaching Black children. On rare occasions, a White teacher will take a stand in support of understanding Black students. Other White teachers usually respond to the commentary with silence. If I endorse the commentary, the teacher will continue with seeking or giving more insight regarding Black children. But if I don't endorse the comments, the teacher is neutralized by the silence. The latter point is especially true if the White teacher is well liked among other White teachers. Thus, silence carries specific capital in preventing White teachers from breaking racial codes and ranks.

Violence

Violence is defined as White teachers' aggressive approaches to diminishing racialized discussions on achieving success with African American students. The basis of this form of violence is the refusal to listen and comprehend information about Black students. Research has highlighted the following times for Whites to just listen when in interracial groups (DiAngelo, 2012):

- When people of color are discussing the sensitive issue of internalized racial oppression.
- When there is need for a less dominant voice from a White person.
- When other Whites have already provided a lot of perspective on a discussion.
- When Whites need to not speak first and most in the discussion.
- When a person of color desires and deserves to have the last word on a topic or subject.
- When a White person is asked to hold back or delay an opinion.

Similarly, additional studies have shown that the following behaviors should be avoided in conversations (Patterson, Grenny, McMillan, & Switzler, 2012):

Controlling

- Coercing others to support a particular way of thinking.
- Dominating the conversation.
- Labeling.
- Stereotyping or categorizing people.
- Calling names.

Attacking

- Belittling the perspectives of others.
- Intimidating others.

Let's look at what happens when White teachers approach discussions about Black children with no regard for these suggestions. On some occasions, Black teachers will speak up in support for the need to be culturally responsive to Black children. Some Black teachers use their same background affiliation to explain their approaches to building solidarity with Black children. Other Black teachers point to the history of race as the reason for understanding racialized ways of teaching Black children. In some cases, both groups of Black teachers will emphasize that understanding Black-White differences is a prerequisite for White teachers to facilitate Black student achievement.

In almost every setting, White teachers respond to these discussions with some form of violence. Some White teachers declare that just by virtue of skin color, Black teachers are automatically effective with Black children. Other White teachers argue that they are being called racists.

Both groups of White teachers framed these discussions as Black favoritism. Much like Whites' views of affirmative action (Wise, 2005), White teachers argue that strategies for Black student success will give Black students unfair advantages. Consequently, White teachers call for identifying strategies that will increase the success of White students.

In assuming this White racial standing, White teachers reinforce the idea that Blacks are unable to have objective views about race (Bell, 1993). They also fail to see how their standing distorts very two important points about Black children and schools. First, Black students are at a disadvantage when denied experiences that are inclusive of their race, culture, and identities. Second, discussions on Black students do not lower expectations for Black student success. Instead, discussions outline specific ways to help Black students succeed in school. However, White teachers take issue with this feedback. The reason is that the feedback is viewed as specific stipulations for understanding Black children to teach them.

Conclusion

In this chapter, an in-depth analysis of the dominant White teaching frame was provided. The crux of the analysis is the frame's influence in a variety of professional development settings. As mentioned, professional development can nurture a growth mind-set within teachers. However, a lack of professional development often stunts teacher effectiveness with students.

In this chapter, we demonstrated how the presence of professional development about Black students was met with Whiteness from White teachers. White supremacy was used to explain White teachers' use of superiority to frame Black children as inferior beings. With fragility, White teachers' invocation of color blindness was connected to the larger White political frame of color-blind racism. Finally, White privilege was discussed with regard to White teachers' insistence on rejecting Black perspectives about Black children. The other side of this privilege is the need for comfortable and convenient approaches to tolerating ideas about Black students.

These actions are not necessarily a consequence of White teachers' moral character. But they are emotionally laden stereotypical performances that cut across location and generation. In this vein, White teachers are White people. To properly frame this connection, remember the indication of no two White people being exactly alike. The same logic applies to White teachers. But White teachers do share an internalized frame of cultural likemindedness that shapes their interactions with Black students.

At the center of the student-teacher dynamic is my chapter 1 primer about race. That chapter provided an in-depth analysis of the history of race. This chapter presented White teachers and Black students as an illustration of how the main partners of American race relations operate in schools.

There is a power dynamic that elevates White teachers' standing in this relationship. The reason is that White teachers carry power that transcends their authority from licensure agencies. As White people, White teachers possess a racial power inherited from the history of extreme White racial oppression of Black people.

This power is rarely subjected to critical analysis or discussion in public school settings. Yet, White teachers' approaches continue to make their mark as best practices for everyone, including Black students. Ironically, Whiteness is still largely unmarked territory for explaining White teachers' supreme, fragile, and privileged orientations toward Black students. The remainder of this book explains how to address these aspects of Whiteness to increase White teachers' effectiveness with Black students.

3

Decentering Whiteness via Awakening to Whiteness

Chapter 2 was a characterization of the racialized mannerisms and behaviors that hinder White teachers' effectiveness with Black children. Notwithstanding, White teachers can overcome these issues to effectively teach African American students. The starting point for this trajectory to effectiveness is decentering Whiteness.

Decentering Whiteness is White teachers' removal of Whiteness as the central focus of their interactions with African American students. Figure 3.1 provides a depiction of this process.

In picture A, note the placement of the white space in the center of the diagram. This placement is parallel to the central focus of Whiteness in American institutions. The reason is that Whiteness often operates as a deeply imbedded, unmarked—but undeniable—influence on American culture. Whiteness often operates as a deeply imbedded undeniable—but unmarked—influence on American culture. In other words, Whiteness is the central part of racial realities of this country.

In picture B, the white space is featured in a different context. Here, the white space is one of four racially labelled categories. In this realm, white spaces are no longer unmarked or unnamed. Whiteness is now one of four racial components of the societal sphere.

To operate in accordance to configuration B, White teachers must develop an awakening to their Whiteness. The term

Decentering Process

Picture A Picture B

Centrality of Whiteness Decentering of Whiteness

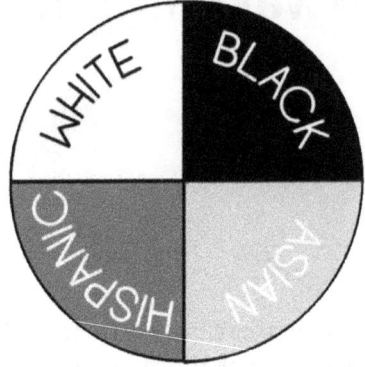

Figure 3.1. Decentering process.

awakening is not used to suggest that White teachers are fully unconscious White people. Rather, White teachers must achieve a heightened awareness of themselves as White people and White teachers.

That is, White teachers must see themselves as White—a vision that requires analysis of membership in the White racial group. The reason is that all White people are born into a world that confers power, control, dominance, and authority on White people (DiAngelo, 2012; Feagin, 2013). Yet, they seldom discuss themselves as being White. White people are not trained to see themselves as members of the White racial group. Consequently, they are unable to critically evaluate their benefits from and complicity in perpetuating Whiteness. Yet, White people still view themselves as being racially superior to other races, especially African American people.

Awakening with White Identity Development

Over the last 20 years, several theorists have suggested identity development as the means to raising racial awareness among White people (Helms, 1990, 1992; Rowe, Bennett, & Atkinson, 1994; Tatum, 2003; Wijeyesinghe & Jackson, 2012). One of the most prominent theories is Janet Helms's "White Racial Identity Development Theory." The origins of Dr. Helms's (1992) theory can be found in her book *A Race Is a Nice Thing to Have: A Guide to Being a White Person or Understanding the White Persons in Your Life.*

In her book, Dr. Helms indicated that White people assume six identity statuses to respond to racial situations in their lives. She categorized the first three identity statuses as Abandonment of Racism. The remaining three statuses are categorized as Defining a Non-Racist Identity. What follows is a description of these statuses.

Category 1: Abandonment of Racism

Stage 1: Contact

The first status, contact, is best described as obliviousness. Here, being White is viewed as the normative standard of society. In addition, White people seldom, if ever, reflect on the meaning of Whiteness. Instead, White people in this stage are oblivious to and clueless about racism. In addition, they are more likely to profess a color-blind identity. They are equally likely to interact mostly with other White people. As a result, White people not only disregard racial differences, but also perceive themselves to be nonbiased people.

Stage 2: Disintegration

At this stage, White people experience increased exposure to and interactions with Black people. With these experiences, they begin to develop an initial awareness of racism and Whiteness. However, these encounters cause White people to experience anger, sadness, and guilt.

Their responses to these emotions are twofold. Some White people deny and resist the reality of racism and Whiteness. Other White people attempt to transition Black people into their approaches to thinking about race. In other words, Black people are encouraged—and sometimes pressured—to disregard race and racism. Overall, many Whites still operate in the disintegration stage in very conflicting ways. For example, White people in this stage may possess a strong desire to be non-racist toward Black people. Yet their actions often still have a racist impact on Black people. Examples of this moral dilemma include but are not limited to

- seeing themselves as accepting of Black people, but opposing their children's marriage to a Black person;
- believing that everyone is equal, but feeling that Blacks receive unfair opportunities for advancement in society;
- acknowledging the history of Black oppression, but opposing Affirmative Action or other programs that seek to remedy this oppression; and
- witnessing racially oppressive acts toward Blacks, but refusing to acknowledge the racial nature of the situation.

Stage 3: Reintegration

During this stage of racial development, White people have replaced guilt and denial with anger and fear. Specifically, White people are more likely to use the "blame the victim" mechanism to address their feelings about racism. In addition, this stage shows their struggles with rejecting racist assumptions about Black people. Instead, they display a reconfirmed belief in White racial superiority.

From this standpoint, White people are more likely to reengage in practices that include but are not limited to

- blaming Blacks for White-framed racial inequalities;
- accepting negative stereotypes about Blacks;
- endorsing Whiteness as the preferred ideology of society;

- living and working in nearly exclusive White environments; and
- building relationships with mostly White people.

Category 2: Defining Non-racist Identity

Stage 4: Pseudo Independence

This stage is characterized by a conceptual understanding of race and racism. Here Whites begin to question previously held beliefs about Black people. They also begin to recognize the ways in which racism was shaped and influenced by White people.

Because of this level of awareness, White people develop a self-centered reflection on Whiteness and racism. Evidence to this effect is seen in Whites who disengage with other Whites. During this time, Whites may also pursue meaningful relationships with Black people. For some Whites, a by-product of cross-racial interaction is a critical examination of the role of Whiteness in their lives. In this context, White people begin to recognize the possible need to personally address racism and Whiteness. However, other Whites define cross-racial interactions by attempting to help Blacks adhere to standards of Whiteness.

Stage 5: Immersion/Emersion

In this stage, Whites undergo an in-depth process of reflection on Whiteness. Specifically, Whites begin to ask questions such as "Who am I racially?" and "What does it really mean to be White in America?" The significance of these questions is twofold. First, this inquiry helps provide Whites with a new way of thinking about their identity as White people. Along those same lines, White people are able to realize that they are indeed racial beings.

Second, this level of questioning can lead White people in this stage to move from a conceptual to experiential understanding of racism. Such a transition can enlighten White people to recognize the ways in which they personally benefit from

Whiteness. Dr. Helms (1992) noted that, at this point, White people are more willing to truly confront their own biases. The significance of this action lies in White people's use of hope and motivation to recognize and respond to Whiteness and racism.

Stage 6: Autonomy

At this stage, White people possess a positive, non-racist orientation toward race. They continually examine their Whiteness to avoid the likelihood of acting with a sense of entitlement. In addition, Whites grow in their motivation and commitment to address racism. As a result, they are less likely to be fearful, intimidated, or uncomfortable with cross-racial interactions. Instead, they are more likely to value diversity and seek understanding of racial, ethnic, and cultural differences.

Fundamentalists, Integrationists, and Transformationists

Another significant White identity development theory is featured in Gary Howard's (2006) book *We Can't Teach What We Don't Know: White Teachers, Multiracial Schools*. Howard provides the first identity development model regarding the racial awareness of White teachers. He specifically purports that White teachers operate in accordance to three distinct identity orientations: fundamentalist, integrationist, and transformationist.

Fundamentalists

Fundamentalists are uninformed about Whiteness. At the same time, fundamentalist teachers are often threatened by people from non-White racial groups. They are frustrated when guided toward reflecting on their own complicity in racism. In terms of schools, fundamentalists argue that all students should be treated in the same way.

Integrationists

Integrationist teachers are more informed on Whiteness and race. They also understand that racial inequality is a contributing factor to racial differences. Yet, integrationists lack an understanding of the systemic nature of racism. As a result, they still feel that "we're all really the same under the skin."

As a result, integrationists struggle to reconcile the differences between their feelings and responses to race and racism. They recognize race without considering the role of Whiteness in creating the oppressive nature of race. When applied to a school context, integrationists use this framework to argue for the assimilation of non-White students into the Eurocentric school system.

Transformationists

Transformationists continually conduct personal explorations of Whiteness. Through this exploration, they begin to understand the oppressive nature of Whiteness. Transformationists are then more empowered to form authentic relationships with non-White people.

Because of this platform, transformationists display a high level of racial awareness of themselves as White teachers. Examples of consciousness include but are not limited to

1. understanding the concomitant relationship between oppression and schools;
2. acknowledging that their beliefs about children result in the success or failure of students;
3. seeing the interrelatedness between knowing themselves, their practices, and their students; and
4. recognizing that the success of minority students is linked to the qualification and preparation of teachers.

The Applicability of Identity Development Theories

Helms (1992) and Howard (2006) provide significant frameworks for analyzing the experiences of White teachers. Helms's work is significant because of her positionality. Specifically, Helms is a Black woman who provides a much-needed non-White perspective on what it means to be White. She also situates Whiteness in the historical context of White-Black relationships. Howard's model shows the ways in which Whiteness spills into the classroom.

Both works are applicable to this book. Their information is premised on White teachers as White people with lives that can be described through the use of their identities. Table 3.1 features an analysis of both identity development theories.

Table 3.1.   Cross-Comparison of White Racial Identity Development Theories

Janet Helms (1992)	Gary Howard (2006)
1. Contact	1. Fundamentalist
2. Disintegration	2. Integrationist
3. Reintegration	Integrationist
4. Pseudo-Independence	Integrationist
5. Immersion/Emersion	3. Transformationist
6. Autonomy	Transformationist

Many White teachers operate along the continuum of contact, disintegration, and reintegration. Many White teachers lack a basic understanding of race and racism. Through further investigation, most of these teachers use the media as the basis for their judgments of African American adults and children. Moreover, these teachers won't acknowledge the parallel between their school's Black-White gaps and the Black-White disparities in this country. For these teachers, racial inequities emanate from what they refer to as trivial racial disparities and differences.

In accordance with disintegration, some White teachers have responded to my work by highlighting their success with cross-racial relationships. For some White teachers, the relationship is described as having a dear friend who is Black. Several White teachers may note their willingness to attend an activity to support a Black child. In sum, these teachers feel that they have had meaningful contact with Black people.

As such, they should now be considered as having an authentic understanding of the racial realities of Black people. Yet, their Black awareness doesn't usually translate into an acceptance of Black children. The reason is that many of these White teachers' judgments of Black children are still based solely on White-framed interpretations.

Experiences with reintegrated White teachers can be best summarized as "blaming the victim." To be exact, these teachers continually blame Black children for their lack of success in school. They usually refuse to acknowledge the relevance of their teaching practices to African American students' issues in school.

Embedded in the "blaming the victim" mantra is a deeper belief in White superiority. This phenomenon is observed in White teachers' use of stereotypes to describe students. Some of their most prominent stereotypical beliefs are, "My Black children don't have any support at home," and "Black parents don't care about education."

In the frame of Howard's (2006) thesis, a large majority of White teachers are categorized as fundamentalists. They are very hostile toward discussions of race. The teachers are also resistant to requests for self-examining their own racial identities as White teachers. For these teachers, all students are the same. Because of this belief, White fundamentalists reject any information that provides specific understandings of the uniqueness of Black children.

Development of White Racial Identity

To develop White racial identities, White teachers must undergo two experiences: "Awakening to White Personhood" and "Awakening to White Teachership." The remainder of this chapter provides a description of these two experiences.

Experience 1: Awakening to White Personhood

The first part of White personhood is for White teachers to see themselves as White people. In essence, their personal vision of Whiteness must be based on four specific sights. The sights are as follows:

- Sight 1: All White people are White.
- Sight 2: All ways of being White are situated in constructed norms of Whiteness that normalize society.
- Sight 3: The normalization of Whiteness has very concrete implications for the lives of all White people.
- Sight 4: Understanding the implications of Whiteness is essential to developing positive White identities.

This book has presented a model that provides White teachers with the foresight for achieving this level of personal, insightful Whiteness. The model consists of two phases: "Becoming a Conscious White Person" and "Becoming a Conscientious White Person." Both phases are centered on research, exploration, acknowledgment, and living. What follows is a description of this model and accompanying phases.

Becoming a Conscious White Person

Researching My Whiteness

White teachers must research their personal lives as White people. The research should begin with consideration of the following question: What does it mean to be White? This inquiry underscores White teachers' current identification with Whiteness. That is, we are able to gain an initial entry into how Whiteness looks inside the minds of White people.

For example, consider a group of White teachers' descriptions of their lives as White people:

- My race never really came into discussions at home. Family was important, but not our race.

- (Family of a professional educator): Household was comparatively color blind. Best friend in sixth grade, Brian Graves (African American).
- I did not learn anything in the home about being Caucasian specifically. My family includes many races, and it is not an issue. I was taught that skin color is just a trait that we all can have differently just like eye color.
- Take care of self. All people are the same. Be who you are not who someone wants you to be. Treat all people how you would want to be treated.
- I don't remember my race being an issue of any kind in the home. Everyone was to be looked at on the same playing field.
- Race was never discussed as it pertains to ourselves. No one ever said, "We are White." Although once in relation to Blacks it was said, "Be glad you were born White."
- Race is not important, because everyone is the same. Judge by character—not looks.
- Being Caucasian was not any better or worse than others; it just was. Everyone is one of God's children.
- We never really talked about race because my mother tried to raise me to see everyone the same and equal. I never thought about being White. I was told we were all Americans (the same).
- We never talked about being "White" or what that meant. My family acted like it meant nothing.
- I did not know about "race" when I was a little girl. We were all equal. There were not race "labels" in Vala.
- My mother and father taught me that I was White and that was that. I was raised to believe that everyone is equal.
- We saw no color—nanny (woman who raised me) was African American.
- I was no better than anyone else. Race and culture were never discussed.
- Parents taught me that all people—regardless of race—are equal in the sight of God. We should never be mistreated because of race.
- Everyone is acceptable and the same. We didn't see race.

- Race was not discussed in the home. Everyone was accepted equally. Do unto others as you would have them to do unto you.

Note the White teachers' emphasis on family influences on their definitions of Whiteness. These teachers were raised to believe that everyone is the same and should be treated with equality. Consequently, they equate equality with the belief that race has no bearing on their lives as White people.

However, this logic does not confirm that race is unimportant to White people. As discussed, race does have meaning in the lives of White people. These responses just reveal the superficiality that disconnects White people from an authentic understanding of their own racial identities. In other words, White people lack an in-depth understanding of how their beliefs and actions are indeed shaped by membership in the White race.

Exploring My Whiteness

White teachers must go beyond their initial thoughts of what it means to be White. My suggestion would be a discussion of the following question: *What is the factor that reinforces White people's limited understanding of their own racial identity?*

The answer, of course, is oppression. If you recall, the first chapter of this book discussed the oppressive nature of Whiteness. Explained now is the role of this oppression in White people's lack of understanding their racial identities. In essence, America has a long history of rationalizing oppression (Feagin, 2013). The strategy has been to blend oppression with bureaucracy. Through the blending, oppression is then presented as an ordinary part of society. This blending contributed significantly to White people's indifferent views of slavery and Jim Crow oppression.

These same patterns of indifference and White superiority are embedded in American organizations and institutions. White people are often socialized to see this structure as a by-product of bureaucracy. As a result, racial disparities are not perceived as being an outgrowth of Whiteness, particularly the racist realities of White racial oppression. In addition, White people do not view Whiteness as a part of their own lives and racial identities.

To address the obliviousness, White teachers should be guided toward achieving deeper interpretations of their Whiteness. In reverting back to the research, consider the following vignette to White teachers (textbox 3.1):

Textbox 3.1

You indicated that Whiteness hasn't impacted your life as a White person. Your reasons for these beliefs are your parents' insistence on the same level of equality among all people. I am asking you to use the following questions to critique this racial socialization:

1. You formed your White racial identity in a White-framed society that has oppressed (use of supremacy, privilege, and fragility to devalue, terrorize, and marginalize) Black people.
   a. What does it mean that your racial identity was formed without any recognition of the racial significance of the White oppression of Black people?
   b. What does it mean that your racial identity was formed without any recognition of how your life as a White person is influenced by the White racial oppression of Black people?
   c. What would it mean if you connected your identity as a White person to the racial significance of the White racial oppression to Black people?
   d. Would this connection cause you to see the racial significance of being White in the context of the White racial oppression of Black people?
      d1. If yes, why and how?
      d2. If no, why not?

2. You formed your White racial identity in a White-framed society that confers White supremacy (superiority, power, dominance, and authority over Black people) on White people.
   a. What does it mean that your racial identity was formed without any recognition of the racial significance of White supremacy?
   b. What does it mean that your racial identity was formed without any recognition of the racial relevance of White supremacy to your life as a White person?
   c. What would it mean if you connected the racial significance of White supremacy to your identity as a White person?
   d. Would this connection cause you to see the racial relevance of White supremacy to your life as a White person?
      d1. If yes, why and how?
      d2. If no, why not?
3. You formed your White racial identity in a White-framed society that confers White privilege (obliviousness to race and White racial oppression) to only White people.
   a. What does it mean that your racial identity was formed without any recognition of the racial significance of White privilege?
   b. What does it mean that your racial identity was formed without any recognition of the racial relevance of White privilege to your own life as a White person?
   c. What would it mean if you connected the racial significance of White privilege to your identity as a White person?
   d. Would this connection cause you to see the racial relevance of White privilege to your life as a White person?

d1. If yes, why and how?

d2. If no, why not?

4. You formed your White racial identity in a White-framed society that confers White fragility (denial and minimization of the significance of race and White oppression) on White people.

   a. What does it mean that your racial identity was formed without any recognition of the racial significance of White fragility?

   b. What does it mean that your racial identity was formed without any recognition of the racial relevance of White fragility to your own life as a White person?

   c. What would it mean if you connected the racial significance of White fragility to your identity as a White person?

   d. Would this connection cause you to see the racial relevance of White fragility to your life as a White person?

   d1. If yes, why and how?

   d2. If no, why not?

Most White teachers are not able to answer these types of questions. That they can't answer the questions is not the problem. The problem is that like White people, White teachers ignore the relevance of the questions to their lives as White people.

Acknowledging My Whiteness

White teachers must acknowledge their status as White people with a limited understanding about race and racism (DiAngelo, 2012; Feagin, 2013). Their limitations are symptoms of White oppression. Born into a culture of White oppression, White people are socialized to ignore the oppressiveness of a White-framed society. Yet, they still inherit and internalize the characteristics of Whiteness. Granted, White people can and do experience issues related to race. In these instances, they are quick to point out the racial significance of the situation. But those issues will not be rooted in the unequal institutionalized racial power that benefits White people.

The more that White people minimize and disregard this system, the more they will unlikely understand how systemic racism functions in this country. Specifically, they will be less likely to recognize the power dynamic of oppression that mediates interactions between Whites and Blacks. For Whites, one implication of this relationship is the insulation from racial stress that plagues Black people. Another implication is the internalized sense of superiority and entitlement that guides White people's responses to matters of race.

White teachers should not use this information as a suggestion to feel guilty about their Whiteness. Instead, they should translate this knowledge into a platform for becoming more informed White people. Here White teachers understand that they and other White people do not have universal life experiences. In other words, White people are racial beings who do not transcend race. Like other people, White people's lives are shaped by race. Unlike others, White people are socially located atop society's racial hierarchy. With this location comes the disproportionate distribution of power, dominance, and control to the White race.

Conscientious White Person

Living My Whiteness

As White teachers develop racial consciousness, they must pursue the second part of White personhood—conscientious White people. Conscientiousness is living with the awareness of Whiteness as only one (not only one) form of cultural legitimacy in this country. The framework for such conscientiousness is featured below.

Framework for Living Whiteness in Conscientiousness

Respecting Racial Differences

White teachers are White people who have high regard for the racial differences of other racial groups. They display a deep understanding of how race creates different life experiences between White people and non-White people.

Accepting Racial Differences

White teachers are White people who understand that racial differences are not deficits—just differences. As such, White teachers are willing to see and name racial differences in ways that maintain the significance of being different.

Valuing Racial Differences

White teachers are White people who see the true worth and significance of the differences among people from other racial groups. The feeling is that there is significance in understanding the need for racial differences.

Exploring Differences

White teachers are White people who do not rely on Whiteness to make sense of the differences from other racial groups. Instead, they take the time and necessary steps to learn the authentic reasons for those differences. They then use those differences to make informed decisions for how to best interact with other racial groups.

To contextualize this framework, let's take a look at a recent professional development on Black culture.

The Talk

During a recent workshop on Black culture, teachers were provided with an article titled "The Talk." The article describes

African American parents' approaches to preparing African American children for interactions with the police. The article featured a cross section of African American parents' explanations of how they conduct "The Talk" with their children. The most common talking points were as follows:

1. Answer all questions in a clear and intelligible manner.
2. Keep your hands in a visible place.
3. Make no sudden moves. Instead, move only when instructed by the police.

Almost all of the Black parents indicated that they did not want to have these discussions with their children. However, they believed that Black children—especially Black males—were perceived as threats within the justice system. Therefore, the parents used "The Talk" to increase their children's chances of surviving encounters with the police.

Many African American teachers provided personal testimonies that reinforced the article. Afterward, many White teachers argued that their parents talked with them about interacting with the police. The teachers then indicated that they had or will have the same discussions with their children. No White teacher could explain the racial significance of their family discussions about the police. Yet many of the White teachers insisted that the "The Talk" applies to every racial group instead of just African American people.

With conscientiousness, these White teachers would have responded to African American teachers in the following way:

Exploring Differences

The White teachers use the article and Black teachers' comments to gain deeper insight about "The Talk." Thought-provoking questions could include but not be limited to the following:

1. What are some specific comments that are made to your children?
2. How do you choose the words and phrases to be expressed to your children?

3. How do you know when it's the best or right time to have "The Talk"?
4. What is the mood and emotion during the discussions with your children?

Through this inquiry, White teachers could experience "The Talk" as a teachable moment about a rite of passage within the Black experience.

Respecting Racial Differences

White teachers display high regard for differences between White people's and Black people's views of law enforcement. *Regard* means realizing that White people and Black people do have extremely different interactions with the police. As a result, White people and Black people have vastly different perceptions on how to interact with the police.

Accepting Racial Differences

White teachers do not view Black teachers' commentary as deficit views about police. They see the views as authentic feelings on guiding their children through a system built on bias, prejudice, and discrimination toward Black people.

Valuing Racial Differences

White teachers appreciate the differences between their perspectives and Black perspectives on talking with children about the police. The appreciation would be seen in their use of the article and commentary—instead of stereotypes—to better understand Black culture.

The revised edition shows White teachers who conscientiously removed superiority and entitlement from their consciousness. They were then able to see themselves as one of two racial groups who have different and valuable perspectives about the police.

Experience 2: Awakening to White Teachership

It is not enough to achieve the realization of White personhood. There is a need for White teachers to understand the racial significance of their identities as White teachers. The identity should be constructed around the following sights:

- Sight 1: White teachers are White people who are socialized by Whiteness.
- Sight 2: White teachers' approaches to teaching are rooted in the normalization of Whiteness.
- Sight 3: Whiteness has very real implications for the teaching practices of White teachers.
- Sight 4: Understanding the socialized normalization of Whiteness is essential to developing positive, multidimensional (open-ended) White teaching identities.

This book presents a model that cultivates this level of White-framed insightfulness within White teachers. The model consists of "Becoming a Conscious White Teacher" and "Becoming a Conscientious White Teacher." Both phases are centered on research, exploration, acknowledgment, and living. In the next section, there is a description of the model and accompanying phases.

Becoming a Conscious White Teacher

Researching Whiteness in My Teaching

White teachers must research the relevance of Whiteness to their roles as White teachers. The guiding questions for this search should be "What does it mean to be a White teacher?" and "How does being White impact your teaching?" This inquiry underscores White teachers' current connection of being White and a teacher. That is, we are able to gain an initial entry into how White teachers connect Whiteness to their teaching.

For example, consider a group of White teachers' descriptions of what it means to be a White teacher:

1. My race has nothing to do with me as a teacher.
2. Why do I need to consider my race when teaching? Should we even consider race when we teach?
3. Nothing. I am teacher of all students.
4. I have never thought about my race—I don't need to.
5. My race is irrelevant. It's my heart that counts as a teacher.
6. Nothing. When I step into a classroom, my "Whiteness" doesn't count. It's my teaching.
7. How should I know? I don't think about my color. I am not racist.
8. That's a question that has no relevance to my work as a teacher.
9. I am so doggoned tired of talking about race. Yes. I am White. But that doesn't have any bearing on how I teach. I love my kids and that's all that should count.
10. I don't see color—I just see kids.
11. Kids are kids—their color has no bearing on me as a White person or teacher.
12. Why would you even ask this question? Teaching is about learning—not my race.
13. I have students from all shapes and colors and I could care less about their color.
14. When you ask, "What does it mean to be a teacher of the human race?" I will answer this question for you.
15. Race doesn't matter—next question.
16. I don't pay attention to my color. I just pay attention to what I need to teach my kids.
17. I strive to be a very good teacher for students of all colors. So why should I look at my race?
18. I am a teacher, not a race.
19. Please don't try to categorize me by my race. Categorize me as Amy—just me.
20. I have never had any problems with my Hispanic children. They all love me. Not my race—but me.

Note the two sets of responses regarding White teachers' perception of the raced aspects of their positions as teachers. Some respondents believed that race is irrelevant to their position as teachers. Several respondents argued that race has no relevance to students.

On the other hand, race was used to signify the insignificance of race. As the main example, several respondents used students' race to minimize the significance of their own identities as White teachers. This approach speaks to White people's use of other races to confirm their racial innocence. Overall, both groups of responses reveal White teachers' deracialization of the meaning of Whiteness to their identities as teachers.

Exploring Whiteness in My Teaching

In this phase, White teachers are guided beyond surface explanations of being White. Discuss the following questions:

- What is the factor that reinforces White teachers' lack of recognizing Whiteness within their teaching?
- What does it mean to be a White teacher in a system that mimics society's oppression of (use of supremacy, privilege, and fragility to devalue, terrorize, and marginalize) Black people?

Now remember that in the White Personhood discussion, similar questions revealed White teachers' lack of personal racial awareness within the broader context of our White society. In this section, the same dynamic is very much at play with a lack of White teacher identity awareness. The other contributing factor to this situation is the unawareness of the oppressive nature of Whiteness within schools.

In essence, Whiteness has always been and is still a pervasive force of oppression in school systems (Dixson & Rousseau, 2005; Ladson-Billings & Tate, 1995; Yosso, 2005). A microcosm of society, schools prioritize White culture over the cultures of other racial groups. For example, schools are based on teaching and learning practices that mirror White-framed depictions of normality. The school curriculum overlooks people of color while upholding positive, sanitized depictions of White people. In addition, research continues to show that all forms of standardized tests are normed on White culture (Ladson-Billings, 1998).

From a humanistic standpoint, White students are still the focal point of academic and social activities and experiences. More recently, White students are often tracked toward gifted and talented and honors programs. Black students, however, are more likely to be placed in general education or special education classes.

Yet, there is virtually no discussion about schools' central emphasis on Whiteness. Instead, schools are viewed as normally and properly White-sanctioned institutions. White teachers frame the bureaucracy as a meritocracy (Villegas & Lucas, 2002).

They continually argue that regardless of race, all students have the same opportunities to achieve success in schools. As long as students work hard, they have the same opportunities to achieve success in school. As long as students take personal responsibility for themselves, they have the same opportunities to achieve success in school. Translation: as long as there is less regard for race, all children have the same opportunities to achieve success in school.

The irony is that White teachers do hold less regard for the race of African American students. The evidence is in the previously discussed supremacy, fragility, and privilege toward African American students. But in a system that disguises Whiteness, White teachers will not automatically examine their regard for Black children. They will not see how their regard contributes to Black children's location on the downside of the Black-White opportunity gap in schools. Their teaching identities will remain constructed around the false premise of the same advantages for students of all racial groups.

In response to their obliviousness, guide White teachers toward a deeper inquiry into the role of Whiteness in their interactions with African American students. Listed below are some questions that should be used for this inquiry.

1. To what extent do you recognize the relationship between White supremacy and your deficit thoughts of Black students?

2. To what extent do you recognize the relationship between White privilege and your dismissal of specific approaches to understanding Black students?
3. To what extent do you recognize the relationship between White fragility and your color-blind thoughts of Black students?

The questions are not designed to pressure White teachers into correct responses about the connection between their race and position as teachers. The questions are a segue into inspiring White teachers into seeing the racialized aspects of their teaching identities.

Acknowledging Whiteness in My Teaching

The acknowledgment of teaching with Whiteness should be situated in the following definition of the term *racism*, which is defined as culturally sanctioned beliefs that, regardless of the intentions involved, defend the advantages Whites have because of the subordinated positions of racial minorities (Wellman, 1977).

In other words, White teachers must acknowledge that they do operate in a system that reflects the broader White racialized society. An excellent analogy that crystallizes the school-society connection is Lisa Delpit's (1988, 2006) culture of power theory.

Delpit argues that schools are a culture of power that shapes the experiences of students. Textbox 3.2 presents the basic tenets and interpretation of her theory.

Textbox 3.2.

Tenet 1: Issues of power are enacted in classrooms.
Adapted Racialized Interpretation: Schools and classrooms possess the power to determine the criteria for intelligence. The criteria are based on textbooks, curricula, and other norms shaped by a White-framed point of view.

Tenet 2: There are codes or rules for participating in power.
Adapted Racialized Interpretation: Students receive access to this power by assimilating into White-framed norms of interaction. Some examples of rule following are speaking, dressing, writing, and thinking.

Tenet 3: The rules of the culture of power are a reflection of the rules of the culture of those who have power.
Adapted Racialized Interpretation: Schools are based on White culture, the most powerful cultural group in the United States.

Tenet 4: If you are not already a participant in the culture of power, being told explicitly the rules of that culture makes acquiring power easier.
Adapted Racialized Interpretation: African American children are not natural inhabitants of the White-framed operations of school. One of the main reasons is that they are taught by White teachers, whose socialization matches the White framing of schools. White teachers make implicit expectations for African American students. The lack of explicit rules creates a cultural breakdown and buildup of tension between these two culturally different groups.

Tenet 5: Those with power are frequently least aware of—or least willing to acknowledge—its existence.
Adapted Racialized Interpretation: White teachers do not recognize the White-framed culture of power within schools and classrooms. Black students do not define school as a culture of power that is rooted in Whiteness. Observe and feel these students' strong visceral reactions to the system's existence.

The acknowledgment of the cultural power of schools does not mean that White teachers are the reason for every school-related failure of African American students. The acknowledgment presents White teachers with the opportunity to analyze their complicity in maintaining the structures that disenfranchise Black students. That is, White teachers can now look closely at how they perpetuate Whiteness and racism during interactions with non-White students. These analyses can inform them of how their identities impact the classroom.

Conscientious White Teacher

Living Whiteness in My Teaching

As White teachers progress toward race-conscious teaching, they must infuse their performances with conscientiousness. Conscientiousness is living with the awareness of Whiteness as only one (not only one) form of cultural legitimacy in the classroom. The selection below presents a framework for demonstrating this conscientiousness.

Framework for Conscientious Identity

White teachers must engage in two actions to develop conscientiousness toward African American students. The actions are abandoning complicity and receiving difference. The next section discusses how White teachers should address these actions.

Abandoning Complicity

White teachers must abandon their complicity in color blindness and deficit thinking. As indicated, these color blindness and deficit thoughts are significant barriers to their effectiveness with African American students. The following section provides insight on how White teachers can address these issues.

Seeing Race. White teachers can benefit in many ways from seeing the race of their African American students. Consider the following story as an introduction to the first benefit. One day, I observed a White teacher stand in front of a class and say, "I don't see color in this classroom." She continued, "I just see humans." Just as the classroom became silent, an African American male yelled, "Then you don't see me."

The students' words mean that by seeing race, White teachers can validate the cultural backgrounds of their African American students. The significance of this benefit is that race is intimately tied to the identities, culture, and heritage of African American people. African American children bring this racialization to schools. Thus, overlooking the significance of race is dismissing a significant part of African American children's identities. As another benefit, seeing race provides White teachers with insight on the ways in which racism impacts African American children. Many African American children experience negative racial situations in schools, especially predominantly White schools. Their stories should be heard, processed, and thoroughly addressed by school leaders.

Unfortunately, African American children often lack a healthy outlet for processing these experiences. On the rare occasions of openly discussing the situations, Black students are viewed by White teachers as "playing the race card." In some instances, White teachers try to convince Black students that race had no role in their racially traumatic experiences. These responses do not decrease the likelihood of African American students experiencing racially stressed situations. Over time, they just learn to internalize their racial oppression.

Finally, when White teachers see race, they can begin to understand the racist nature of the color-blind ideology. Simply put, color blindness does not end racism. To understand the essence of this simplicity, let's take a complex look at color blindness and White people. An ideal color-blind society is based on the belief that race is not an issue. This belief works well for White people, who are not racialized in negative or disadvantaged ways. Black people, on the other hand, regularly experience race-based difficulties in their lives.

Thus, White people are almost always in the position to respond to racial stress in two ways. One way is to ignore the racism with color blindness. The second way is to use color blindness to deny the daily racial issues of African American people. Simply put, color blindness does not end racism. White teachers who understand this dynamic are better able to address racism in their classrooms.

Dismantling Deficits. White teachers must address deficit thinking in two specific ways. First, they must continue to look closely at how Whiteness plays out in their school culture. The reason is that, although well intentioned, many White teachers are unaware of the deeper pathological dimensions of their schools. These dimensions do influence their identities and practices in the classroom. Without examining this culture, White teachers remain immersed in the web of deficit ideologies that shortchange African American students.

Second, White teachers must realize that African American students do bring capital to school. *Capital* is defined as the ways in which goods and resources are used to achieve upward mobility. There are three major forms of capital. *Economic capital* is money, property, and other assets. *Social capital* is characterized as the networks of connections, influence, and support that are based on group membership and contacts. *Cultural capital* describes the shared process and exchanges within a specific community. The next chapter provides a comprehensive review of the cultural capital of Black children. For now, this chapter argues that this capital must be viewed as an asset to African American children's schooling experiences.

Receiving Difference

White teachers are now able to demonstrate receptiveness to African American students. Receptiveness is a multi-pronged approach to affirming African American students. The section below presents receptiveness in terms of racial awareness and racial affirmation.

1. Racial Awareness: White teachers realize that race is an influential factor of African American students' responses to schools. They also consider the ways in which schools

contribute to the racial identity development of African American students. The awareness prompts White teachers to further reflect on how their racial socialization impacts African American students' experiences in the classroom.

2. Racial Affirmation: White teachers move beyond the need to use Whiteness as the only criteria for teaching African American students. They are receptive to ideas and resources that are culturally relevant/responsive to African American students.

Conclusion

This chapter made an argument for decentering Whiteness to occur within White teachers. The main part of my case is for White teachers to awaken to the personal and professional realization of having White identities. The awakening will require White teachers to pursue a personal identity development toward seeing themselves as White people. The point of the professional identity development is realizing that the Whiteness in the White person shapes the Whiteness in the White teacher.

This approach to identity development allows for Whiteness to become a positive part of White teachers. But awakening via White identity development should not become a stagnant process. As White people, White teachers are intimately linked and complicit in a historical arrangement of dominance that routinely favors White over other racial hues. Therefore, awakening to Whiteness should be a reoccurrence of ever-developing identity development analyses within White teachers. This process should further nurture an ever-developing application of racial awareness toward African American students. In the next chapter of this book, this discussion becomes a part of the culturally specific framework for teaching African American students.

4

A Relational Passport to Black Student Achievement

The first part of this book was spent on analyzing Whiteness, White teachers, and White orientations to teaching. With this chapter, the focus shifts to providing White teachers with a framework for teaching African American students. This requires a description of Blackness as it relates to Black children.

Blackness is a shared set of experiences that have created a culturally relevant, socio-emotional bond among Black people. The experiences are as follows:

1. There is an African experience and an American experience that have historically shaped the Black existence in America.
2. Black people have a heritage of sharing the African experience and American experience within and between generations of Black people.
3. Over time, history and heritage have created a racial identity development experience that is unique to Black people.

The only way for White teachers to truly grasp these points is by seeing their daily relevance to African American children. When the first Blacks arrived in America, they brought a rich West African heritage with them (Nobles, 1972). Over time,

Black people encountered experiences that altered certain aspects of their African heritage (Nobles, 1972, 1974, 1980). But African heritage continues to anchor the lives of African American people (Asante, 1987; Boykin, 1983; Nobles, 1985).

For example, A. Wade Boykin (1983) articulated nine Afrocentric dimensions of Black culture that are rooted in the West African tradition.

Afrocentric Dimensions of Black Culture

- Spirituality: the belief that religious forces are always at play in the lives of people. As a result, life situations happen for very significant nonmaterial reasons.
- Harmony: the belief that a person's actions are linked to his/her environment.
- Affect: the integrated demonstrations of heightened levels of sensitivity to the expression of emotions and feelings.
- Verve: a psychological preference for variability and intensity in stimulation, especially in movement.
- Movement: an orientation to life that is based on the coordinated interconnectedness of rhythm and music.
- Communalism: a social interdependence of people that prioritizes the group over the individual.
- Expressive Individualism: the development of a distinctive and often spontaneous style of self-expression.
- Orality: the emphasis on using speaking as an aural model of communication.
- Social Time Perspective: The belief that the actual event is more important than the time for starting the event.

These descriptions underscore Africa's relevance as the original home culture for Black people. The point here is that Black culture is not a manufactured, adapted version of Eurocentric ideals. Instead, Black society is very much influenced by African-based values, attitudes, traditions, and beliefs.

That said, the question now becomes "What does it take for Blackness to become a significant part of how Black children are taught by White teachers?" The answer: cultural relevance. By now, most educators have heard of cultural relevance. But this chapter will still provide a few well-researched definitions of this term.

1. *Cultural relevance* is "a pedagogy that empowers students intellectually, socially, emotionally, and politically by using cultural referents to impart knowledge, skills, and attitudes" (Ladson-Billings, 1994, pp. 17–18).
2. *Cultural relevance* is a pedagogy that uses cultural knowledge, prior experiences, frames of reference, and performance styles of ethnically diverse students to make learning more relevant to and effective for culturally diverse students (Gay, 2000).

These descriptions of cultural relevance will not be redefined. Instead, they will be discussed in accordance to mindfulness and responsiveness—ideas that point to the recurring White-Black theme of this book.

Responsiveness is the ability to draw from African American students' backgrounds to effectively teach and reach them. Mindfulness is the mind-set needed to effectively maintain the background as the guide for addressing African American students. With a developed White racial identity, White teachers must envision the following level of mindfulness:

1. Blackness is embraced by White teachers as the central focus of understanding African American students. That is, Black culture is the main lens for understanding how to connect Black children to achievement.
2. Whiteness is placed in a twofold configuration to endorse the centrality of Blackness. First, White teachers' backgrounds are placed in the background. Second, White teachers' backgrounds are the supportive—not deciding—part of establishing common ground with African American students.

Overall, mindfulness and responsiveness must be integrated into all aspects of White teachers' interactions with Black children. The remainder of this chapter highlights this process for relationship building.

A Relational Passport to Black Student Achievement

An important part to the schooling experiences of African American students is relationships with teachers. My use of the term *relationship* denotes a mutually respectful connection between teachers and students. In the sections below, I present a framework specifically for White teachers to use for achieving this connection with African American students.

The Principle

What Must White teachers Be Mindful of to Build Authentic Relationships with African American Students?

White teachers must realize that Black students operate with a highly interpersonal regard for cross-racial encounters. A significant aspect of this regard is a focus on culturally sensitive connections. In school settings, such connections must be made with teachers. Listed below is research-based support for this principle:

- When African American students know they are cared for, it means they are in relationships with teachers (Noddings, 1992).
- African American students are more influenced by authority figures, such as teachers, than dominant culture students (Sizemore, 1981; Vasquez, 1988).
- Teachers' perceptions of what African American children can do are often stronger than African American chil-

dren's perceptions of what they can do (Slaughter-Defoe & Carlson, 1996; Ware, 2002, 2006).

- Whereas White students attributed success to their own abilities, Black students are more likely to link success to their connection with teachers (Mooney & Thornton, 1999).
- Unlike White students, African American students cite student-teacher relationships as the most important dimension of school climate (Sizemore, 1981; Slaughter-Defoe & Carlson, 1996).

Why Is This Understanding Specific to African American Students?

From an Afrocentric perspective, African American children's need for relationship is rooted in a communal emphasis on the group instead of the individual. Consequently, they enter school with a strong social expectation for experiencing a similar connection to teachers.

A powerful rationale of the Americanized perspective is featured in *Young, Gifted, and Black: Promoting High Achievement among African-American Students* (Perry, Steele, Hilliard, 2004). Here Theresa Perry draws an insightful parallel between Blackness in schools and Blackness in America. Listed below are the key points of her comparison.

- Being a member of a racial caste group brings with it some challenges for making an ongoing commitment to achievement.
- Society's ideology of intellectual inferiority also fundamentally affects commitment to achievement over time.
- African Americans are the only racial group to be the subject of a persistent, well-articulated, and unabated ideology about their mental incompetence.
- Schools do not have spaces that are intentionally organized to forge identities of African American students as achievers.
- Schools do not provide spaces that intentionally buffer African American students from the day-to-day experiences

of racism in the school or from the explicit and subtle impact of the ideology of Black intellectual inferiority.
- Schools are not likely to have a narrative that is counter to the narrative of "openness and opportunity," which talks about Black achievement in the face of constraints and limits.
- Schools make few attempts to systematically organize occasions to create desire, to inspire hope, and to develop and sustain effort optimism or to socialize students to the behaviors that are necessary for them to be achievers.
- There is little to no discussion about how racism in and out of schools affects effort optimism.
- African American parents are the first generation of African Americans to navigate racism in a supposedly "open and integrated" society. Yet they may still struggle with passing these skills on to their children (p. 105).

Collectively, Afrocentric and Americanized perspectives make relationship building a highly racialized prerequisite to African American student success. As such, White teachers must use this cultural relevance to make meaningful connections with these students.

The Approach

How Can White Teachers Translate This Mindfulness into Successful Relationship Building with African American Students?

Successful relationship building entails White teachers' achievement of solidarity with African American students. *Solidarity* is defined as culturally relevant closeness between White teachers and African American students. To achieve this level of closeness, White teachers must apply humble insight, comprehensive listening, and empathetic interpretation toward Black children. In the sections that follow, a detailed description of each application is provided.

Humble Insight

Humble insight is White teachers' commitment to recognizing African American students in their entirety. To understand this context for recognition, consider the opening activity of my workshop "Seeing African American Students":

First, provide White teachers with the chart below (table 4.1):

Ask the teachers to identify the examples that are commonly observed among their African American students. They must then assign a positive rating (+) or negative rating (−) to the examples. Nearly all of these examples are common among African American students. In addition, most of the examples receive negative ratings (see table 4.1).

Then engage teachers in a discussion of the chart. Explain that the chart provides examples of Communalism (column A), Movement (column B), Verve (column C), Expressive Individualism (column D), Orality (column E), and Affect (column F). Also discussed is the Afrocentric relevance of these dimensions to African American children. After this discussion, the teachers slowly but surely develop a positive view of the examples.

The point is that these characteristics represent the humanity of Black children. As such, much of Black children's humanization can be attributed to the richness of their race-specific cultural experiences. Thus, to relate to African American children, White teachers must step back far enough to see Blackness for all of its humanity.

Comprehensive Listening

Comprehensive listening is the use of listening to understand African American students. One part of understanding is getting to know African American students. Here teachers learn about Black students—their families, friends, hobbies, preferences, fears, interests, and aspirations. The intent is to learn about the personal aspects of African American students' lives. In addition, teachers can share their common experiences.

Table 4.1.

Column A	Column B	Column C
-1. Will watch out for each other right away.	-1. Grand, full-body movements.	1. Love rhythm and movement with learning.
-2. Will mostly stick together and take/back up for each other.	-2. Would rather be moving than sitting.	-2. Will drum on tables while learning.
-3. Will defend one another.	-3. Can't sit still, like to dance, kinesthetic learners.	-3. Will get restless after sitting at desks a long time.
-4. Will engage in excited conversations at lunch or in the halls.	-4. Like activities that have a lot of movement.	4. Respond favorably to activities that require energy and thinking.
5. Prefer to eat/walk/work within the African American group.	-5. Project a certain flow in their movement.	5. Can focus on their work while looking at what others are doing.
6. Black students are very close friends and want to sit next to other African American students in class.	-6. Like drama, acting out in plays—planning dancing, etc.	-6. Can multitask with energy.
7. So many seem to know each other's family and relatives—The Hang Out.	-7. Always drumming, tapping, sing out.	-7. Have higher levels of environmental responsiveness.
8. Doing things based on family or friend behaviors.	-8. Musically/rhythmically inclined.	
-9. When one Black student says something, that student will turn to another Black student for validation and vice versa.	-9. Can easily dance/tap out complex patterns and rhythms	
10. Will often respond as a group to the teacher's instruction.	-10. Often out of seat without permission.	

Column D	Column E	Column F
-1. Distinct walk/gait—even if rule says to walk a certain way.	1. Full of elaborate stories—need to communicate—talk.	-1. Tend to be more emotional about discipline.
-2. Walk with "swag" (puffed-up image).	2. Love to relate personal stories.	-2. Strong emotional responses to criticism and praise.
3. Very clean dress, matching accessories.	-3. Prefer to talk rather than write.	-3. React emotionally to teacher instruction or peer responses.
-4. Displays of very distinct dress/hairstyles.	4. Love to talk and do activities that involve talking to partners, groups.	-4. Use a high level of emotion, especially when explaining an idea.
5. Will use their clothes and hair to show their confidence in being different.	-5. Shout out frequently.	-5. Act out emotions when a teacher asks them to follow directions or stay quiet.
-6. Can express themselves like no other.	6. Volunteer answers in whole group.	-6. Communicate with intensity when contributing to group discussions.
-7. Don't normally like to go with the flow, fit in.	-7. Has a need to answer the loudest (and first).	-7. Quick to get upset.
-8. Will use certain ways to make sure they are heard.	-8. Tend to think out loud.	-8. Will react very personally to most things related to themselves.
-9. Constant use of physical gestures when talking and walking.	-9. Louder expression for all to hear.	-9. Will take things very personally.
	-10. Often verbally communicate needs / feelings in a spontaneous way.	

But basic commonalities do not lead to the common ground that is often missing between White teachers and African American students. Common ground is based on White teachers' willingness to satisfy Black students' pressing need to be heard by teachers. Such urgency often entails school-related situations that involve teachers.

Let me give you a classic elementary school example. An African American male is bothering another student. The other student responds to the African American male by saying, "You're stupid." A back-and-forth name calling develops into a heated exchange between the two students.

The White teacher intervenes and stops the exchange. She then asks both students to explain the reason for the name calling. After hearing both perspectives, the White teacher reprimands both students. Because of starting the disturbance, the African American male also loses recess.

The African American male attempts to but is denied an opportunity to know why he is being denied recess. The White teacher is not required to provide the African American male with an explanation. But suppressing the African American male's voice determined the following outcome: the African American male yelled and screamed "You're not fair!" "You don't like me!" and "I hate this class!" The White teacher then calls security to remove the African American male from the classroom.

The White teacher knew the African American male student—but not in a way to elicit the desired response to the punishment. As such, let's consider a hypothetical. The White teacher did indeed take the time to listen to the African American male. In addition, the teacher explained the reason for denying recess to the African American male student. There's no guarantee that the African American male wouldn't show any disappointment about the teacher's decision. After being heard, the African American male would be less likely to become belligerent toward the teacher.

The main idea is there are significant benefits to listening to African American children. First, a culturally relevant listening ear convinces Black children that their thoughts, ideas, and feelings are important. Second, listening is the segue to helping Black children feel safe, cared for, and respected in school. Third, African American children know that at least one adult in the school cares about them. This level of care causes African American students to think of the classroom as a nonjudgmental and supportive environment.

Having acquired this connection, Black children are more likely to work toward living up to teacher expectations.

From an academic standpoint, these students will work harder for teachers who listen to them. They will also follow teachers' procedures and guidelines for discipline. African American children are also more likely to talk through the major issues with teachers.

Empathetic Interpretation

Empathetic interpretation is the use of accurate information to make sense of situations that may warrant empathy. Empathy and interpretation are two significant components to enhancing White teachers' relationships with Black students. Yet White teachers often profess to show more empathy than they actually do for students of color (Delgado, 1996; Marx & Pray, 2011). Their display is termed false empathy. This empathy is based on judgments and assumptions that emanate from misinformed perspectives, prejudices, and biases of the student. In the end, the teacher marginalizes and pathologizes the student.

Here's a representative sample of how false empathy influenced a White teacher's interaction with an African American student: During the first semester of the school year, Valisha excels in Betty's science class. She participates in class discussions. Her work is always submitted in a timely manner. Valisha also follows all classroom procedures. In short, Valisha is a model student.

After the Christmas holidays, Betty notices a change in Valisha's behavior. Valisha is now withdrawn from class. She fails to complete all assignments. Once a model student, she is now failing to follow class procedures.

One day, while talking to the counselor, Betty learns that Valisha's parents were going through a marital separation. As a result, Betty's attitude changes toward Valisha. She extends the time allowed for Valisha to complete assignments. In addition, Valisha is now mostly warned for displaying inappropriate behavior.

Consequently, Valisha continues to underperform in Betty's class. She gives little effort toward completing assignments. She has also now become defiant toward Betty's expectations for following class procedures.

I learned this information upon being asked to help Betty connect with Valisha. According to Betty, the following logic influenced how she approached Valisha:

1. Valisha's parents are going through a separation, which will remove father from the home.
2. Fatherless families are a horrible part and problem within African American communities.
3. It is horrible for children to experience a parental separation, especially with the removal of the father from the home.
4. Valisha must be having horrible experiences with her parental separation and having no father in the home.
5. The parental separation and fatherlessness must be the main cause of Valisha's negative behaviors in my classroom.

Here we see the negative impact of false empathy on a White teacher's response to an African American student. Drawing from White perspectives on Black families, Betty makes two major assumptions about Valisha. First, Valisha will no longer have a father figure in her life. Second, Valisha will now have a negative home life. Because of these assumptions, Betty responded to Valisha's behavior with low expectations. Said another way, Betty pathologized Valisha and called it empathy.

Now balance Betty's interpretation with outcomes of a discussion between Betty, Valisha, the counselor, and Valisha's mother and father. Valisha's parents were briefly separated but reconciled their relationship. The separation had no bearing on Valisha's behavior in Betty's class. The crux of the matter was Valisha's unhealthy attempt to gain the interest of a male student.

The student had a reputation for associating with girls who had no interest in school. Consequently, Valisha decided that after Christmas, she would dumb down to getting his attention. Sure enough, Valisha began the spring semester with a continuation of excellence in her classes. But she was unfocused and defiant in Betty's class. The reason is that Valisha and the male student were both in Betty's classroom.

Let's consider another version of this situation. Here Betty talked to Valisha and learned that her performance was indeed influenced by her parents' separation. What would be an empathetic interpretative approach for supporting Valisha? Based on my work with White teachers, I propose a four-step model for empathetic interpretation. Within the model is an empathetic interpretative approach to relating to Valisha.

Step 1: The White teacher identifies the situation that may warrant the need to empathize with the Black student.

Description: Betty has learned that Valisha's performance is impacted by her parents' separation.

Step 2: The White teacher considers the situation from a realistic but hopeful perspective.

Description: In the original narrative, Betty made assumptions about the relevance of parental separation to Valisha's behavior. In this narrative, Betty may still make the same assumptions regarding Valisha's situation. Therefore, I suggest she use the following guide to reconsider that thought process:

A. **Valisha's parents are going through a separation, which will remove the father from the home.**
   Questions for Reconsideration
   - What evidence suggests that Valisha will live with her mother?
   - What evidence confirms that Valisha's father will no longer have a presence in the home?

B. **Fatherless families are a horrible part and problem within African American communities.**
   Questions for Reconsideration

- What evidence shows that fatherless families are an issue in African American communities?
- What evidence supports the rationale for equating a fatherless family with no father in the home?

C. **It is horrible for children to experience a parental separation, especially with the removal of the father from the home.**

Questions for Reconsideration

- What evidence suggests that parental separation is an overwhelmingly horrible experience for children?

D. **Valisha must be having horrible experiences with her parental separation and having no father in the home.**

Questions for Reconsideration

- What evidence suggests that parental separation has created a horrible home life for Valisha?
- What evidence suggests that living without a father has created a horrible home life for Valisha?

E. **The parental separation and fatherlessness must be the main cause of Valisha's negative behaviors in my classroom.**

Questions for Reconsideration

- What evidence suggests that parental separation is the sole cause of Valisha's underperformance in Betty's classroom?

With this reflection, Betty would be less likely to pathologize Valisha's experience.

Step 3: The White teacher engages the Black student in more discussions about how he/she is affected by the situation.

Description: Betty revisits the parental situation with Valisha. This time, Betty determines the extent to which Valisha is affected by her parents' separation.

Step 4: Using the discussions as a guide, the White teacher applies the most appropriate level of sympathy and compassion toward the Black student. The focus of the empathy is the

overall welfare of the Black student. Listed below are the main components of this process:

A. Building the Black child's self esteem
B. Building the Black child's confidence to manage the situation
C. Maintaining expectations for the Black child to fulfill school-related obligations

Description: Betty feels for and with Valisha. She is available to Valisha on an as-needed basis. She still insists that Valisha resumes participation in all aspects of class. She only accepts assignments that are submitted on time. Valisha would be reacclimatized to following the classroom guidelines. Suffice it here to say that Valisha would be required to be an accountable student.

These steps may or may not inspire Valisha to return to her original performance in science. But what is for sure is Betty's informed application of care and concern toward empathizing with Valisha. Such an approach highlights a culturally relevant use of empathy to be used by White teachers to connect with African American students.

The Sample

What Other Evidence Shows Relationship Building as an Effective Way for White Teachers to Connect with African American Students?

A few years ago, I was asked to assist a high school with recruiting Black students into Advanced Placement (AP) courses. The principal indicated that a number of Black students were qualified for enrollment in the courses. However, they were not taking advantage of enrollment opportunities.

After accepting the invitation, I looked at the achievement data for African American students. I found that 40 Black students had the grades to enroll in AP courses. Of this population, there were 17 African American males and 23 African American females. This population consisted of 14 sophomores, 16 juniors, and 10 seniors. All of the students had excellent grades and at least a 3.5 GPA.

Excited, I immediately coordinated one-on-one interviews with the students. Over a three-week period, I conducted the interviews to determine the students' reasons for not enrolling in AP courses. The outcomes of the interviews are as follows:

- 17 students had never heard of AP courses.
- 8 students were just not interested in AP courses.
- 15 students were informed that AP courses were stressful. Therefore, they didn't want to add challenging courses to their schedules.

After sharing the results with the principal, I was asked to develop at least three recommendations for recruiting the students into AP courses. I would also discuss the plan with Becky, a White female assistant principal who was primarily responsible for curriculum and instruction.

I invited the students to an "AP Meet and Greet"! I would use the event to apprise the students of AP courses. In addition, the students would then be asked to attend one additional session on registering for AP courses for the upcoming school year.

Only 15 African American students attended the "AP Meet and Greet." I explained the AP program to the students. The students also attended the second session. But their questions had little to do with either registration or clarification. The students spent the session explaining their fears and concerns with enrolling in AP courses. In their minds, AP courses were specifically designed for White students.

The students reasoned that White students represented the majority of the student enrollment in AP courses. They also provided numerous examples of how White students were routinely treated better than Black students. One of the African American girls stated, "There is no way in hell that an AP teacher would see me as an equal to the White kids in those classes!"

During my return flight home, I continued to try and make sense of the students' testimonies and perceptions of AP courses.

Upon landing at the airport, I finally made the connection—race was the reason for low Black student enrollment in AP courses. As such, a conventional "Just Do It" response would not convince these African American students to enroll in AP courses. I needed to use a relational approach to get the students to agree to this commitment.

The following week, I refocused my initial intentions into a culturally relevant approach for recruiting African American students into AP courses. Specifically, I developed four discussions on Blackness, success, and achievement. Each discussion, which consisted of two sessions, was characterized by the following theme: Because of Black people's brilliance, Black students belonged in courses that emphasized excellence in achievement. Listed below are the key points for these discussions.

Discussion 1: "Education, Success, and Pathways"

Students were informed that because of their race and intelligence, they belong in AP courses. They were then engaged in developing pathways to success. The pathways were their ideas of the different ways in which they could achieve success in and beyond high school.

To put structure to strategy, I provided the students with the following pieces of butcher paper:

a short piece of paper
a long piece of paper

The students wrote "Short-Term Success" on the short piece paper. They wrote "Long-Term Success" on the long piece of paper. The students listed the activities conducive to temporary success on the "short-term" paper. Their "long-term" papers featured the activities that would lead to permanent success. A variety of responses were listed on both pieces of paper.

Upon comparing the responses, the students noticed a significant difference between the papers. Nearly all of the activities on the "long-term" papers required the achievement of an education. But the majority of the activities on the "long-term" papers did not require any level of education.

Through this activity, the students learned that short-term paths don't lead to long-term success. Long-term paths are designed to elicit short-term success.

Most important, education is a long-term but worthwhile endeavor.

Discussion 2: "The Gifts, Dreams, and Hopes of Black Legacy"

I started the session by presenting the students with the following quote:

> Bringing the gifts that my ancestors gave, I am the dream and the hope of the slave. I rise I rise I rise.
>
> — Maya Angelou "Still I Rise" (Angelou, 1978)

I then asked students to identify the words that resonate with them. The top three words were *gifts*, *dream*, and *hope*. Using their words as a guide, we explored the historical legacy of the Black experience in America. We reviewed pictures, readings, and quotes from the slavery, segregation, and Jim Crow eras.

The images and words informed the students of Blacks' use of perseverance and pride to overcome their struggles in America. Because of this legacy, they, as African American students, represented the gifts, dreams, and hopes of the Black race. As such, they must use this legacy to improve their lives with an advanced education.

Discussion 3: "Excellence in Black"

The students and I discussed the ways in which Black people have excelled in America. We talked about Blacks who succeed in different genres and industries. Students also reviewed pictures and quotes from famous Black Americans such as James Baldwin, Madam C. J. Walker, Harriet Tubman, and Mae Jemison.

They were especially impressed with Charles Drew's story. Evidence to this effect could be seen in our spirited discussion around Dr. Drew's quote on excellence. It reads: *"Excellence of performance will transcend artificial barriers created by man."*

I asked the students to share their perspectives about the quote. The students immediately deduced that race has no bearing on the ability to achieve excellence. One student yelled, "I'm just as good as any White student at this school." Another student responded by saying, "Word. Any student for that matter!" All of the students nodded in agreement.

I purposely steered the discussion toward educational excellence. The reason is that I wanted the students to feel that Black excellence transcended sports and entertainment. Overall, my goal was for students to see that, as Black people, they already possess the ability to excel in achievement.

Discussion Four: "Young, Gifted, and Black Is Where It's At"

This discussion focused on spotlighting the excellence in the students. I first provided students with a copy of Nina Simone's song "To Be Young, Gifted and Black" I used the lyrics to inform students that success is waiting for them. We discussed the need to first believe that they really possess the "it" factor to be successful. To sustain this point, I provided the students with the following chart visual (see table 4.2):

Table 4.2.

Time	Mind	Pedigree
Young	Gifted	Black
Prime	GPA	Royalty

I then challenged the students to organize the words into belief statements regarding their youth, intelligence, and race. Here are some examples from the activity.

Young (Youth)

- "It is my time to shine and I will do so with excellence."
- "I'm in the prime of my life to do anything I want to do."

- "John is the name, prime time for success is the game."
- "Time will never be up for my pursuit of achievement."

Gifted (Intelligence)

- "With my mind, I will continue to show Great Passion for Academics."
- "I am smart, and I got the GPA to prove it."
- "My mind is not a waste, but a way to pace myself as I do what I set out to do."
- "My mind and GPA is what will pave the way to achievement."

Black (Race)

- "I'm not more royal than anyone, but respect my pedigree."
- "I come from royalty, meaning I am destined to succeed."
- "I am the pedigree that represents hopes and dreams."
- "I can do what I see with my pedigree."

The students shared and responded to each other's sentences. They also realized that "Young, Gifted, and Black" was not just a title. The phrase was also a worldview that could propel them to greatness and achievement.

* * *

At the conclusion of the last session, Becky and I planned to talk with the students about AP courses. Becky opened the discussion by talking about AP courses. But we quickly sensed nervousness among the students. Becky then stopped talking and asked the students to share their feelings.

The students indicated that because of the sessions on Blackness, they realized that they were worthy of being in AP courses. Yet they still did not know enough about the courses. The students were therefore unsure of whether or not they could succeed in an AP environment.

Immediately after the meeting, Becky asked me to come to her office. As soon as I arrived at her office, she said, "Mack, I get it now." She continued, "Now that I've met the students and with me being the only White person in the room just now, all of our talks about race and these students make better sense to me."

Becky then stated, "We can't just expect most of our Black students to just go into AP courses." She further said, "We must create an entry for them to get into AP."

I then said, "Great! What are you thinking, Becky?"

Becky responded by saying, "We must add a step that will further show these Black students that they do indeed belong in AP!" Just prior to the Christmas break, we determined that the students needed to experience AP courses.

At the beginning of the second semester, Becky and I guided students through two activities. The first activity was classroom observations. Becky arranged for the students to make six 30-minute observations of the AP course that interested them. She or I accompanied the students on the first three observations. The students completed the remaining three visits by themselves.

During each observation, the students took notes of course activities. Becky then debriefed each student, offering additional ideas for the next observations. The second activity was a mixer. For two hours, our students talked with students who were enrolled in AP courses. They also talked with AP teachers about expectations and best practices for achieving success in their classes.

After the students completed these activities, Becky and I talked with them about AP courses. Four students indicated that they were no longer interested in enrolling in AP courses. The remaining 10 students indicated that they would sign up for AP courses.

Becky then coordinated sign-up times with the students' counselors. The students met with their counselors and received additional information about their preselected AP courses. Afterward, they signed up for AP courses.

This achievement highlights the importance of cultural relevance to recruiting African American students into advanced courses. I originally pursued this goal in the context of convenience. Specifically, I informed the students that, given time and availability, they should seize the opportunities to enroll in AP courses.

After listening to students, I shifted the focus to ability. Here the message was that the students were Black intellectuals and therefore belonged in AP courses. Use of the latter perspective required the development of relationships between the students and me.

As a Black person, I already had the credibility to form close connections with the students. But I also knew that my Blackness must be used to connect with the students in solidarity. That's why I structured the activities and interactions around humility, understanding, and empathy. Listed below are some explanations of how these approaches factored into my solid connections with the students.

Empathetic Interpretation

The students alluded to the notion of the school being a site of White-framed oppression. In addition, this viewpoint played a factor in their decision to enroll in AP courses. As a Black person, I felt the need to empathize with the students. But I did not tell the students that I understood their feelings. Instead, I changed my focus to connecting to the students, with the by-product being enrollment in AP courses.

Listening for Understanding

From the beginning, I realized that availability of enrollment would not lead to the placement of African American students in AP courses. The solution would be to listen to the students. After listening to their racialized concerns about AP courses, I developed sessions that emphasized Blackness.

Each session consisted of opportunities for students to share their ideas and feelings about the activities. I also listened carefully to see how they internalized the main ideas of our discussions. I incorporated this feedback into planning each follow-up session. This approach allowed me to connect the students to the identity of Black achievers.

Seeing with Humility

During the first two sessions, the students would enter the room and start discussing topics related to their personal lives. My first instinct was to restrict their engagement to discussions related to Blackness. Due to our age difference, I did not see the relevance of those discussions to the sessions.

But then I reconsidered the discussions from a cultural perspective. The students displayed the African American cultural tendencies of social and verbal interactions. As such, it would be counterproductive to minimize a characteristic that was a part of their way of expressing Blackness.

Consequently, the students and I termed the beginning of the remaining sessions as "Family Fellowship Minutes." For the first five minutes, the students engaged in personal discussions with each other. Afterward, they transitioned into participating in the session activities. The more I participated in the fellowship, the better I became at linking the fellowship activities to the sessions.

To further grasp the relevance of these approaches, let's consider some background information. The White-framed foundation of schools is based on individualism, competition, and goal orientation. In contrast, the African-centered concept of communalism places emphasis on togetherness and cooperation.

Operating within a White-framed environment, I initially sought to satisfy the inquiry of "How do I get African American students into AP courses?" In words, I needed to connect the students to the school objective of increasing African American students in advanced courses. Once I came to my Black senses, my new focus was "How do I connect with African American students in ways that lead them to see that their brilliance belongs in AP courses?" Consistent with communalism, I was now placing more importance on bonding with the students than leading them toward AP course enrollment.

The same cultural shift is evident in Becky's involvement in the project. As a White person, Becky's cultural frame of reference was goal orientation. As a prime example, her response to the first session was "So are the students ready to enroll in the courses?" But as our conversations became more racialized, I observed a change in her consciousness, too.

Based on our conversations, I would not say that Becky became a deeply informed White person. I do believe that she became mindful of her Whiteness to the point of seeing the racial significance of our work with the students. Becky's mindfulness resulted in the idea of early student exposure to AP courses.

The effectiveness of this step can be traced to Becky's achievement of solidarity with the students. She used our initial conversations as a guide for how to talk to African American students. She then used her own interactions with the students to determine how to see, listen, and empathize with them. Consequently, the students eventually viewed Becky as a caring adult instead of their original title for her—"White Lady AP."

Conclusion

The best way for White teachers to internalize this chapter is through the lens of proximity. The essence of relationship building is negotiating closeness and distance between two or more people. This agreement is extremely fragile, especially when constructed across racial differences. When those racial differences are White teachers and Black children, connections must be used to negotiate an authentic teacher-student relationship. To be exact, the White teacher–Black student relationship must be developed through the teacher's push for solidarity. Professional solidarity can be best established by accepting only the very best from African American students. Personal solidarity entails learning and embracing the cultural characteristics that Black children bring to classrooms. The strengthening of such bonding will only come through the maintenance of culturally relevant respect, understanding, sensitivity, and trust by White teachers.

5

A Behavioral Passport to Black Student Achievement

The introduction marked the initial discussion of discipline and African American students. In particular, statistics were used to highlight the ways in which African American children are categorized in accordance to behavior. What I have found is that much of these behavioral issues occur in classrooms with White teachers. As such, this chapter presents a framework for White teachers to use to establish a positive disciplinary relationship with African American children.

The Principle

What Must White Teachers Be Mindful of to Build Positive Behavior within African American Students?

White teachers must realize that Black children's responses to authority (redirection) are highly influenced not just by the position of the person—but the person in the position.

Why Is This Understanding Specific to African American Students?

African American students' emphasis on the person is related to the Afrocentric theme of harmony. As mentioned, harmony is African Americans' need to be harmoniously united with their environment. Drawing from this perspective, I purport that discipline for Black children is more than the issuance of consequences from teachers to students. Discipline is a highly personal negotiation of harmony between two people.

The presence of White teachers adds a significant cross-racial dynamic to this equation. Race influences White teachers' responses to disciplinary situations pertaining to African American students. In due regard, African American students hold race-based perceptions of White teachers' approaches to addressing them during disciplinary situations. As a result, White teachers' personal characteristics will influence African American students' responses to disciplinary situations.

The Approach

How Can White Teachers Translate This Mindfulness into Building Positive Behavior within African American Students?

To build positive behavior, White teachers must understand power and authority through the eyes of African American students. Power is the ability to redirect the behavior of African American students. As certified figures of authority, White teachers wield the power to make commands and directives toward African American students.

Authority is the legitimacy to influence and shape the behavior of African American students. For White teachers, this level of authority is legitimated by how well they negotiate trust, respect, and understanding with African American students. To fully understand this negotiation, White teachers must consider the following questions:

1. Trust
   - Do Black students trust that my use of discipline is designed to make them better people?
2. Understanding
   - Do Black students understand the logic behind my approaches to resolving the disciplinary issue?

3. Respect
   - Do Black students feel that I hold some level of regard / respect for their views of the disciplinary situation?
   - Do Black students feel that I see the humanity inside their views of the disciplinary situation?
   - Do Black students feel that I still see them as human beings?

In other words, White teachers must work to become authoritative figures in the lives of African American students. The next section features my culturally relevant framework of authoritativeness.

Dimension 1: Cultural Consideration

Cultural consideration is the ability to see the context for the behaviors of African American students. White teachers must understand the different aspects of Black students, by law, Black children are Black students who are required to get an education. By design, Black students are Black children. In this role, they are brothers and sisters, sons and daughters, and nieces and nephews. They are also friends and companions. The latter role greatly influences their behaviors within schools.

Let's consider a situation that depicts a common White teacher response to the overlap between these identities. Beth is on afternoon bus duty. She notices Candice, a Black fourth-grader, standing over Keesha, a third-grade student.

Beth walks over to investigate the situation. The gist of the investigation is as follows:

Beth: What's your name?

Candice: Candice.

Beth: Who's your teacher?

Candice: Ms. Jenkins.

Beth: Why are you standing over this student?

Candice: I told her to stop bothering my cousin because . . .

Beth (interrupting Candice): Because it looks to me, young lady, like you're taking matters into your own hands by bullying.

Candice: No, I'm just telling her that she can't be messing with my cousin.

Beth: Your job is not to tell anything. That's why I'm here. We have zero tolerance for any type of violence. (*Beth points to a designated area.*) Now go and sit by the bench. (*Beth directs Candice to the bench.*)

(*Candice begrudgingly walks toward the designated area. She then murmurs a response to Beth.*)

Candice: You're not being fair.

Beth: Excuse me?

Candice: You won't listen.

Beth: Okay, bullying and disrespect—that's it. Now I'm taking you to the principal.

Candice: What did I do?

(*Candice refuses to follow Beth's request. The principal is called to the bus area to escort Candice to the office.*)

Here we see a common White teacher response of inconsideration of the context surrounding African American students. Beth's first response to the situation was to separate Candice the student from Candice the cousin. Because of this separation, Beth was unable to see the multidimensionality of Candice. In the end, Candice was seen as a disrespectful bully who needed to be corrected by the principal.

The implication from this narrative is for White teachers to consider the multidimensionality of African American students. Just dealing with the student role doesn't provide White teachers with the authority to influence African American students. White teachers must also acknowledge the out-of-school roles that shape the lives of African American students.

In this case, Candice the student is not what caused her to confront Keesha. Candice the cousin is what influenced her decision to protect her cousin from the harm of another student. Regardless of outcome, Candice was committed to being her cousin's cousin in all places—even the zero tolerance environment of schools.

Acknowledging this context does not mean that African American students are exempt from rules. In fact, I've observed an authentic contextual understanding lead to resolution between White teachers and Black students. To that end, reconsider the previous situation with the following revision:

Beth: Why are you standing over this student?

Candice: I told her to stop bothering my cousin because she shouldn't be messing with her.

Beth: Okay. So I see that you love your family. Not a problem. I see you. But at this moment, the way in which you're showing love for this problem is not acceptable.

Candice: But she shouldn't be messing with my cousin.

Beth: And you're right. But if you attempt to mess with her, then you're wrong. And two wrongs don't make a right. So here's what we're going to do. I want you to step away from this student.

(Candice refuses to step away from the student. Beth still reiterates her point to Candice.)

Beth: Candice, you're saying that you love your cousin. Right?

Candice: Yes.

Beth: Then show her that you mean it by not doing something that will cause you to be in trouble at school. I'm going to say this again—step away from the student.

(Candice begrudgingly steps away from the student.)

Beth: Now let me say this again. I see you and hear you when you say that you love and want to protect your cousin. Trust— I love and will protect my cousins, too. But I need you to hear me when I say that there's a much better way to show love and protection for her at school. *(Beth points at herself.)* And that way is to let me, the right person at the school, do the loving and protecting for your cousin in this situation. So sit right here and I will do some investigations.

(Candice begrudgingly sits in the designated area. Beth then talks to Keesha.)

The significance of the revised model is threefold. First, Beth acknowledged and acted on Candice's need to be seen as a cousin. Evidence to this effect was the continual recognition of the significance of family in all places.

This awareness did not weaken Beth's disciplinary stance. Because of that recognition, Beth was not relegated to the familiar White role of trying to overpower Black children into submission. She was now in a better position to address Candice's behavior with authority.

She acquired enough authority to shift Candice's disposition regarding the situation. Beth's ability to maintain this legitimacy was not based on her investigation of the situation. Instead, Beth was seen by Candice as applying a fair assessment of both students' actions. As a result, Candice would more than likely understand—not necessarily agree—why her actions may result in an office referral.

Another equally significant consideration is reading the culturally sanctioned behaviors of African American students. In *Are Black Kids Worse? Myths and Facts about Racial Differences in Behavior* Russell Skiba and Natasha Williams (2014) argue that Black children are not worse behaved than students from other racial groups. But when viewed through a subjective lens, African American student behaviors are rated more negative than the behaviors of other students.

One reason is that some of these culturally sanctioned behaviors are consistently misinterpreted by White teachers. As mentioned, many African American student behaviors are a reflection of being conditioned in an Afrocentric culture. White teachers often read African American students' affect as confrontational, threatening, and aggressive. The same words are used to characterize displays of orality and expressive individualism. Black students' displays of verve are defined as hyperactivity.

Another prime example of misinterpretation is movement. Against the backdrop of White-framed movement, stylized movements have been central to the Black American experience (Neal, McCray, Webb-Johnson, & Bridgest, 2003). For many African American males, these culturally sanctioned movements range from posturing to performance. Collectively, the movements are used to convey a ritualistic sense of pride and strength in Black masculinity. Yet in a White-framed society, the movement styles of African American men are often characterized in negative ways.

In school settings, I often see African American males' movements framed by White teachers from a deficit perspective. For example, walking is one of the most distinguishing styles of movement among African American male high schoolers. The visual for this stylized movement is as follows: tilted head, bent posture, slanted or dipped knees (Neal, McCray, Webb-Johnson, & Bridgest, 2003). The addition of dragging a foot creates a stroll that is a rite of passage from Black boyhood to Black manhood. On the other hand, White male adolescents walk with an erect posture, straight head, and synchronized movements. Now consider both movements in the scenario below (see textbox 5.1).

Textbox 5.1. The Stroll

Ricky, an African American male, strolls into Ms. Jensen's classroom. Ms. Jensen immediately says, "Ricky, come in here ready to work."

Ricky responds to Ms. Jensen by saying, "I am serious. What are you talking about?"

Ms. Jensen then retorts, "You're walking in here like you don't care about this class."

Ricky sighs and then takes his seat.

A few minutes later, Jerod, another African American male, strolls into the classroom. Ms. Jensen immediately states, "Not again!"

> Jerod says, "What are you talking about, Ms. J?" He continues, "I just got here."
>
> Ms. Jensen replies, "You're walking in here like you don't want to learn!"
>
> Prior to taking his seat, Jerod says, "I've got my book, paper, and pencil!" He continues, "So what makes you think I don't want to learn?"

Fortunately, neither Ricky's nor Jerod's exchange with Ms. Jensen resulted in disciplinary removal. But these exchanges do take place in an environment that upholds White-framed orientations for movement. In this context, the discussions show how Black-framed styles of movement can present problems for African American male students.

Therefore, White teachers must learn why the concepts of orality and movement reflect a legitimate culture instead of deviations from normality. Through this process, these teachers will be better able to avoid deficit interpretations of African-centered expressions. They will then be able to embrace Black students' behavioral diversity in affirming ways. Without affirmation, African American students will "become alienated from the schooling process because schooling often asks children to be something or someone other than who they really are. . . . It asks them to dismiss their community and cultural knowledge. It erases things that the students hold dear" (Ladson-Billings, 2001, p. xiv). In short, Black student culture will continue to be prone to being characterized as behavioral disorders in White teacher classrooms (Webb-Johnson, 2002).

To that end, consider a culturally affirming version of "The Stroll." Here Ms. Jensen holds affirming views of Ricky and Jerod. For example, she views the stroll as a legitimate form of movement for both students. As a result, both boys are treated as regular students with culturally distinct approaches for entering the classroom. In addition, these stylized movements neither disrupt the learning environment nor diminish the students' standing in the classroom.

Table 5.1. Disciplinary Narratives

Aquanetta Jackson	
Seventh Grade 10 Discipline Referrals Most Referrals Classified as Disrespect Major Issue: Talking Back to Teacher Referring Teacher: Goodwin	**Goodwin's Perspective on Referrals** "Aquanetta is a bright student. But she lets her disrespect get in the way of her potential. She will not respect my authority as her teacher. So she is removed."
Aquanetta's Perspective on Referrals "A lot of times I react the way I do with Mr. G because he acts like he don't want to hear me. And yes, I use my hands to emphasize what I want to be heard. I do this especially when he acts like he don't want to hear me. And then I get accused of being disrespectful and we (Black students) get treated like criminals. But when White students do something in the class, they are looked at like angels. And then when you get to the office, you don't get a chance to say anything. That's cause White teachers will try to act as if nothing ever happened, especially when they did or said something in a wrong way to us. So the best thing for me to do is get my feelings out open on the spot and when I get to the office, too."	
Janae Seals	
Ninth Grade 6 Discipline Referrals Most Referrals Classified as Defiance Major Issue: Refusal to Follow Directions Referring Teacher: Jolley	**Jolley's Perspective on Referrals** "If I say go up, Janae will go down. If I say go East, you know she's going West. So at some point, I'm forced to tell her to go away, as in the principal's office."
Janae's Perspective on Referrals "The thing with Ms. Jolley is this—she just wants me to do what she says without listening to what I'm trying to tell her. So I just refuse to listen to her. Sometimes, I won't do my work and she'll kick me out! And she don't want me to say nothing about how I feel! And Ms. Jolley and the other White teachers in this school wonder why Black students get loud with them sometimes. That's because we sometimes feel that being loud is the only way that we can make them feel us about the situation."	
Marcus Bell	
Eleventh Grade 7 Discipline Referrals Most Referrals Classified as Disruption Major Issue: Disrupting Class Referring Teacher: Claxton	**Claxton's Perspective on Referrals** "Smart, but disruptive force in motion—that's how I see Marcus. He can be compliant. But most days, he is a major disturbance to the classroom."
Marcus's Perspective on Referrals "I don't have a problem with Ms. Claxton correcting me—I really don't. It's just the way that she and these other White teachers go about doing it. You don't have to loud talk me to do it. Because every time she does that with me, what do you think I do? Exactly. Because a lot of these White teachers talk about being fair, but that's just talk when it comes to Black students. But as soon as we say something back, they ready to shut us up with a referral. How's that fair? But I'm not going out like that. I already know that nobody in this school is gonna talk on my behalf or see my side of the story. So anytime I feel like it, I am going talk up for myself to let others know that they can't just play me."	

Another important disciplinary consideration for White teachers is the role of emotions in African American students' behavior. The major disciplinary issue in schools for which principals request my assistance is between Black students and White teachers. My first response to this dilemma is to ask both groups about their disciplinary issues with each other. Table 5.1 lists views from three African American students and the White teachers who wrote disciplinary referrals about them.

These narratives depict the ways in which emotion factors into disciplinary situations between African American students and White teachers. The presence of emotion is not the root cause of these situations. The lack of acknowledging emotion is the issue. Table 5.2 features an analytical depiction of the situation.

To end this cycle, White teachers must acknowledge the emotional life of African American children. To that end, consider the framework found in tables 5.3, 5.4, and 5.5 as context for African American students and emotion.

This framework provides a multifaceted perspective on the emotionality of African American students. From a Black people perspective, emotions distinguish the distinction and together-

Table 5.2. Dyadic Interpretation of Disciplinary Situations

Dyad	Summary
Presence of Power	The White teacher uses power to exert control over and silence the African American students. As a result, the African American student feels that he/she has no voice in the situation.
Absence of Voice	
Presence of Emotion	Denied a voice, the African American student displays anger, frustration, and disrespect toward the White teacher. These responses denote the student's lack of respect, trust, and understanding regarding the actions of the White teacher.
Absence of Respect	
Presence of Labeling	The White teacher ignores the African American student's feelings. The African American student is labeled as disrespectful and removed from the classroom.
Absence of Student	

Table 5.3. The Emotionality of African American Students

Part I
Emotion as Need for Connection

Harmony	
Afrocentric Perspective	**African American Student Perspective**
African Americans seek to be harmoniously conjoined with their environment.	All three students express a willingness to cooperate with teachers who treat them with fairness, dignity, and respect. On the other hand, they resist teachers who do not respect them.
Americanized Perspective	
African American people often view some life situations through the lens of racial justice. They feel that the only way to achieve a sense of wholeness in these situations is through equal treatment by other people.	**Sample Statements** • "I don't have a problem with Ms. Claxton correcting me—I really don't. It's just the way that she and these other White teachers go about doing it. You don't have to loud talk me to do it." Marcus • "The thing with Ms. Jolley is this—she just wants me to do what she say without listening to what I'm trying to tell her. So I just refuse to listen to her." Janae

Communalism	
Afrocentric Perspective	**African American Student Perspective**
African Americans prioritize social connection over individualized achievement.	Denote how all three students talk about themselves in the context of group identity. They define their quest for respect in the context of other African American students at the school. In a way, these sentiments purport a racial and psychological connection to the African American student population.
Americanized Perspective	
African American people have been historically inclined to "stick up" and "stick with" each other to maintain a strong sense of racial pride and solidarity within their racial group.	**Sample Statements** • "And Ms. Jolley and the other White teachers in this school wonder why Black students get loud with them sometimes. That's because we sometimes feel that being loud is the only way that we can make them feel us about the situation." Janae • "Because a lot of these White teachers talk about being fair, but that's just talk when it comes to Black students. But as soon as we say something back, they ready to shut us up with a referral. How's that fair?" Marcus

Table 5.4. The Emotionality of African American Students (continued)

Part II	
Emotion as Need for Expression	
Orality	
Afrocentric Perspective	**African American Student Perspective**
African Americans use speaking and talking as the primary modes for purposeful communication.	A common theme in the written descriptions is African American students' willingness to speak out about their feelings of being mistreated by the teachers.
Americanized Perspective	**Sample Statements**
African American people use varying levels of verbal communication to simultaneously be heard by and informative to other people.	• "And yes, I use my hands to emphasize what I want to be heard. I do this especially when she acts like she don't want to hear me." Aquanetta • "But I'm not going out like that. I already know that nobody in this school is gonna talk on my behalf or see my side of the story. So anytime I feel like it, I am going to talk up for myself to let others know that they can't just play me." Marcus
Affect	
Afrocentric Perspective	**African American Student Perspective**
African Americans place a strong emphasis on expression that is filled with emotions and feelings.	The African American students convey a strong sense of emotion about their feelings regarding the situation. Their conviction is seen in the passionate ways in which they justify their responses toward the teachers.
Americanized Perspective	**Sample Statements**
African American people have historically used emotion to draw attention to the seriousness of their feelings regarding situations and issues.	• "And she don't want me to say nothing about how I feel! And Ms. Jolley and the other White teachers in this school wonder why Black students get loud with them sometimes." Janae * "But I'm not going out like that. I already know that nobody in this school is gonna talk on my behalf or to see my side of the story. So anytime I feel like it, I am going talk up for myself to let others know that they can't just play me." Marcus

Table 5.5. The Emotionality of African American Students (continued)

Part IIII Emotion as Need for Recognition	
Expressive Individualism	
Afrocentric Perspective	**African American Student Perspective**
African Americans have strived to maintain a distinct personality and identity.	The African American students are intent on being heard. The lack of acknowledging their feelings intensifies this need for recognition. **Sample Statements** • "That's because we sometimes feel that being loud is the only way that we can make them feel us about the situation." Janae • "And yes, I use my hands to emphasize what I want to be heard. I do this especially when she acts like she don't want to hear me." Aquanetta
Americanized Perspective	
African American people have used speech, movement, and appearance to maintain a distinguished existence in a society that has historically marginalized Blackness.	
Social Time Perspective	
Afrocentric Perspective	**African American Student Perspective**
African Americans view the mood of the event as being more important than the time of the event.	The scenarios showed students who refused to see if they would be able to share their side of the story at a later time. They immediately expressed their anger about the disciplinary situation. **Sample Statements** • "I already know that nobody in this school is gonna talk on my behalf or to see my side of the story. So anytime I feel like it, I am going talk up for myself to let others know that they can't just play me." Marcus • "And then when you get to the office, you don't get a chance to say anything. That's cause White teachers will try to act as if nothing ever happened, especially when they did or said something in a wrong way to us. So the best thing for me to do is get my feelings out open on the spot and when I get to the office, too." Aquanetta
Americanized Perspective	
When needed, African American people replace "clock time" with the freedom to determine the "starting time" for how they will interact with their surroundings.	

ness among African American students. Emotions influence the expressiveness within African American students' speech and conversation. Emotion is also the litmus test for determining African American students' adherence to time or the timing of the event. Simply put, emotion is a culturally relevant determinant of African American students' being.

The latter point is especially true with regard to disciplinary situations between Black students and White teachers. When Black children are ignored, emotion puts them in a constant state of rage. When recognized, the emotions within Black children can be used as an invaluable source of reasoning.

Through consistent practice, Mr. Goodwin used this information to become an effective responder of disciplinary issues with Aquanetta. As an example, look closely at Mr. Goodwin's stance in the following situation:

The Accusation

Mr. Goodwin: Okay, class! Good morning!

Class: What's up?

Mr. Goodwin: What's up is your quiz for today!

Class: Aah!

Mr. Goodwin: Moving on. Clear your desk of everything except for your pencil.

(Students remove materials from their desk.)

Aquanetta: I can't find my pencil. Do you have my pencil, Todd?

(Todd ignores Aquanetta. She then screams out about the pencil.)

Aquanetta (screaming): Mr. G, tell this boy to give me my pencil!

(Mr. Goodwin begins to distribute the quizzes to students.)

Mr. Goodwin: Okay, class, here comes your quizzes.

(Aquanetta now becomes angry with Mr. Goodwin.)

Aquanetta (screaming): Okay, so it's like that! Well, you must not want me to take this test, Mr. G!

Mr. Goodwin stops passing out quizzes and stares at Aquanetta. He slowly mouths "I hear you, Aquanetta." He then continues to distribute the quizzes to students. Aquanetta then makes another remark regarding the pencil. Mr. Goodwin responds by asking a student to distribute the quizzes to the students who do not have a quiz.

With one hand on his left ear, he mouths "Aquanetta, I hear you. I hear you!" Afterward, Mr. Goodwin summons Aquanetta over to his desk. He provides Aquanetta with a pencil and directs her to take the quiz. At the end of class, Mr. Goodwin dismisses every student except Aquanetta. He then proceeds to engage her in the following conversation:

Mr. Goodwin: Aquanetta, do not make false accusations in this class.

Aquanetta: You don't know that he didn't have my pencil.

Mr. Goodwin: Aquanetta, do not make false accusations in this class.

Aquanetta: Well, the next time I don't have a pencil . . .

Mr. Goodwin (interrupting Aquanetta): You will look for your pencil and then come and see me if you can't find your pencil. Again, you do not make false accusations in this class. Make A's not accusations.

Aquanetta: So are you saying that I should just let somebody steal from me?

Mr. Goodwin: No. You should say something—as long as you have the evidence to back up what you feel.

Aquanetta: Hmm . . .

Mr. Goodwin provides Aquanetta with a pass for her next class. He then reiterates that she is expected to not make false accusations about other students.

Here we see Mr. Goodwin's approach to addressing an outburst from Aquanetta. That Aquanetta failed to quickly comply with Mr. Goodwin was not an issue. The reason is that Mr. Goodwin continued to acknowledge the emotion behind the outburst. He was then able to channel the emotion into a form of reasoning.

In other words, Mr. Goodwin did not discard Aquanetta's feelings. He used her anger as a starting point for discussing her feelings. Specifically, he impressed upon Aquanetta the need to reconsider her false accusation about another student, hence the importance of White teachers' understanding emotion to become authoritative figures for African American students.

Dimension 2: Cultural Synchronization

At this point, I have described the context for proactively considering and responding to African American students' behavior. I will now discuss synchronization as an approach to misbehavior with African American students. Cultural synchronization is the alignment of a teacher's actions with the background culture of students (Irvine, 2002). The main premise of this paradigm is race. White teachers and White children are able to connect across the unstated White-framed subtleties of school. But this same connection is usually nonexistent between White teachers and Black children.

Therefore, congruence is especially relevant to White teachers' effectiveness in addressing the willful misconduct for African American students. As such, I am proposing a verbal, vocal, and visual approach to addressing these disciplinary situations with African American students. The section below provides a synchronized description of this model.

Verbal (Verbalization)

Key Emphasis: Words

Verbalization is the use of culturally congruent communication to respond to disciplinary situations with African American students. Such communication is based on the unscripted and unrestricted expression of information between African American people.

Vocal (Vocalization)

Key Emphasis: Emotions

Vocalization is the use of an emotionally laden tone to enhance the communication regarding disciplinary situations with African American students. As mentioned, emotions are a significant part of Black culture. A significant reason is that relationships among Black people consist of authentic expressions of emotions and feelings.

Visual (Visualization)

Key Emphasis: Demeanor

Visualization is the display of a demeanor that reinforces the words and tone for disciplinary situations with African American students. The essence of demeanor is that, from birth, African Americans are inherently attuned to the social cues within Black culture. As a result, they are very adept at reading nonverbal forms of communication.

The significance of this model lies in the racialized ways in which verbal discourse plays out in Black culture and White culture. White people often use linear- and logic-based forms of indirect expression to communicate with people (Kochman, 1981). In this context, White-framed orality is also marked by a protocol defined by turn-taking procedures.

Black people's communication is an interrelated combination of two sets of expression (Hale, 2001). On the one hand, Black communication is an authentic and direct approach to express information with people. At the same time, Black communication patterns are also infused with demonstrative displays of animation and emotion that are nested in overlapping speech. These communication patterns are practiced during African American parents' interactions with their children.

I have witnessed the ways in which White-framed and Black-framed communication differences shape disciplinary moments between White teachers and Black students. To illustrate this point, I will present three enactments of actual disciplinary moments involving White teachers and Black students. I will then describe how the White teachers' reactions reflect common reaction patterns among White teachers in similar situations.

I will then provide a Black-framed reenactment of the vignettes. The purpose of the revised vignettes is twofold. Drawing from Black culture, I depict plausible Black teacher responses to these situations. I then connect those responses to the larger pattern of Black teacher reactions to similar situations with African American students. I also show how the responses embody the verbal, vocal, and visual approaches to disciplinary situations with African American students. The examples are not designed to provide White teachers with scripts for addressing disciplinary issues with Black children. Rather, the information is a framework for establishing culturally relevant disciplinary relationships with African American students.

White-Framed Vignettes: The Originals

Vignette 1—Elementary School: "The Bonus Word"

Grade Level: Grade 4

Synopsis: Ms. Jones (White teacher) responds to Marshall's (African American student) desire for a specific word during a spelling test.

Ms. Jones: Okay, class. Let's get ready for our spelling test. Take out your pencils and let's begin.

(Ms. Jones announces the first word for the students.)

Ms. Jones: Okay, the first word is *germ*.

Marshall: What's the bonus word?

Ms. Jones: Class, we know that the bonus word is not given until the end of the test. Besides, if I give the bonus word now, then you won't have a bonus word at the end of the test.

Marshall: Man!

(Ms. Jones ignores Marshall's outburst.)

Marshall (in an angry voice): I want the bonus word.

Ms. Jones (in an agitated voice): Marshall, I just explained the rule.

Marshall (throwing a fit): Man, I want the bonus word now! Give it to me!

Ms. Jones: That's enough—I said. Be quiet or go take your test with the principal.

(Marshall slams his pencil on the desk and refuses to take the test.)

Marshall (screaming): I hate you, Ms. Jones!

Ms. Jones: What did you say?

Marshall: I hate you and this stupid school!

Ms. Jones: That's it! Leave now!

(Marshall kicks the desk and heads to the principal's office.)

Vignette 2—Middle School: "The Problem"

Grade Level: Grade 7
Synopsis: Ms. Robinson (White teacher) summons Katrina (African American student) to the hall for ridiculing another student.

Ms. Robinson: Katrina, you have no right to make fun of Sharon.

Katrina: Well, she thinks that she's all that, because she makes good grades.

Ms. Robinson: She is smart and you shouldn't make fun of her.

Katrina: Well . . .

Ms. Robinson: Well, you know that our character word for this month is *support*—meaning we support each other in this class.

Katrina: Okay.

Ms. Robinson: And if you belittle Sharon again, I'm going to move you.

Katrina: If you move me, we are going to have a problem.

Ms. Robinson: Come with me. We are going to the office.

Vignette 3—High School: "The Look"

Grade Level: Grade 11

Synopsis: Mr. Livingston (White teacher) addresses Rishanna (African American student) for not being prepared to take a quiz.

Mr. Livingston: Okay, let's get prepared to take our weekly mathematics quiz.

Rishanna (whispering to Janice): Janice, can I borrow a pencil?

Janice: Here.

Mr. Livingston: Girls, be quiet now!

Rishanna: Ay, Mr. Livingston—look I'm just asking the homey for a pencil.

Mr. Livingston: But that's not what you were supposed to be doing. And you know the rules—come to class prepared with all materials for learning.

Rishanna: I do have my materials. I just needed a pencil.

Mr. Livingston: A pencil is a material. And without it, you are not ready to take the test.

Rishanna: Well, the fact that I'm trying to get a pencil should tell you that I'm ready to take your test.

Mr. Livingston: You know what—I'm not wasting any more time on this matter. Just turn around and get ready for the quiz.

(At this point, Rishanna turns around, but refuses to take the quiz.)

Mr. Livingston: You know what—just leave!

Rishanna: Gladly!

Black-Framed Vignettes: The Revisions

Vignette 1—Elementary School: "The Bonus Word"

Grade Level: Grade 4

Synopsis: Ms. Jones (African American teacher) responds to Marshall's (African American student) desire for a specific word during a spelling test.

Ms. Jones: Okay, class. We have a spelling test for today. Take out your pencils and let's begin.

(Ms. Jones begins to call out the words to students.)

Ms. Jones: Okay, the first word is *germ.*

Marshall: What's the bonus word?

(Ms. Jones stares at Marshall for two minutes. She then continues with administering the spelling test to the class.)

Ms. Jones: I got your bonus word! Next word, *jump.*

Marshall (in an angry voice): I want the bonus word.

Ms. Jones: Okay, Marshall. You want the bonus word—you got it: L-I-S-T-E-N! Now listen and pay attention. Because I ain't the one.

Marshall: Man!

(Marshall stops taking the test. Ms. Jones stares at him while announcing the spelling words to students. As she moves closer to Marshall, he resumes taking the spelling test.)

Ms. Jones: Now that we are at the end of the test, here's your bonus word—the word *best. (Ms. Jones looks at Marshall.)* We must all be at our very best.

Vignette 2—Middle School: "The Problem"

Grade Level: Grade 7

Synopsis: Ms. Robinson (African American teacher) summons Katrina (African American student) to the hall for ridiculing another student.

Ms. Robinson: Katrina, you have no right to make fun of Sharon.

Katrina: Well, she thinks that she's all that, because she makes good grades.

Ms. Robinson: I hear you. But I don't feel you. What I'm feeling is what makes you think you can just hurt someone else's feelings?

Katrina: Well . . .

Ms. Robinson: Well, here's the deal—you can do what I say or you can do what I say. But you're gonna do what I say.

Katrina: Well, I think Sharon needs to hear this, too. Or we going to have a problem.

Ms. Robinson: Maybe in another world. But the only problems in Robinson's world are the math problems that you are gonna copy from the board. (*Ms. Robinson points to the dry erase board in the classroom.*) Now get back in the classroom and focus on learning what's going to help you.

(*Ms. Robinson points to the class, directing Katrina to go back to her seat. Katrina, who is upset with Ms. Robinson, begrudgingly walks back to her seat.*)

Vignette 3—High School: "The Look"

Grade Level: Grade 11

Synopsis: Mr. Livingston (African American teacher) addresses Rishanna (African American student) for not being prepared to take a quiz.

Mr. Livingston: Okay, everybody. Let's get prepared to take our weekly mathematics quiz.

Rishanna (whispering to Janice): Janice, can I borrow a pencil?

Janice: Here.

Mr. Livingston (looking at Janice and Rishanna): Class, I know that I don't hear any voices in the classroom.

Rishanna: Ay, Mr. Livingston—look I'm just asking the homey for a pencil.

Mr. Livingston (pointing to himself): Okay. Well, look here—I'm telling you that I know that I don't hear any voices in this classroom.

(As students quietly gather test materials, Mr. Livingston retrieves the quiz. He then distributes quizzes to students. When he approaches Rishanna, he provides her with the quiz and a pencil. Attached to the quiz is a post-it note that reads "Next time, have all of your materials—pencil included!" He then distributes the quiz to the remaining students.)

Analysis

These enactments feature responses that are common among White teachers' approaches to disciplinary situations with African American students. The White teachers drew from logic and rules to expect compliance from African American students. For example, Ms. Jones used patience as her logic for telling Marshall to wait for the bonus word. Ms. Robinson's response to Katrina was rooted in the need for respect among students. Finally, Mr. Livingston reminded Rishanna of the inability to succeed without being prepared for class.

Despite these explanations, the African American students still believed that their actions were legitimate. Evidence to this effect is seen in their refusal to acquiesce to the teachers' requests. As a result, all three students were removed from the classroom.

Disciplinary removal was nonexistent in the vignettes involving African American teachers. The reason is that the African American teachers used culturally synchronized approaches to addressing the students. In the section below, I connect these approaches to my verbal, vocal, and visual model for culturally responsive discipline.

Verbalization—Directness in Words

All three African American teachers used a communicative style that was compatible to African American students. A clear illustration of this point is the straightforward style of speaking that is highly valued in Black culture. For example, consider the following verbal exchange between Ms. Jones and Marshall:

Marshall: What's the bonus word?

(Ms. Jones stares at Marshall for two minutes. She then continues with administering the spelling test to the class.)

Ms. Jones: I got your bonus word! Next word, *jump!*

Marshall (in an angry voice): I want the bonus word.

Ms. Jones: Okay, Marshall. You want the bonus word—you got it: L-I-S-T-E-N! Now listen and pay attention. Because I ain't the one.

Note the way in which directness textured Ms. Jones's commands. She is clear in her direct expectations for Marshall. Her responses are consistent with African American teachers' usage of verbal comebacks in ways that resonate with African American students.

Another feature of Ms. Jones's direct discourse is culturally congruent warnings. As an example, consider her statement "I ain't the one!" The significance of this statement is twofold. The statement conveyed a demand for Marshall to follow directions. In this demand, she also expressed an unwavering expectation to be respected as the teacher.

In "The Problem," Ms. Robinson relied on dialect and language to emphasize a point to Katrina. I present the exchange below as evidence:

Katrina: Well . . .

Ms. Robinson: Well, here's the deal—you can do what I say or you can do what I say. But you're gonna do what I say.

Ms. Robinson's response depicts the colorful ways in which language is used in Black communities. On the surface, her response suggests that Katrina has a choice in the matter. But in reality, her only choice is to follow the directions of the teacher.

Another example of Black dialect is featured in Mr. Livingston's approach to redirecting Rishanna toward the quiz. Here's the exchange that initiated the redirection.

> *Rishanna:* Ay, Mr. Livingston—look I'm just asking the homey for a pencil.

> *Mr. Livingston (pointing to himself):* Okay. Well, look here—I'm telling you that I know that I don't hear any voices in this classroom.

The phrase "that I know that I don't hear any voices" was a direct way of telling Rishanna to remain quiet. The other implied message was that the only person in a position to not be quiet is Mr. Livingston.

Vocalization—Authenticity in Tone

In each vignette, the teachers used a twofold emotional approach to set the tone with students. First, the teachers acknowledged the students' emotions. For example, Ms. Jones used humor to respond to Marshall's emotions. Remember that in "The Bonus Word," Marshall insisted on quickly receiving the bonus word. Ms. Jones's first response was "I got your bonus word!" Her second response to the request was to spell the word *listen*. Readers outside of Black culture may detect a sense of harshness in her responses. But within the Black community, these comments are viewed as humorous. They also reinforce Ms. Jones's insistence on announcing the bonus word at the end of the test.

Another example of acknowledging emotions was "I hear you." Ms. Robinson used this statement to show her attentiveness to Katrina. But the next sentence "But I don't feel you" indicates that Ms. Robinson did not agree with Katrina's views. She instead wanted Katrina to hear her expectations for respecting all students.

Second, teachers used emotions to emphasize specific points with their students. In the section below, I list some of the teachers' emotion-laden responses to students.

Jones's Emotionality

- I got your bonus word! Next word, *jump*.
- Okay, Marshall. You want the bonus word—you got it: L-I-S-T-E-N! Now listen and pay attention. Because I ain't the one.

Robinson's Emotionality

- Well, here's the deal—you can do what I say or you can do what I say. But you're gonna do what I say.
- Maybe in another world. But the only problems in Robinson's world are the math problems that you are gonna copy from the board (Ms. Robinson points to the dry erase board in the classroom). Now get back in the classroom and focus on learning what's going to help you.

Livingston's Emotionality

- Class, I know that I don't hear any voices in the classroom.
- Okay. Well, look here—I'm telling you that I know that I don't hear any voices in this classroom.

The common thread within these responses is the cultural relevance of emotions. Like most Black teachers, these teachers understood the role of emotions in addressing African American students. The basis of this understanding is that African American children emphasize the emotional aspects of the school environment. In return, they expect teachers to have and show emotion.

The power of emotion in this context manifests in resolving disciplinary issues with African American students. Without emotion, teachers have only the power to control African

American students' behavior. With emotion, teacher reprimands reflect care and concern for African American students. The latter point explains why the disciplinary situations were handled without disciplinary removal.

Another culturally relevant explanation is the emotional state of the African American teachers. In my opinion, two categories of emotions can be used to classify teacher responses to disciplinary issues with African American children. The categories are coercive emotions and cooperative emotions. Coercive emotions galvanize teachers to use punitive measures to respond to unwanted African American student behaviors. In my opinion, the following coercive emotions influenced White teachers' ineffective responses to issues with African American students:

- anger
- frustration
- annoyance

When teachers experience cooperative emotions, they search for positive solutions to resolve issues with African American students. The most commonly observed cooperative emotion for achieving this harmony is disappointment. I consistently observe African American teachers express disappointment in African American students' misbehavior. Yet disappointment is still filled with significant cultural capital in terms of the Black teacher–student relationship. The reason is that disappointment strengthens Black teachers' resolve to nurture the excellence within African American children.

Visualization—Sincerity in Demeanor

Demeanor was a contributing factor to the African American teachers' responses to African American students. In many instances, coercion and consequences are often used to force African American students into compliance. But the vignettes showed the relational stance that is a part of African American teachers' responses to African American students. Examples that typified this demeanor are as follows:

- Ms. Jones: Now that we are at the end of the test, here's your bonus word—the word *best*. (*Looking at Marshall.*) We must all be at our very best.
- Ms. Robinson: Maybe in another world. But the only problems in Robinson's world are the math problems that you are gonna copy from the board (*points to the dry erase board in the classroom*). Now get back in the classroom and focus on learning what's going to help you.
- Mr. Livingston: Next time, have all of your materials— pencil included! (Attached note.)

These responses are consistent with research on African American teachers' responsiveness to discipline with a no-nonsense demeanor. Beneath this exterior is a warm interior that provides the following comforts for African American students:

- Allowing African American students to feel a sense of acceptance during disciplinary moments.
- Working to ensure that African American students give appropriate responses during disciplinary situations.
- Helping African American students to see that the disciplinary situation is not designed to get them.

The focus of these disciplinary aims is expectations and success instead of the quickest route to disciplinary removal.

The Sample

What Other Evidence Shows Construction of Authority as an Effective Way for White Teachers to Address Discipline with African American Students?

Teacher support is an important aspect of my consulting career. A significant part of the support is facilitating White teachers' disciplinary effectiveness with African American students. The section below provides a representative example of my numerous experiences with helping White teachers acquire authority with this group of students.

Step 1

Bob, the school principal, hires me to help a teacher effectively address disciplinary issues with African American students. During the previous two school years, she has written 371 disciplinary referrals on students. Of this number, 343 disciplinary referrals were written on African American students. Of this number, 277 referrals were written on African American male students.

In an effort to reduce the referrals, Bob moved the teacher from teaching eighth grade to teaching sixth grade. The idea was that the teacher would experience fewer issues and referrals with younger African American students. However, within the first month of this school year, the teacher has written 27 disciplinary referrals about African American students. Based on this evidence, Bob concluded that the teacher did not know how to address African American students.

Step 2

I hold a preliminary meeting with Pamela Piland, the White teacher who would be supported by me. After we exchange pleasantries, I begin to talk with Pam about her challenges with African American students. Here's an excerpt from the conversation:

> *Hines:* So tell me—what are your main behavioral challenges with the African American students?
>
> *Pam:* Well, let me first of all say that I love all of my students.
>
> *Hines:* Okay.
>
> *Pam:* But this year, I keep having the same issues with my African American students.

Hines: Yes. That's why I'm here.

Pam: It's not all of them. But it's just a big issue already and we're still in the first semester of the school year.

Hines: Well, what do you feel is the main cause or causes of your issues with African American students?

Pam: I don't want to sound racist.

Hines (interrupting): Pam, just be honest and tell me what you think.

Pam: Okay. Well, a lot of my African American students come from poverty and single-parent homes. So, it's just that I don't think that they can behave.

Thus, operating from a White frame, Pam feels that external issues are the main cause of her disciplinary issues with African American students. I don't judge Pam in accordance to her views. Instead, I suspend my thoughts until engaging her in future conversations about the issue.

Step 3

I take three steps to enhance my readiness for supporting Pam. First, I review disciplinary records to identify possible patterns related to her issues with African American students. I then conduct classroom observations to investigate her interactions with African American students. The final step is interviews with African American students to gain their perspectives on Pam's practices. The sections below provide the outcomes of these actions.

Action 1: Review of Disciplinary Record

My investigation of Pam's disciplinary record showed that most of her referrals were written about African American students from her first and fourth periods. In addition, a disproportionate number of the referrals were written on African American males. Moreover, the major categories of these referrals were disrespect, defiance, and class disruption.

Action 2: Classroom Observations

Over the course of four days, I observed Pam's six classes. During my observations, I discover that her first period has the highest number of African American students. Her fourth period consists of a high number of African American males. The section below features observed incidents between Pam and African American students.

Critical Behavior Incidents (First Period): Incident 1. At the beginning of class, Pam greets students. She notices that an African American student is playing with his pencils. The following scenario presents her approach to addressing this student:

Pam: Tyree, don't start.

Tyree: What?

Pam: Don't start—that's what!

Tyree: I'm not doing nothing.

Pam: Okay now.

Tyree: Man!

Pam: Did you just hear me?

Tyree: Man forget this.

Pam: That's it.

(Ms. Pam sees the security officer in the hallway. She directs the security officer to remove Tyree from the classroom.)

Pam: Okay now. Where were we?

Jason: Why did you kick him out?

Pam (pointing at Jason): You're next! Now silence!

(Jason puts his head on the desk and goes to sleep.)

Critical Behavior Incidents (First Period): Incident 2. The bell rings to end first period. The students pack their belongings to go to their next class. Suddenly, Pam says, "Wait, I didn't tell you all to pack up your stuff." She continues, "You don't move until I say move!"

Many African American students sigh in disbelief. Then Jared, an African American male, stands up and moves to the door. Pam then yells, "Get back here, Jared!" Jared pauses and then leaves the classroom. Pam rushes to the door and says, "Jared, get back here and stop disrespecting my rules." Jared ignores Pam and continues to walk down the hallway.

Critical Behavior Incidents (Fourth Period): Incident 1. Pam talks with students about their performance on a recent quiz.

> *Pam:* Some of you did not do well on the quiz, because you won't pay attention. It's like you don't care about your life. You've got to get an education.
>
> *Jeannetta:* Ms. P, we care about ourselves.
>
> *Joe:* We just don't understand your teaching.
>
> *Pam:* If you all would pay attention, we wouldn't be in this predicament.
>
> *Jeannetta:* Well, a lot of times, we can't even ask you questions about what you're teaching us.
>
> *Pam:* I can't make you learn.
>
> *Jeannetta:* But you can act like you want us to learn.
>
> *Pam:* Jeannetta, how dare you disrespect me?
>
> *Jeannetta:* Ain't nobody disrespecting you!
>
> *Pam:* Watch your tone, young lady!
>
> *Jeannetta:* I'm not watching anything. I just want to learn from what you teach.
>
> *Pam:* Leave!
>
> *Jeannetta:* What did I do?
>
> *Pam:* I said go to the office or I'll call security!
>
> *(Jeannetta walks out of the classroom and slams the door.)*

Critical Behavior Incidents (Fourth Period): Incident 2. Pam is reviewing least common denominator with students. During the lesson, several issues arise between Pam and African American students.

Pam: Okay, class. Who can tell me about the term LCD?

Josh: You mean LSD?

(The class laughs.)

Pam: What did you say?

Josh: Nothing, Ms. P.

Pam: No. I heard you. But I want to hear you say it again.

Josh: Oh, lord. Here we go again.

Pam: If you keep on disrupting class, the only place you're going to go is back in the sixth grade.

Josh: Huh, that's what you think.

(Pam stops the lesson and walks to her desk. She buzzes for security to remove Josh from the classroom.)

Action 3: Student Interviews

I conducted interviews with African American students who were involved and not involved in the critical behavior incidents. The section below provides the essential findings from the interviews.

Involved African American Students (First Period)—
Tyree's Expression:

Man, when I go to that lady's class, I'm like whatever. 'Cause it's like man her tone and she be yelling and screaming like we dumb or something. I'm just tired of it. I ain't gotta take that from her.

Involved African American Students (First Period)—
Jared's Insight:

Hines: What was that about? Why did you ignore Ms. P?

Jared: I walked out of Mrs. P's class, because I can't keep being late for language arts class. I am already behind in that class and he won't let you in if you're late.

Hines: Did you talk to Ms. P?

Jared: Man, I mean excuse me, Dr. Hines, I tried to explain that to her. But she won't listen. And last week, I came back to her class to get a pass when I couldn't get into language arts. And she told me "it's not my problem" and wouldn't give me a pass. So I'm not going out like that again.

Involved African American Students (Fourth Period)— Jeannetta's Feelings:

It's like half the time, we don't understand what she's saying. And most days, when you ask her something, she just goes off on you. And I'm like look I'm just trying to understand where you coming from. You know. So I just felt some type of way and that's why I got mad at her.

Involved African American Students (Fourth Period)— Josh's Quote:

Ms. P is a good teacher. But she just keeps going on and on and won't let things go. I was just playing. But she tried to shame me and I just clapped back at her.

Uninvolved Students (First Period)—Michelle:

I think Ms. P is a good teacher and some of the Black students do give her a hard time. But she just gets so mad and then starts going off on them. And they yell back and get sent to the office.

Uninvolved Students (First Period)—Marcus:

It's hard to learn in there when she has problems with Lyrica, Fredrica, Tyree, and Jared (African American children). Everybody in the class knows that she doesn't like them. And I think that's why they be always arguing with each other.

Uninvolved Students (First Period)—Daniqua:

Sometimes we (Black children) do be giving her a hard time. But then sometimes she's just mean to us, especially Tyree. But when she's in the mood, she will try to teach us.

Uninvolved Students (Fourth Period):

Hines: Thanks for talking to me.

Students (in unison): You're welcome.

Hines: So what did you think about what happened in class on today?

Shenay: You talking about Jeannetta and Josh?

Vanessa: That's all the time.

Carlos: Well, sometimes with Jeannetta and all the time with Josh.

Hines: What do you mean?

Golden: Well, it's like she loves to teach.

Vanessa: But she don't want to listen to the people that she is teaching.

Hines: What do you mean?

Vanessa: She don't really try to understand your side of the story.

Shenay: So some of us ignore her.

Carlos: But my homey Josh get off the chain with her when she don't wanna hear what he's saying.

Hines: Gotcha.

After completing these tasks, I conclude that two factors contribute to Pam's disciplinary issues with African American students. First, Pam does not acknowledge the emotionality of her African American students. Second, she lacks the cultural insight to effectively de-escalate disciplinary moments with these students.

Step 4

I meet with Pam to discuss the findings from the disciplinary review, observations, and student interviews. I do not provide specific results from these actions. The reason is that I believed Pam would view the results as an attack on her character. This level of White fragility could also prevent Pam from feeling confident about my ability to support her. As such, I decided that after earning Pam's trust, I would share all of the feedback with her.

Using the findings as a guide, I engage Pam in developing a plan of action for addressing her African American students. First, through extensive discussions, we develop two behavioral objectives. Pam would learn to minimize and avoid unnecessary disciplinary issues with African American students. She would also be able to address the willful misbehavior of African American students.

After completing this process, Pam and I developed a four-part, first-person agreement to the objectives. The agreements are as follows:

1. Ability—I will commit to developing a holistic understanding of situations that lead to conflict with my African American students.
2. Stability—I will work to be the stabilizing force of disciplinary situations with African American students.
3. Durability—I will persevere through disciplinary moments with African American students.
4. Humility—I will view suggestions as opportunities to enhance my approaches to addressing disciplinary issues with African American students.

I then facilitate Pam's steps toward eliciting the desired behaviors from her African American students. What follows is a description of these experiences.

Phase 1: September 2015–November 2015

In the beginning, the basis of our work consists of knowledge, skills, and disposition. From a knowledge standpoint, Pam and I discuss the relevance of Whiteness to her disciplinary responses with African American students. Pam is initially resistant to acknowledging her Whiteness. She feels that race has no relevance to her interactions with African American students.

In response, I remind Pam of the humility aspect of the agreement. I then engage Pam in specific readings about Whiteness. Afterward, Pam and I review the feedback from her African American students. Listed below are examples of these discussions:

Jared, an African American male, stands up and moves to the door. Pam then yells, "Get back here, Jared!" Jared pauses and then leaves the classroom. Pam rushes to the door and says, "Jared, get back here and stop disrespecting my rules." Jared ignores Pam and continues on to his next class.

Example 1: Addressing Emotion (First Discussion)

Hines: Pam, why do you think that Jared stands up?

Pam: Because he is disrespectful and doesn't listen.

Hines: And his reason for leaving the classroom and refusing to answer you?

Pam: Again, he's disrespectful and won't listen.

I introduce Jared's feedback to the discussion:

Hines: What was that about? Why did you ignore Ms. P?

Jared: I walked out of Mrs. P's class, because I can't keep being late for language arts class. I am already behind in that class and he won't let you in if you're late.

Hines: Did you talk to Ms. P?

Jared: Man, I mean excuse me, Dr. Hines, I tried to explain that to her. But she won't listen. And last week, I came back to her class to get a pass when I couldn't get into language arts. And she told me "it's not my problem" and wouldn't give me a pass. So I'm not going out like that again.

Example 1: Addressing Emotion (Second Discussion)

Hines: Pam, look carefully at Jared's feedback and tell me what you see.

(Pam reads the feedback and then shares her views with me.)

Pam: I just see defiance and disrespect.

Hines: I don't see that.

Pam: Well, what do you see?

Hines: I see a student that doesn't feel heard. And because the student doesn't feel heard, he is ignoring you.

Pam: But don't you think that by ignoring me, he is being disrespectful?

Hines: Yes. But do you understand where the disrespect is coming from?

Pam: I feel like you are defending this Black student.

Hines: No. What I'm trying to do, Pam, is get you to see how the lack of acknowledging emotion is impacting the way in which Jared sees and responds to you.

While Pam sits silent, I further explain that as a White person, she has been socialized to only consider White-framed perspectives. As a result, she is oblivious to the impact of the emotion-laden perspectives of her African American students.

To further expound on this point, I engage Pam in a discussion of the relevance of emotion to Jeannetta's response to her teaching. To expand on this point, I engage Pam in a discussion of the relevance of emotion to Jeannetta's response to her teaching.

Example 1: Addressing Emotion (Third Discussion)

Hines: Let's look at your exchange with Jeannetta.

Pam: Well, what's there to look at, Dr. Hines? She was extremely disrespectful to me!

Hines: Again, Pam. Look at how race influenced the outcome of the situation.

Pam: Why do I need to consider race?

Hines: Because as a White person, you are trained to believe that race doesn't matter. But it does—to you and to Jeannetta.

Pam: Huh?

Hines: Look at these statements.

> *Jeannetta: Ms. P, we care about ourselves.*

> *Jeannetta: Well, a lot of times, we can't even ask you questions about what you're teaching us.*

> *Jeannetta: But you can act like you want us to learn.*

> *Jeannetta: Ain't nobody disrespecting you!*

> *Jeannetta: I'm not watching anything. I just want to learn from what you teach.*

> *Jeannetta: What did I do?*

Hines: You see this commentary as disrespect.

Pam: Well, if it's not that, then what is it?

Hines: These comments highlight the emotion drive responses of an African American student who feels ignored by you. So it's not a situation where she is just making these statements out of the blue. As with many African American people, she is just saying "Listen to me and value my humanity. See the worth in what I'm trying to explain to you." Her choice of words may be raw. But they are an expression of her authentic efforts to convey her issues to you.

Pam: Okay. So tell me what to do?

Hines: Listen and realize that emotion is a very, very important part of understanding the needs of Jeannetta, as well as other African American students.

Pam: So are you saying that all of my Black students are exactly alike?

Hines: No. I am saying that when it comes to needing to be heard, your African American students will use similar displays of emotion to be heard by you.

Example 2: Embracing Synchronization (First Discussion)

> *Hines:* Pam, let's look back at the exchange below between you and Josh.
>
>> *Pam: Okay, class. Who can tell me about the term LCD?*
>>
>> *Josh: You mean LSD?*
>>
>> (The class laughs.)
>>
>> *Pam: What did you say?*
>
> *Hines:* Think about your response "What did you say?"
>
> *Pam:* Well, I knew what he said. I just wanted to make him admit it.
>
> *Hines:* What were you trying to accomplish with that?
>
> *Pam:* I wanted him to see that a 12-year-old has no business making that type of comment in class or anywhere for that matter.
>
> *Hines:* Okay.

I then provide Pam with the following narrative:

> Ms. P is a good teacher. But she just keeps going on and on and won't let things go. I was just playing. But she tried to shame me and I just clapped back at her.

Example 2: Embracing Synchronization (Second Discussion)

> *Hines:* Pam, look at Josh's perception of you and the situation.
>
> *Pam:* Well, like I said—a 12-year-old has no business discussing LSD in school. That's just so inappropriate.
>
> *Hines:* Okay. I hear you. But in keeping in line with our objectives, there's a way to simultaneously make your point and keep African American students in class.

Pam: Do you mean just ignore that type of behavior?

Hines: No. I mean respond in ways that are more attuned to your African American students.

I use this exchange to introduce cultural synchronization to Pam. I then provide a preliminary review of how to use the verbal, vocal, and visual model with African American students. We then brainstorm possible culturally synchronized responses to Josh's LSD comment. Sample comments are as follows:

Humorous Statements

- I got your LSD!
- Okay, so you got jokes! You better be serious when you take your test, which will include LCD!
- Pay attention, Josh! Or I'm a think that you're on LSD!

Direct Statements

- Josh, you know that I didn't mention anything about LSD!
- Josh, I am not the one to talk to about LSD! LCD—then we can talk!
- I know that you just didn't mention what I think that you mentioned in my class.
- Yes, which stands for Listen, Sit, and Do not use those initials in this class again.

After reviewing these responses, I inform Pam how to add vocal and visual dimensions to the culturally congruent communication. For the next two months, I provide Pam with verbal, vocal, and visual responses to addressing recurring discipline issues with African American students. The textboxes below show an e-mail exchange between us in response to her request for disciplinary assistance with African American students (see textboxes 5.2–5.5).

Textbox 5.2

From: Pam Piland <PPiland@education.net>
To: Mack Hines <hines@yahoo.com>
Sent: Wednesday, October 7, 2015 4:45 PM
Subject: Help, Dr. Hines!!!!
Dr. Hines,

Hope you are well. I want to share a situation I had with an African American female in my first-period class. Yesterday, I was talking with a student about classroom rules and her phone went off. She knew it was against school rules but said it was her mother. I said, "Okay, go outside and quickly make the call. But when you get back, your phone comes to me." After taking the call, she came back and would not give me the phone! I was so pissed that I sent her to the office and she was put in ISS for the rest of the day. I sent her to the office because she was so rude about the situation.

What I want to know from you is how could this Black student be this way with me? I let her take the call and she still acted like a spoiled brat afterward.

Also, what was a more "synchronized" way for me to handle this situation—now and in the future? What are your suggestions for preventing this issue from becoming a major problem between me and this student?

Textbox 5.3

From: Mack Hines <hines@yahoo.com>
To: Pam Piland <PPiland@education.net>
Sent: Thursday, October 8, 2015 8:45 AM
Subject: Re: Help, Dr. Hines!!!!
Hi, Pam.

I just received and read your e-mail. Here are my views on the situation with the African American student. I want to commend you for your response to the student's need to talk with her mom. At the same time, I want to push your thinking about the rest of the situation.

First, is it that the student was being a "spoiled brat" or that your emotion caused you to see the student in a negative light? I am going to go with the latter point. I believe that anger is what pushed you to immediately send the student to the office. I also feel that disappointment—not anger—should have determined your response to the student. This emotion may have caused you to view the African American student as being unappreciative of your graciousness. From there, you would see that lacking appreciation is what caused the student to disregard your expectations for the classroom.

By considering this perspective, you will be better prepared to consider the following question:

- How do I reintegrate this African American student back into my classroom?
- This question is contingent upon your response to this question: Do I allow this student's behavior to throw me off track in terms of how I actually see her?

By this, will you allow the African American student's response to form your final thoughts of who she is? Or will you see this student for what she could become by receiving guidance from you?

Of course, my opinion is that the student receives guidance from you.

My suggestion:

1. Find the African American student and have a "heart to heart" talk as soon as possible.
2. Use the previously discussed verbal, vocal, and visual approach to address the student.

Verbal Suggestions

Use direct, straightforward language to make the following points:

- You have guidelines for cell phones in your classroom.
- All students will follow those guidelines.
- Students will be addressed when they do not follow those guidelines.

Vocal Suggestions

Remember that we talked about the culturally responsive ways of using emotion with African American students. Based on your e-mail, I suggest that you stress the following points in an emotional way:

- You were gracious enough to allow her to take the call.
- You displayed this gesture because you recognized the seriousness of the phone call.
- You also displayed this gesture because you do care about the overall welfare of your students.
- Your kindness will not be mistaken for weakness.

Visual Suggestions

Remember that we talked about displaying a demeanor of concern and conviction. Your concern lies in setting students up for success in your class.

Your conviction is that you will push students to live up to your expectations.

Lastly, remember that African American students view authority through the person and not just the position. So you need to make the response about you and the student. The student needs to understand that you are the rule, law, and policy in the classroom. As such, the student must respect you.

At the same time, your response is also based on concern for the student. Yes, you want the student to stop using the cell phone in class. The need for discontinuing this behavior is not just about being in compliance with rules. Through talking with you, the student needs to see that this experience is about being a person of character and integrity.

Let me know if you need more feedback.

I'll talk to you soon.

Sincerely,

Dr. Hines

P.S. Lastly, as long as you are *genuine*, your use of these suggestions will help the student to see your concern for her.

Textbox 5.4

From: Pam Piland <PPiland@education.net>
To: Mack Hines <hines@yahoo.com>
Sent: Wednesday, October 14, 2015 12:45 PM
Subject: Response to Dr. Hines

Dr. H,

I put all of your suggestions into action with the student. At first, she copped an attitude. But I remembered your word "genuine." I tried to be as professional and authentic as I possibly could. She eventually listened to me and did most of her work.

THANK YOU!!!!

Question:

I'm still a little unsure of how to handle this student.

Your thoughts?

PP

Textbox 5.5

From: Mack Hines <hines@yahoo.com>
To: Pam Piland<PPiland@education.net>
Sent: Friday, October 16, 2015 7:23 AM
Subject: Re: Response to Dr. Hines
Pam,
Great job with this student!

You feel unsure because you haven't learned to connect with this student yet. As I said over and over, it takes time to gain authority with African American children. The MAIN thing is that you remembered to be *genuine*! I will continue to help you understand how to resolve your issues with our African American students. For now, just continue to reflect on what you have learned from this experience.

Have a good day and great weekend!
Sincerely,
Dr. Hines

Phase 2: December 2015–February 2016

Pam and I have now read and discussed extensive research on Whiteness and other concepts related to race. As a result, she has developed a nuanced understanding of how race influences her disciplinary issues with African American students. Evidence to this effect is seen in her willingness to reflect on approaches used specifically to respond to African American students.

Yet she still needs assistance on how to best engage African American disciplinary issues. As a result, Pam and I begin to co-construct approaches to responding to the issues. We identify an incident or issue with African American students. Initially, I would initiate the majority of the solutions to the issues. Now, Pam and I co-construct approaches to elicit the desired behaviors from African American students.

One way is for Pam to propose a solution to be used with African American students. We then discuss the feasibility of the solution. Another approach is for me to offer an idea for addressing the misbehavior. Whereas Pam would instantly use my suggestion, she now considers the usefulness of the approach for her African American students.

Let's look at an example of how this collaboration played out in Pam's classroom (see textboxes 5.6 and 5.7).

Textbox 5.6

From: Pam Piland <PPiland@education.net>
To: Mack Hines <hines@yahoo.com>
Sent: Tuesday, February 9, 2016 9:15 AM
Subject: An Issue

Dr. Hines, I want your opinion on a situation that has been happening since last week. I have some African American students—3 girls and 3 boys—who gather in my classroom during their lunch period. One of the girls is Jeannetta. One of the boys is Josh.

My only problem with this situation is this: The students stay in my classroom until about 10 minutes left for lunch. Then they rush to lunch, and Josh and Jeannetta are late coming back to my class.

The other day, I stopped my two students at the door and told them about their behavior. Josh just walked off from me. And both students are still late coming back to my class from lunch.

Since working with you, I am trying to think out of the box with handling these situations.

But I'm not going to lie—right now, I am thinking about stopping the students from loitering in my classroom.

PP

Textbox 5.7

Tuesday, February 9, 5:45 PM

Mack Hines: Pam, just read your e-mail. Let's think this through. First question—what do you ultimately want from Josh and Jeannetta?

Pam Piland: I want my students to get back to my class on time.

Mack Hines: Why do you want them to get to class on time?

Pam Piland: Obviously so they won't interrupt class.

Mack Hines: And that's it?

Pam Piland: No. Because one of the rules is for ALL students to return to class in a timely manner.

Mack Hines: Okay, rules established. Check. What else?

Pam Piland: Okay. I see where you're going with this. Not just rules but concern for student.

Mack Hines: BINGO!

Pam Piland: I've got to show these students that I care about them and insist that they live up to my expectations.

Mack Hines: So how can you communicate these thoughts to both students?

Pam Piland: Let me think about it and get back to you.

Mack Hines: Cool!

Over the next two days, Pam and I engage in phone discussions about the best approach to address the situation. The section below provides the most important excerpt from those conversations (see textbox 5.8).

Textbox 5.8

Pam: I am going to pull both students to the side and talk to them.

Hines: Good start!

Pam: In a very straightforward way, I will say something to the effect of enjoying having their company in class and that I'm humbled that they see my class as a safe haven. But that I need them to better manage their time and get back from lunch in a timely manner.

Hines: Pam.

Pam: Yes.

Hines: Let's go back to the verbal part of the verbal, visual, and vocal approach. How are you aligning "company in class" and "class as safe haven" as directness with Black students?

Pam: Honestly. I feel like it is kind of harsh to just come right out with it.

Hines: Pam, as we've discussed, African American students expect you to act with authority to get authority. For many of these students, that authority is based on saying what needs to be said about a situation.

Pam: But I just . . .

Hines: Look—I understand that you need to feel comfortable in your skin. At the same time, I encourage you to remember that you're working with students who are socialized from a different communication style than you as a White person.

Pam: I know. I was direct when I dealt with the phone situation. It just wasn't comfortable.

Hines: Okay. Well, here's my take—you can't let these students continue to return late to your class. We both know that the students have perceived you as being a nagger. And if you revert to being indirect, they will return to viewing you in that way.

Pam: Well, maybe I should practice directness with some of my friends or loved ones.

Hines: Do whatever it takes to gain the confidence to directly address this situation with these two students. The main thing is that they must know and see that you care enough to address this issue with them.

Pam: Okay. Bye.

Hines: Keep in touch.

The following week, Pam addresses the situation with her African American students. The section below presents the results from her actions (see textboxes 5.9–5.12).

Phase 3: March 2016–May 2016

The date is April 16 and I am in the midst of my 35th observation of Pam's class. Pam is teaching a lesson on fractions. After reviewing the lesson, she transitions the class to independent practice. As she starts individual student discussions, Josh yells, "Hey, Ms. P, I got a problem."

At this point, I am a little nervous about what will be the end result of this situation. On the one hand, Pam has matured in her consideration and responsiveness to African American students. For example, as a result of Jared's feedback, Pam now makes timely dismissals of her classes. After our review of Jeannetta's feelings, she now provides detailed explanations of lessons and assignments.

Textbox 5.9

From: Pam Piland <PPiland@education.net>
To: Mack Hines <hines@yahoo.com>
Sent: Friday, February 19, 2016 6:45 PM
Subject: Decision with Students
Dr. Hines,
I decided to address these students in a direct way. I started by telling them that I don't have a problem with having them in my class. But I made both of them aware of my real issue: the lateness. I directly said, "I cannot and will not have you making late returns from lunch." I also said, "I expect more from you and better from you. I care for you." And I said it in a way to let them know that I meant it. I ended by telling them, "It's my job to hold you accountable for being the best that you can be. And I will do it." Well, after that talk, Josh and one of the other boys stopped coming to my room.

As for Jeannetta, she and the other students still come to my class for lunch. For the first three days, they visited my class for only 5 minutes. Yesterday, they stayed in my class for the first 20 minutes of their lunch. But for all three days, she's returned from lunch on time!

Textbox 5.10

From: Mack Hines <hines@yahoo.com>
To: Pam Piland <PPiland@education.net>
Sent: Friday, February 19, 2016 7:45 PM
Subject: Re: Decision with Students
Pam, great news!!! My suggestion is that you still reiterate this expectation to Jeannetta and Josh. By the way, what's the deal with Josh?

Textbox 5.11

From: Pam Piland <PPiland@education.net>
To: Mack Hines <hines@yahoo.com>
Sent: Friday, February 19, 2016 8:36 PM
Subject: Re: Decision with Students
Off and on. He's was actually on time on Monday, Tuesday, and Thursday. He was late on Wednesday and Friday. I sent him to the office on Wednesday, because I just needed someone else to talk to him about being on time. On Friday, I just pulled him to the side and told him that he must be on time to my class. I reiterated that he has to live up to my expectations.

Textbox 5.12

From: Mack Hines <hines@yahoo.com>
To: Pam Piland <PPiland@education.net>
Sent: Friday, February 19, 2016 10:55 PM
Subject: Re: Decision with Students
Great! Remember, that this is a process, Pam. The most important thing for you to do is two things. Keep reviewing the main points from all of our discussions on African American students. Also, continue to tailor the discussions to your African American students.

I think you are comfortable with the vocal and visual. But you must continue to embrace the need for directness to your African American students.
Again, great job and I will see you next Tuesday.
Sincerely,
Dr. H

But she still has a somewhat tenuous relationship with Josh. Therefore, her response to him will play a significant role in the outcome of this situation. Despite my concerns, I cautiously observe the scenario unfold in the following manner:

Ms. Pam: Yes, Josh. How can I help you?

Josh: Can I go get a drink of water?

(The class laughs.)

Ms. Pam: Get to work, Josh, and I'll think about it.

Josh (eyes rolling): Come on, now! I'm thirsty!

Ms. Pam: I have a thirst that will only be satisfied when you get to work.

Josh: Oh, Lawd!

Pam continues to observe students' work. She stops by Josh's desk to look at his work. *(She then informs him to go and get some water. As he walks to the door, she provides him with one additional directive.)*

Ms. Pam: Josh.

Josh: Yes, Ms. P.

Ms. Pam: Make it quick! My thirst is still not satisfied.

(Josh sighs. Yet he quickly gets water and returns to the classroom.)

Here we see Pam's effectiveness in addressing a disciplinary moment with an African American student. One indicator of success is addressing the issue without disciplinary removal. Another measure of success is engagement through consideration and synchronization. From a considerate standpoint, Pam's most important line was "Yes, Josh. How can I help you?" This question communicated a readiness to acknowledge Josh's emotions. This response also prevented Pam's response from leading to a hostile exchange with Josh.

An equally significant part of the scenario was Pam's response to Josh's request for water. If you recall, Pam responded to Josh's thirst with her own thirst for hardworking students.

The synchronization of this reply lies in the eloquent and humorous expression of nonnegotiable expectations for student achievement.

During my visit, I observed Pam use similar responses to resolve other disciplinary moments with African American students. These outcomes offer some explanation for her fewer disciplinary referrals with this student population. The results also highlight Pam's growth and maturity in interacting with Black children in her classroom.

Zone of Disciplinary Development for White Teachers

A useful way of analyzing Pam's success is Lev Vygotsky's (1978) Zone of Proximal Development. Vygotsky defined Zone of Proximal Development as "the distance between the actual development level as determined by independent problem solving and the level of potential development as determined through problem solving under adult guidance or in collaboration with more capable peers" (p. 86). In other words, a child's development consists of two levels. The level of actual development is characterized by the child's ability to independently perform the task. At this level of potential development, the child can complete the task through scaffolding from an adult or competent peer.

Scaffolding is the support needed to facilitate the child's learning experiences (Bodrova & Leong, 2007). The task remains the same throughout the scaffolding process. But as the child grows in completing the task, less guidance is needed from other individuals (see figure 5.1).

My work with Pam can be termed a Zone of Disciplinary Development for White Teachers. This zone consists of three levels. The levels are as follows: Surface Understanding, Proximal Consciousness, and Competent Effectiveness (see figure 5.2). Using Pam as my example, I describe these levels in the next section.

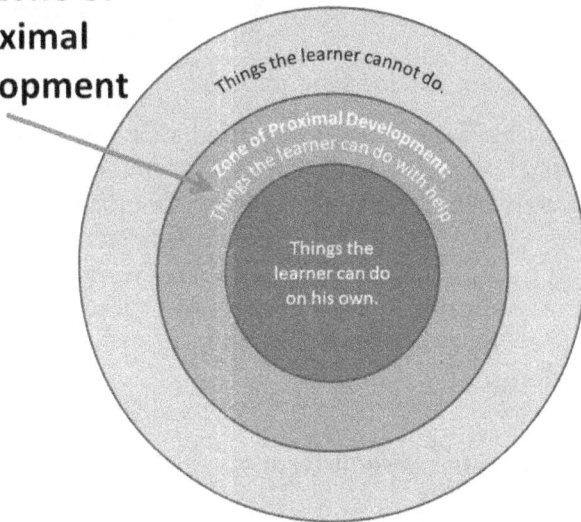

Figure 5.1. Zone of Proximal Development. "The Zone of Proximal Development." Cuppacocoa. http://www.cuppacocoa.com/the-zone-of-proximal-development/

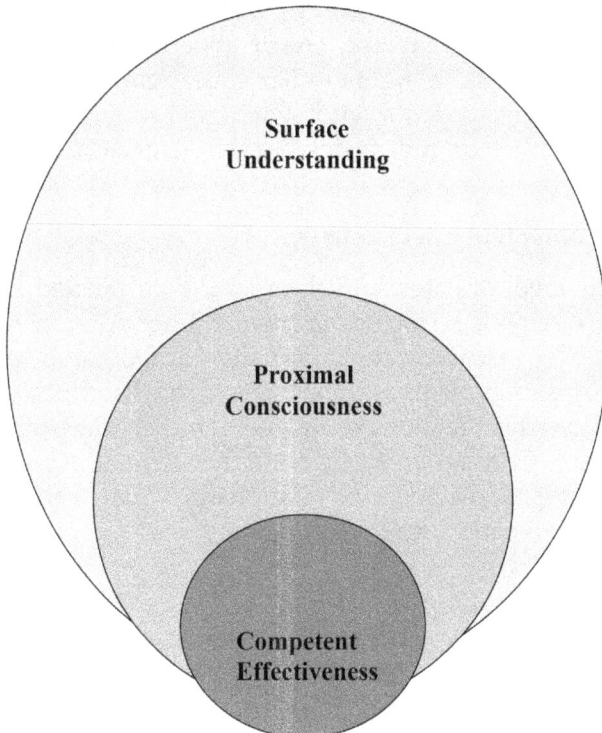

Figure 5.2. Zone of Disciplinary Development for White teachers.

Level 1: Surface Understanding

Under guidance, Pam developed an awareness of her Whiteness. I also provided her with insight on becoming considerate of and synchronized with African American students. But at this point, these teachings did not have enough time to influence her thoughts on disciplinary issues with African Americans students. As a result, Pam continued to look to me for specific ways of solving disciplinary problems with her African American students.

Level 2: Proximal Responsiveness

At this point, Pam still needed support on what to do when faced with disciplinary issues with African American students. As a result, I mentored and monitored her progression through these issues. As a mentor, I engaged Pam in discussions on thought processes conducive to positive change in African American students' behavior. The next step was for me to monitor her use of these thoughts in her classroom. As Pam became proficient in consideration and synchronization, I continued to provide guidance on redirecting African American students.

Level 3: Competent Effectiveness

At this level of actual development, Pam needed little support in resolving disciplinary issues with her African American students. The main reason is that she earned the authority to command respect in disciplinary situations. In effect, consideration and synchronization became her lens for interpreting Black misbehavior. Consequently, Pam and her African American students developed disciplinary relationships that were based on harmony, connection, and community.

The Practical Application

Directions: Use this section to analyze your applications of behavior building approaches toward African American students.

Considering Roles

1. Describe the disciplinary situation in need of role consideration.
   a. What steps did you take to identify the situation in need of role consideration?
   b. Were the steps used for identification based on an informed understanding or uninformed understanding of Whiteness?
   c. Were the steps used for identification based on an informed understanding or uninformed understanding of Blackness?
2. How did you use role consideration to address disciplinary situations with African American students?
3. What were the authoritative aspects of the application?
4. What were the overall results of the application?
   A. Did the results enhance your ability to acquire the authority to shape the behaviors of African American students?

If yes, why?

1. What is your evidence of effectiveness?
2. What was it about you that contributed to the effectiveness?
3. What was it about the African American student that contributed to the effectiveness?
4. How can you translate your findings from the use of role consideration into an even more effective response to African American students in similar situations?

If no, why not?

1. What is your evidence of ineffectiveness?
2. What was it about you that contributed to the ineffectiveness?
3. What was it about the African American student that contributed to the ineffectiveness?

4. How can you use your findings from the use of role consideration to make modifications that elicit the desired behaviors from the African American student?

Considering Culture

1. Describe the disciplinary situation in need of cultural consideration.
   a. What steps did you take to identify the situation in need of cultural consideration?
   b. Were the steps used for identification based on an informed understanding or uninformed understanding of Whiteness?
   c. Were the steps used for identification based on an informed understanding or uninformed understanding of Blackness?
2. How did you use cultural consideration to address disciplinary situations with African American students?
3. What were the authoritative aspects of the application?
4. What were the overall results of the application?
   A. Did the results enhance your ability to acquire the authority to shape the behaviors of African American students?

If yes, why?

1. What is your evidence of effectiveness?
2. What was it about you that contributed to the effectiveness?
3. What was it about the African American student that contributed to the effectiveness?
4. How can you translate your findings from the use of cultural consideration into an even more effective response to African American students in similar situations?

If no, why not?

1. What is your evidence of ineffectiveness?
2. What was it about you that contributed to the ineffectiveness?
3. What was it about the African American student that contributed to the ineffectiveness?
4. How can you use your findings from the use of cultural consideration to make modifications that elicit the desired behaviors from the African American student?

Considering Emotion

1. Describe the disciplinary situation in need of emotional consideration.
   a. What steps did you take to identify the situation in need of emotional consideration?
   b. Were the steps used for identification based on an informed understanding or uninformed understanding of Whiteness?
   c. Were the steps used for identification based on an informed understanding or uninformed understanding of Blackness?
2. How did you use emotional consideration to address disciplinary situations with African American students?
3. What were the authoritative aspects of the application?
4. What were the overall results of the application?
   A. Did the results enhance your ability to acquire the authority to shape the behaviors of African American students?

If yes, why?

1. What is your evidence of effectiveness?
2. What was it about you that contributed to the effectiveness?
3. What was it about the African American student that contributed to the effectiveness?

4. How can you translate your findings from the use of emotional consideration into an even more effective response to African American students in similar situations?

If no, why not?

1. What is your evidence of ineffectiveness?
2. What was it about you that contributed to the ineffectiveness?
3. What was it about the African American student that contributed to the ineffectiveness?
4. How can you use your findings from the use of emotional consideration to make modifications that elicit the desired behaviors from the African American student?

Use of Synchronization

1. Describe the disciplinary situation in need of cultural synchronization.
   a. What steps did you take to identify the situation in need of cultural synchronization?
   b. Were the steps used for identification based on an informed understanding or uninformed understanding of Whiteness?
   c. Were the steps used for identification based on an informed understanding or uninformed understanding of Blackness?
2. How did you use cultural synchronization to address disciplinary situations with African American students?
3. What were the authoritative aspects of the application?
4. What were the overall results of the application?
   A. Did the results enhance your ability to acquire the authority to shape the behaviors of African American students?

If yes, why?

1. What is your evidence of effectiveness?
2. What was it about you that contributed to the effectiveness?
3. What was it about the African American student that contributed to the effectiveness?
4. How can you translate your findings from the use of synchronization into an even more effective response to African American students in similar situations?

If no, why not?

1. What is your evidence of ineffectiveness?
2. What was it about you that contributed to the ineffectiveness?
3. What was it about the African American student that contributed to the ineffectiveness?
4. How can you use your findings from the use of synchronization to make modifications that elicit the desired behaviors from the African American student?

Conclusion

This chapter presents a model of cultural relevance for bridging the disciplinary gap between White teachers and Black children. White teachers have the right to address Black children for misbehavior and other disciplinary issues. But these teachers neither cannot nor shouldn't attempt to punish poor behavior out of Black children. That approach does not work.

White teachers must understand a contextual understanding of how discipline and authority work within Black culture. This comprehension should be reflectively applied toward building desired behavioral expectations within Black children. Although time consuming, this approach is the difference between controlling Black behavior and eliciting behavior that shows respect for the authority within White teachers.

6

An Instructional Passport to Black Student Achievement

Much of the current focus of classroom instruction is on the location of the school and subject matter of the teacher. But the true meaning of teaching and learning is who and how. To determine how to teach students, teachers must first know who they are teaching. This chapter explains why this concept is the basis of determining White teachers' instructional effectiveness in teaching African American students.

The Principle

What Must White Teachers Be Mindful of in Order to Deliver Effective Instruction to African American Students?

White teachers must realize that Black children excel in learning environments that are congruent to the lived experiences of Black people.

Why Is This Understanding Specific to African American Students?

In order for teaching and learning to lead to Black student achievement, Black students must experience a familiar environment. A familiar environment makes students comfortable enough to pursue achievement. For Black children, familiarity lies in the opportunities for these students to bring and see elements of their culture in schools.

The importance of this level of familiarity cannot be understated. The reason is that, like most American institutions, the education system is culturally responsive to White culture. Schools mimic this value system by embracing ways of thinking and knowing that affirm White families and children.

As a result, White teachers are often uncomfortable with the prevalence of Black students' cultural tendencies in classrooms. Unlike Black teachers, White teachers are far less likely to see the educational value of Black children's home life experiences. Simply put, Blackness is not legitimized within the culture of schools.

As such, White teachers must still be educated on the power of allowing Black students to learn with Blackness. This approach is a matter of teacher enlightenment. For Black children, learning while Black is a cultural necessity. In the end, both rationales can create a stronger teaching and learning relationship between White teachers and Black students.

The Approach

How Can White Teachers Translate This Mindfulness into Delivering Effective Instruction to African American Students?

The most meaningful approach to teaching African American students is culturally relevant teaching. Drawing from extensive research, this term is defined as the use of Blackness to create meaningful learning experiences for African American students. The underlying tenet of this instructional approach is cultural orientations to drawing these students into the learning environment.

White teachers must take three steps to demonstrate this level of instructional engagement with African American students. The steps are background, common ground, and then higher ground. The section below provides a theoretical and practical explanation of these steps and further explains these steps.

Part 1: Theory

Step 1: Background

In *Black Children: Their Roots, Culture, and Learning Styles,* Dr. Janice Hale-Benson states that "Black people participate in a coherent culture that shapes their cognitive development and affects the way they approach academic tasks and the way they behave in traditional academic settings" (1986, p. 21). The essence of Dr. Hale-Benson's viewpoint is the relationship between culture and cognition. That is, thinking and learning are socially located and mediated by culture (Gordon & Armour-Thomas, 1991; Vygotsky, 1978).

If you recall, we referenced the relevance of Black culture to the relational and behavioral needs of African American children. The central point of these analyses was Black cultural dimensions. The other side of this analysis is the relationship between these dimensions and home and community. In other words, African American homes tend to be culturally structured environments of verve, communalism, orality, affect, spirituality, social time perspective, harmony, movement, and expressive individualism (Boykin, 1983, 1995). As a reference point, here are four examples that are prominently featured in research on Black culture.

Example 1: Movement.   A hallmark of many African American homes and communities is movement. A critical part of this socialization is the rhythmic life orientation that shapes Black patterns of speech and activity. Such rhythm also includes unique kinesthetic displays of coordinated gestures and movement.

Example 2: Communalism.   African Americans tend to be socialized in communities that strongly emphasize interdependence (Boykin, 1995). Here Black lives are socialized toward each other instead of aligned with objectives (Boykin, 1986). Within a communal orientation, significant importance and attention are attached to connections and relationships. As a result, social bonds are a salient factor in the everyday lives of African American children.

Example 3: Verve.   Verve is of great value to African American people. The reason is that African American homes often serve as reservoirs of high levels of physical stimulation (Boykin, 1983). Many familial activities are filled with varying levels of intensity, variability, and density. Intensity is the liveliness and loudness of behavior. Variability is characterized as the variety within activities. Density is depicted as the simultaneous presence of stimulating elements within the environment. Stimulation refers to the number of stimulating elements or activities simultaneously present.

Example 4: Orality.   Orality is best described as an array of communication styles within African American homes and communities. Historically, African Americans have relied on the spoken word as an important means of communication. Three facets of oral communication that stand out are call-response, tonal semantics, and signification.

Call and response is a back-and-forth exchange of information. The speaker makes a call to the audience. The audience, in turn, responds to the speaker.

Both the call and response always serve several purposes. First, the communication affirms the significance of the shared knowledge. Second, the active participation creates a communal bond between the speaker and audience. Third, active participation affirms the significance of the content.

Tonal semantics is the use of rhythm and voice to add emphasis and meaning to word usage. In this context, the voice is used "like a musical instrument with improvisations" (Smitherman, 1977, p. 134). At the same time, rhythm gives the voice an acoustical expression and demeanor.

Another key characteristic of tonal semantics lies in the vocal arrangement of words for meaning. Depending on the speaker's vocal tone and rhythm, words and phrases can carry a variety of meanings. In addition, words with different or a repetitive tone convey the importance of specific situations.

Signifying is the playfully aggressive use of sarcasm to make comments about someone's behavior (Smitherman, 1977). The crux of this method of communication is that "[i]t is a culturally approved method of talking about somebody. Since the signifier employs humor, it makes the put-down easier to swallow and gives the recipient a socially acceptable way out" (Smitherman, 1977, p. 134). This form of verbal dueling is often seen and heard between family and friends within African American communities.

There are two functions of signification. The directive function consists of sharing someone else's commentary in ways that arouse anger and disbelief. The depreciative function involves the signifier's use of wit to arouse embarrassment and shame within the listener.

Overall, these and the other dimensions represent unique patterns of socialization that sustain shared belief systems among Black people. African American children acquire this socialization through tacit cultural conditioning. Over time, this orientation causes Black children's life experiences to crystallize into a cognitive Black personality. That is, Black children display culturally conditioned ways of thinking, behaving, and feeling. Table 6.1 provides a profile of African American children's personality.

Table 6.1.   Profile of African American Children's Personality

Characteristic	Personality
Orality	African American children are both word dependent and verbally expressive.
Communalism	African American children are more oriented to people than things.
Movement	African American children display a rhythmic and coordinated orientation to life.
Affect	African American children are highly sensitive to emotions and feelings.
Verve	African American children are very attuned to situations that involve multiple stimuli.
Expressive Individualism	African American children value uniqueness, adaptation, and spontaneity.

This profile presents a much-needed, authentic view of African American children. But viewpoints are just the beginning for White teachers. White teachers must stretch authentic insight into actions and authentic understandings of African American children.

Central to this goal is engaging African American students in venues outside of school. The significance of such engagement is twofold. First, non-school settings remove the chain of command that creates asymmetrical power relationships between White teachers and Black students. Second, Black churches and other Black-framed cultural landmarks provide invitations into Black-framed cultural immersion experiences. Both benefits provide White teachers with insight on why background makes Black lives matter to African American children.

Step 2: Common Ground

Common ground is a customization of the curriculum to the backgrounds of African American children. Achievement of this level of customization requires two critical understandings. First, African American children enter schools with a cognitive Black personality. Because of this personality, African American children display culturally conditioned learning preferences in classrooms. Table 6.2 features a profile of the learning preferences that have been observed within African American children.

Drawing from this profile, teachers make curriculum modifications that address the instructional needs of African American students. At this point, change is developing lessons and activities that reflect African American ways of knowing, understanding, and representing information. *Knowledge* is defined as ensuring that content holds some relevance to African American students' lives. Understanding entails allowing African American students to process information from a culturally framed perspective. Representation consists of examples that are framed by African American students' worldviews.

Table 6.2.   Profile of African American Children's Learning Preferences

Characteristic	Preferences
Orality	African American children rely on word meanings and expressions to make sense of learning situations.
Communalism	African American children are highly responsive to teaching and learning that involves bonding and connecting with others in a socialized context.
Movement	African American children thrive when presented with opportunities to learn in movement-friendly learning environments.
Affect	African American children thrive in academic tasks that are tailored to the inclusion of emotions and feelings.
Verve	African American children respond favorably to learning environments that allow for intense levels of task stimulation and task variation.
Expressive Individualism	African American child are comfortable with being able to maintain distinct perspectives on information.

Step 3: Higher Ground

Higher ground is the deliverance of instruction in ways that match the needs of African American students. Based on my observations, I have found that the tenets of African American culture can be translated into effective instructional strategies for African American students. Table 6.3 highlights some strategies that have been consistently used to increase Black students' engagement and achievement.

By using these approaches, teachers are taking into account the learning styles that emanate from the socialization of African American children. As a result, they can enhance African American student achievement in a variety of ways. In other words, teaching and learning take place in environments that connect with the lived experiences of African American children. That same environment is also ripe for the inclusion of African American students' perspectives on information.

Through these experiences, African American students become active participants in their own learning. One of the most significant displays of involvement is critical thinking. Here African American students become producers of knowledge

Table 6.3. Instructional Strategies for African American Student Achievement

Characteristic	Preferences
Orality	The teacher cultivates a learning environment that showcases speaking as a performance. In addition, because their verbal abilities are viewed as strengths, African American students employ various modes of oral expression.
Communalism	The teacher emphasizes interdependent approaches to student achievement. In this context, African American students are able to support and be supported in acquiring information.
Movement	The teacher formats activities to include different levels of purposeful movement. In addition, academic tasks are structured within a variety of highly rhythmic expressiveness conditions.
Affect	The teacher emphasizes the emotional value of information. The teacher also affirms the emotions and feelings of African American students.
Verve	The teacher creates an arousing learning environment that offers task variation and task stimulation. For example, African American students acquire information in a variety of stimulating formats with varying levels of intensity.
Expressive Individualism	The teacher creates activities that facilitate African American students' understanding of concepts in novel and unique ways.

instead of just knowledge consumers. They are then able to transfer content learned in this context to real-life situations.

Part 2: Theory into Practice

Ms. Rosenell Jackson is an African American third-grade teacher who facilitates high achievement among African American students. In fact, her African American children earn the highest standardized language arts test scores among third-graders within the school. This year, she has a class of 20 students. Of this population, she has eight African American students. The remaining demographics consist of six Hispanic students and five White students. Here is a sample lesson that was designed to intentionally engage the African American students in her classroom.

Lesson Objective

- The students will be able to describe fantasy and reality in their own words.
- The students will be able to identify elements of fantasy and reality in a story.

Standard

Students understand, make inferences, and draw conclusions about the structure and elements of fiction and provide evidence from text to support their understanding.

The Lesson

Ms. Jackson opens the lesson with the following statement: "Okay class. Today we are going to start talking about fantasy and reality."

Drawing from Black culture, she then uses call-and-response communication to describe the difference between the two genres. The following dialogue highlights her commentary to students:

Ms. Jackson: When I say *fantasy*, you say "not real." And when I say *reality*, you say "real." Ready?

Class (in unison): Yes!

Ms. Jackson: Fantasy!

Class: Not real!

Ms. Jackson: Come on, class, and say it like you mean it!

Class: Not real!

(At this point, four African American students are standing while responding to Ms. Jackson.)

Ms. Jackson: That's what I'm talking about! Reality!

Class: Real!

Ms. Jackson: Fantasy!

Class: Not real!

Ms. Jackson: Reality!

Class: Real!

Ms. Jackson: Good, good, good! Okay, kids, have a seat.

Ms. Jackson then draws from African American vernacular to reiterate the differences between fantasy and reality. She uses the following dialogue to revisit the genres.

Ms. Jackson: Okay, we are going to do another back and forth on fantasy and reality. But this time around, when I say *fantasy*, you say "That ain't real!" And when I say reality, you say "Now I know that's real!" Ready?

Class (in unison): Yes!

Ms. Jackson: Fantasy!

Class: That ain't real!

(The same four African American students are standing while responding to Ms. Jackson.)

Ms. Jackson: Reality!

Class: Now I know that's real!

(Ms. Jackson continues the call and response with a high level of rhythm, emotion, and feeling.)

Ms. Jackson (emphasizing first syllable fan*):* Fantasy!

Class: That ain't real!

Ms. Jackson (emphasizing first syllable re*):* Reality!

Class: Now I know that's real!

Ms. Jackson (emphasizing fantasy*):* It's fantasy!

Class: That ain't real!

Ms. Jackson (emphasizing syllables ality*):* It's Reality!

Class: Now I know that's real!

Ms. Jackson: Fantasy for one!

Class: That ain't real!

Ms. Jackson: Reality, please!

Class: Now I know that's real!

After completing the call-and-response exercise, Ms. Jackson writes the students' following responses on the board:

- Real.
- Not real.
- That ain't real.
- Now I know that's real.

Ms. Jackson leads the students in a choral reading of each response. She then asks, "Students, look on the board, as I read the words to you." Ms. Jackson reads the four statements to the students. She then asks, "What word did you continue to hear me read?" Without hesitation, several African American students yell, "Real."

Ms. Jackson then says, "That's right! Real." Ms. Jackson then asks, "What does the word *real* mean to you?" The students provide a variety of answers related to authenticity. Many African American students gave stories instead of definitions about *real*. Here's an example given by an African American female student:

> You know like one time we was going to my grandma's house. My brother asked my mama to stop at McDonald's. My mama said, "Where's your McDonald's money?" Me and my cousin started laughing.

An African American male provided the following story:

> Every night before I go to bed, me and my daddy say our prayers. I like the part when we have to say "I pray to the Lord my soul to keep." 'Cause that's how I know that God is real.

After discussing *real*, Ms. Jackson connects the term to fantasy and reality. She says, "Boys and girls, believe or it not, your answers about *real* go right along with fantasy and reality." Ms. Jackson then puts the following chart on the board (see table 6.4):

Table 6.4.   Fantasy versus Reality

Fantasy "That Ain't Real."	Reality "I Know That's Real."
1. Make Believe	1. Not Make Believe
2. The story happens but can't really happen.	2. The story happens and can really happen.
3. The characters are not real.	3. The characters are real.

After discussing the characteristics of fantasy and reality, Ms. Jackson reads a story below to the students called "The Man and the Bushes":

Once upon a time, there was a man who lived on a farm with his wife and two kids. His job was to trim bushes for the city. One day, while trimming bushes, a voice spoke to him. The voice said, "Why are you cutting me?" The man looked around but did not see anybody.

As he started to finish trimming the bush, the same voice said, "Don't do it!" He looked around, but he still didn't see anyone. He then picked up his hedge trimmer to continue with trimming the bushes.

Before he could start, he again heard, "Don't cut these bushes!" He looked in the bush and saw a ghost! The ghost pointed at the man and said, "Don't cut these bushes!"

"Yikes," the man screamed. He then dropped his hedge trimmer and ran to his truck. He then called his wife and told her about seeing a ghost. His wife told him to stay away from those bushes.

As the man was driving home, the ghost appeared in his truck. The man started to scream. The ghost then said, "Calm down—I am not going to hurt you." The ghost continued, "I just want to talk to you."

After calming down, the man said, "Then talk." The man continued, "And be real with me." The ghost then said, "The real deal is that I eat the bush to stay alive."

The man then took the ghost to some bushes in the country. When they arrived at the new bushes, the man said, "You can live here." The ghost thanked the man and then asked, "Why must you cut the bushes where I lived?" The man replied, "Because I work for the city." He continued, "And by cutting city bushes, I can make a living." He then drove back to cut the bushes in the city.

Ms. Jackson and students discuss the story. Ms. Jackson then says, "Let's take a look at what's fantasy and reality about this story." The students then complete several activities on differentiating fantasy from reality.

Activity 1. Ms. Jackson provides each student with scissors, glue, and a worksheet (see table 6.5).

Table 6.5.   Activity 1 Worksheet

Fantasy	Reality

Ms. Jackson then provides students with the following directions:

FROM FANTASY TO REALITY

1A. Cut and glue the first *fantasy* strip onto the *fantasy* side of the chart.
1B. Cut and glue the first *reality* strip onto the *reality* side of the chart.
2A. Cut and glue the second *fantasy* strip onto the *fantasy* side of the chart.
2B. Cut and glue the second *reality* strip onto the *reality* side of the chart.
3A. Cut and glue the third *fantasy* strip onto the *fantasy* side of the chart.
3B. Cut and glue the third *reality* strip onto the *reality* side of the chart.

FROM REALITY TO FANTASY

4A. Cut and glue the fourth *reality* strip onto the *reality* side of the chart.
4B. Cut and glue the fourth *fantasy* strip onto the *fantasy* side of the chart.
5A. Cut and glue the fifth *reality* strip onto the *reality* side of the chart.
5B. Cut and glue the fifth *fantasy* strip onto the *fantasy* side of the chart.
6A. Cut and glue the sixth *reality* strip onto the *reality* side of the chart.
6B. Cut and glue the sixth *fantasy* strip onto the *fantasy* side of the chart.

Students complete the activity in 40 minutes.

The students then discuss their charts in groups. Afterward, Ms. Jackson and the students discuss one reality strip and then one fantasy strip. They continue this sequence until they discuss all of the strips.

To bring closure to the lesson, Ms. Jackson gives students two post-it notes. The heading on one post-it note reads "Fakest." The heading on the other post-it note reads "Realest."

To bring closure to the lesson, Ms. Jackson writes *realest* and *fakest* on the board. She then says, "Let's talk about these words." She asks, "What was the fakest part of this story?" She continues, "Or what really seemed like a fantasy to you?"

Ms. Jackson then asks, "What was the realest part of this story?" She continues, "Or what really seemed like reality to you?"

With raised hands, the White students and Hispanic students wait to receive permission to respond to both sets of questions. African American students blurt out a variety of answers. Ms. Jackson facilitates the different response patterns between the Black students and other groups of students.

Analysis

The purpose of this analysis is to describe the role that African American culture plays in Ms. Jackson's lesson on fantasy and reality. Overall, orality was the central dimension of this lesson. Ms. Jackson used various forms of verbal communication to engage African American students in reality and fantasy.

A significant example is her use of the term *real* in the context of African American vernacular. As mentioned, Black vernacular English consists of a variety of pronunciations and grammatical structures. In Black communities, *real* is a word that is infused with this English structure. Some of the most common Black-framed statements about real are as follows:

- "Keep It Real!"
- "Be Real with Me"
- "On the Real"
- "For real"
- "You ain't real!"
- "I know that's real."

Collectively these statements emphasize authenticity in ways that convey realistic meaning to African American people.

Ms. Jackson used this African American linguistic approach to connect *real* to the lesson. At the start of the lesson, she used the Black-framed call-and-response approach to link fantasy and reality to *real*. In the first back-and-forth sequence, the students answered her calls of fantasy and reality with *not real* and *real*. But in the second back-and-forth sequence, the students broadened their responses to "That ain't real" and "I know that's real." In addition, many African American students uttered these phrases to Ms. Jackson in a standing position. This level of engagement highlighted a connection between these statements and the cultural experiences of these students.

In observing the remainder of the lesson, it was noted that African American students had a strong need to use orality to learn the difference between fantasy and reality. For instance, consider the initial class discussion on the meaning of *real*. For the most part, African American students provided stories to convey their background knowledge of *real*. Ms. Jackson drew from these referents to show her African American students that the term is central to differentiating reality from fantasy. She further contextualized the lesson by reading a story, another African-centered oral tradition. Other Black cultural dimensions were threaded throughout the lesson. These dimensions are summarized in the section below.

Verve

The back-and-forth engagement of fantasy and reality immersed African American students in multiple stimuli at the same time. Through this experience, African American students were required to quickly focus their thinking on multiple examples of both genres. The African American students were able to better internalize—not memorize—the differences between fantasy and reality. At this point of the lesson, these students were also able to better connect both concepts to the term *real*.

Affect

Affect was evident in Ms. Jackson's emotional use of the term *real* to set the stage for the lesson. The call and response with the students consisted of high levels of emotion to emphasize the connection between real and reality and fantasy. Emotion was also used to encourage and affirm African American students.

Also embedded in this exchange were tonal semantics. For example, she used tone and pitch to stress the first syllable for *fantasy* and *reality*. She then used the same vocal approach to stress the second syllabic sounds of *fantasy* and *reality*. Her voice is what gave more emphasis and meaning to both words. Ms. Jackson's vocal usage contributed to African American students' responses to her calls from a standing position.

Note that Ms. Jackson did not use every cultural dimension to facilitate African American students' involvement in the lesson. The reason is that culturally responsive instruction doesn't necessitate the use of all aspects of Black culture to teach African American students. However, White teachers must still learn when and how to use African American students' cultural backgrounds to engage them in classrooms.

The Sample Case Study

What Other Evidence Shows Engagement as an Effective Way for White Teachers to Deliver Instruction to African American Students?

At the end of a recent school year, I was asked to support two seventh-grade math teachers' work with African American students. During my discussions with the principal and curriculum specialist, I learned that their African American students yielded the lowest math scores on state standardized tests. These students also had the lowest math averages of the students in these teachers' classrooms.

As a result, I was asked to enhance the teachers' mathematical effectiveness with African American students for and beyond the following school year. I pursued this goal through class observations and a review of standardized test data. During the last two months of school, I conducted six classroom observations of each teacher. The commonalties for both classroom observations were as follows:

A. Both of the teachers were White females. One teacher was named Patricia Stenson. The other teacher was named JoBeth Rizendine.
B. Both classrooms featured a small number of African American students.
C. A majority of the classroom content focused on mathematical problem solving.
D. Both teachers displayed the following sequence to deliver instruction to students:
   1. The teachers wrote the math objective on the board.
   2. They announced the objective to the students.
   3. Patricia would demonstrate the concept on the overhead projector. JoBeth would use the Smartboard to illustrate the concept for students.
   4. Neither teacher's presentation entailed their moving around the room to check for student comprehension.
   5. Both teachers talked for a majority of the demonstrations. They asked very few questions to check for student comprehension.
   6. After delivering the presentation, the teachers issued worksheets to students. The students were expected to individually complete the assignments.
   7. The teachers circulated the room only when students requested their assistance.

After conducting the observations, I reviewed standardized test data for the teachers' current classes. I found that most of the African American students failed to meet proficiency in areas related to mathematical problem solving. I then reviewed a sample seventh-grade standardized mathematics test book. I noticed that over half of the test questions were featured in a problem-solving context.

Next, I coordinated a meeting with the principal, the teachers, and the school's leadership team. I explained that the classroom factors contributed to the underperformance of African American students. Specifically, the teachers' instructional practices lacked cultural responsiveness and engagement.

I then proposed to conduct a series of professional development sessions with the teachers. The sessions would be organized into the following categories: Understanding the Cultural Context of Whiteness and Understanding the Cultural Context of Blackness. I would use the Whiteness sessions to enlighten the teachers on how their race influenced their practices with African American students. The Blackness sessions would provide teachers with the cultural insight on teaching African American students.

Many leadership team members were dismayed at my findings and proposition. Both teachers argued that the causes of African American students' underperformance were located outside of the classroom. For example, Patricia stated that many of the African American students lived in impoverished environments. As a result, they probably lived in families that didn't value education. But when I asked for proof of Patricia's assertions, she was unable to verify her claims.

JoBeth and I had a slightly different discussion. The gist of our discussion was captured in the following exchange:

JoBeth: There's nothing wrong with the way we teach math.

Hines: It's not about right or wrong, Ms. Rizendine.

JoBeth: Then what's it about, Dr. Hines?

Hines: Effective or ineffective.

JoBeth: Okay, then what does this have to do with race or African American students?

Hines: Your approaches to math are not reaching African American students. And your test data also shows the lack of effectiveness with Black children.

JoBeth: And . . .

Hines: It is important for you to understand how your position as a White person contributes to your approaches to teaching these students.

JoBeth: So now I am a racist?

Hines: That's not what I said.

The principal stops the discussion. He then says, "Listen, we all have opinions." He continues, "But the main thing is our African American students are not doing well in middle-level math." He concluded, "And Dr. Hines is here to help you work through this issue."

A few days later, I received the following e-mail from the principal:

Dr. Hines,
    I have spoken with the leadership team and we have decided to move forward with having you work with us.
    We only want you to train the teachers on Black students.
    If you agree to this condition, then you can start on May 27, the day after Memorial Day.
    Thanks and I look forward to hearing from you.
    Kyle Belcher
    Principal

I was extremely disappointed with the decision to avoid race discussions with the teachers. At the same time, I still wanted to do something to have a positive impact on the teachers' African American students. Therefore, I accepted the offer to work with the school.

Starting on May 27, I provided the teachers with a series of professional development sessions on African American students' success. What follows is a time line of the events that highlights my specific approaches to support these teachers.

May 2014–June 2014: Background

I used my first meeting to engage both teachers in a discussion on culturally responsive teaching for African American students. Patricia was somewhat attentive to my descriptions and explanations of cultural responsiveness. However, JoBeth questioned the relevance of race and culture to teaching African American students. She argued that because each child is different, race shouldn't factor in how children learn in school.

During the second meeting, I introduced the concept of background to the teachers. I explained that teachers must understand the cultural backgrounds of their African American students. JoBeth asked me to justify my assertion. I responded by explaining that African American children's background is different from the culture of schools.

I then asked the teachers to describe the culture of the school. Both teachers were initially perplexed by this question. Patricia then said, "I think that the culture of school values education." She continued, "We also believe that all children can learn." JoBeth then said, "As long as the parents value education."

I then said, "Okay, so how would you describe the cultural characteristics of your African American students?"

JoBeth quickly stated, "Again, race doesn't matter, Dr. Hines!" She continued, "We believe that all kids can learn regardless of race."

I replied, "But you have not answered my question." I continued, "What are some of the behaviors that are very prevalent among most or all of your African American students?"

Patricia then said, "Well, Dr. Hines, I have never really thought of African American students as a race." She continued, "Like Jo said, we just see them as students."

I used Patricia's response as the perfect opportunity to guide the teachers into a critical analysis of African American culture. To put structure to strategy, I engaged the teachers in a review of the dimensions of Black culture. I then said, "Your homework is to take the next few days and think about the African American students who have been in your classroom." I continued, "I would then like for you to identify as many students as possible who displayed behaviors that matched the definitions of the dimensions."

The last part of the homework was for the teachers to describe the specific behaviors that fit the dimension descriptions.

As requested, the teachers brought their homework assignment to our next session. Table 6.6 presents their reflections on African American students.

After the teachers reviewed their sheets, they were provided with additional examples of the African American cultural dimensions. We then developed a profile of African American students who attended their classrooms (see table 6.7).

After we discussed the profile, I explained that these characteristics are a direct link to learning preferences for African American students. Before I could explain the linkage, both teachers wanted to further discuss the profile.

Patricia said, "I still don't see why this profile is so specific to Black culture." She continued, "Isn't it possible for a White child or child from any other race to show these behaviors?"

JoBeth then stated, "I personally feel that you are saying that every Black child in this country acts in the same exact way."

I responded to both views by providing an explanation of the cultural relevance of the profile. Specifically, I explained that the profile reflects patterned behaviors that are prevalent within African American culture. In this context, African American people endorse the cultural dimensions in varied ways. But the essence of the dimensions lies in their reflection of the Black experience in this country. As such, children from other races are not likely to display these dimensions in their entirety.

Instead of moving forward with learning preferences, I decided to end the session. I informed the teachers to take some time to review all of our discussions. We would then resume our discussions within a week.

At this point, I was concerned about the direction of the professional development sessions. I believed that JoBeth refused to embrace any aspect of the discussions. My perception of Patricia was that she wanted to benefit from the sessions. However, she needed a rationale for doing so.

I then had an idea. I believed that the teachers could benefit from interacting with African American students outside of the school. Such interactions could possibly provide the teachers with a real-world understanding of their African American students.

Table 6.6. Teacher Identification of African American Student Behaviors

	Patricia	JoBeth
Spirituality	• My African American students are most likely to mention God as a factor in their lives.	• Now that I think about it . . . • Some of my African American students . . .
Harmony	• Big picture thinkers.	• N/A
Affect	• Wear their feelings on their sleeves. • You know their feelings right away. • Highly emotional and sensitive about everything.	• Take everything way too personal. • Too much emotion at times when expressing themselves to me and other students. • Great at multitasking. • Talking to one and listening to another.
Verve	• Seem to be enthralled by carnival-like atmosphere in classrooms.	
Communalism	• Stick together no matter what. • Seem more into lessons when they can work with other students.	• They operate more like a family. • Will defend each other even when the other Black student is wrong.
Orality	• Can be loud at times. • Want to talk. • Correction—must talk. • Extremely verbal.	• Loud. • The most talkative group of students. • React favorably to certain words. • Very slang oriented.
Movement	• Loves to move around the classroom. • Move a lot in seats.	• Will tap and work at the same time. • Often enter room dancing and singing.
Social Time Perspective	• Many of my African American students get lost in the assignment. It's like the timer doesn't mean anything to some of them.	• N/A
Expressive Individualism	• My Black children are not followers (unless it's another Black child). They have a kind of stand-outish-like attitude and demeanor. • Want to be the main attraction.	• My Black girls have these elaborate hairstyles and clothing. It's almost like a costume. • I remember that I had this Black male who always walked into class with a drag. I thought he had a physical disability. Then one day, I saw him walking across the school yard without a limp. I approached him and asked, "Hey why don't you walk into my classroom in this manner?" His response, "Because I got a reputation to protect even when I'm in the classroom."

Table 6.7. Profile of African American Students

Dimension	Description
Harmony	African American students have big picture thoughts about life situations.
Orality	African American students are verbally expressive children.
Communalism	African American students have stronger preferences for people than things.
Movement	African American students need movement in their lives.
Affect	African American students are sensitive and attuned to the ways in which others perceive them.
Verve	African American students are much affected by multiple things happening in the learning environment.
Expressive Individualism	African American students value the freedom to be unique.

During the next meeting, I proposed the plan to the teachers. I was delighted to find both teachers in agreement with the proposition. Neither teacher was comfortable with making visits to the African American students' homes. But they were receptive to participating in events that were a part of the lives of these students.

Suddenly, Patricia said, "This past year, one of my African American parents offered several times for me to visit her church."

I then responded, "See if that offer still stands."

Patricia said, "Oh the offer has always been standing and still is!" We laughed and then decided to attend that and another African American church. The teachers also agreed with my suggestion to attend at least two nonreligious events.

The Black Church Experience

We attended one traditional and one nontraditional African American church service. The section below features my summary of the Black cultural relevance of the church visits.

Spiritual Relevance (Spirituality)

The main theme of both church services was devotion to God. Throughout the service, congregants were called to testify to the power of God. One particular moment was observed during the traditional pastor's discussion of the election. The pastor's commentary on the election was as follows:

> Look, it doesn't really matter if Obama or Romney wins the November election. That's 'cause God is the real president! God is the leader of the free world and all worlds for that matter! But y'all don't hear me, though.

Affective Relevance (Affect)

Congregants continued to show strong emotional responses to God. For example, prior to the traditional pastor's sermon, the choir sang "God Is My Everything." Toward the middle of the song, the lead singer gave an emotion-filled testimony about the role of God in her life. Some people in the audience stood up and shouted "Amen," "Sing girl!," and "Tell your story." Other people begin to scream and shout.

After the choir finished singing the song, the pastor approached the podium. However, he could not start to deliver his sermon to the audience. The reason is that some congregants were still screaming and shouting. Other congregants were giving personal testimonies about God.

As another example, the nontraditional pastor gave a sermon titled "What Has He Done for Me Lately?" The sermon was derived from Janet Jackson's classic song "What Have You Done for Me Lately?" The difference is that the pastor was challenging the audience to realize that God has already done enough for them. He made this point with the following commentary:

> Now back in the day, we shook our hips when Janet asked us to think about what others have done for us. But you shake your head in trying to figure out what God has done for you. Where they do that at? Now if you really want to show God that you recognize him, stand up. If you are proud of what God has done for your life, stand up.

In response to the pastor's directions, the congregants stood up and praised and shouted God's name.

Communal Relevance (Communalism)

Both pastors fostered a sense of connectedness among the congregants. In the nontraditional church, the pastor directed participants to participate in a talk-and-hug moment. Here participants had to exchange hugs with two unfamiliar people. After exchanging hugs, participants were directed to talk about the value of God in their lives.

As a traditional example, the pastor informed congregants to link arms in groups of four. The congregants talked about why they attended the church service. They also discussed what they wanted to learn from the church service.

Socialized Relevance (Social Time Perspective)

The talk-and-hug moment was supposed to last for exactly one minute. The pastor needed 10 minutes to restore order in the church. The reason is that the congregants talked with and hugged an average of about five people. The congregants' behavior reflects African Americans' tendencies to be motivated by the mood instead of the time frame of the event.

Oral Relevance (Orality)

Traditional Church Service. The pastor's sermon was filled with orality. One example of this type of discourse was call and response. For example, the pastor directed the technology person to show a slide of Philippians 1:27.

> Only, conduct yourselves in a way worthy of the gospel of Christ, so that, whether I come and see you or am absent, I may hear news of you, that you are standing firm in one spirit, with one mind struggling together for the faith of the gospel.

The pastor then engaged the church in the following call-and-response exchange:

Pastor: When I say *standing firm,* I want you to say *in one spirit.* When I say *struggling together,* you say *faith of gospel.*

Audience Member: Holy glory!

Pastor: Standing firm!

Audience: In one spirit!

Pastor: Struggling together!

Audience: Faith of gospel!

Pastor: Y'all don't hear me. I say *standing firm!*

Audience: In one spirit!

Pastor: Struggling together!

Audience: Faith of gospel!

Pastor: We are standing firm in one spirit for the faith of the gospel.

(The audience erupts in praises and cheers.)

Nontraditional Church Service. The pastor used different props to symbolize the importance of God. For instance, he showed the congregants an empty pizza box. He then provided the following commentary:

> Church, this here is an empty pizza box. But without a pizza, it's just a box. But with a pizza in the box, the box carries on a whole new meaning.

An audience member yells, "Make it plain, pastor."

> Now your life is like that pizza box. Not saying that you need pizza. (*The audience laughs.*) I'm saying that you need God in your life. (*The pastor's voice rises.*) You need Jesus in your life. The lily of the valley. The alpha and the omega. (*The pastor's voice reaches a crescendo.*) God, Jesus, lily, valley, alpha, and omega. Get it in your life! Get him in your life. (*The audience again erupts in shouts and cheers.*)

Vervistic Relevance (Verve)

A variety of activities transpired at the same time. For example, the preacher of the traditional service completed the sermon. He then conducted an altar call for members who were interested in joining the church. The altar call was extended to those who were in need of prayer. While the pastor prayed for these congregants, the choir sang a song. The pianist played music. A designated group of church leaders prayed at the back of the church. These activities maintained the high level of stimulation that was initiated by the sermon and previous singing.

With regard to the nontraditional service, the deacons collected tithes from the audience. As they passed the collection plate to congregants, the choir sang several songs. The pastor made remarks such as "It's more blessed to give than to receive" and "Bring the tithes to the storehouse." A group of praise team dancers danced on stage.

Response to Church Events

At the end of each church service, I invited Patricia and Jo-Beth to share their feelings with me. Here's an excerpt from a discussion about one of the church services.

Traditional Church Service Discussion

Hines: So what did you think about the church service?

Patricia: Everyone was so upbeat and lively!

JoBeth: It seemed like a lot of chaos to me. But it was good to see some of our students in church.

Patricia: I agree.

Hines: Well, tell me what you thought about the pastor's sermon.

Patricia and JoBeth: Well . . .

Hines: This only works if you are honest.

JoBeth: I'll just say it. We thought he was very loud. Why did he need to yell?

Hines: I don't think that he was yelling.

Patricia: Well, what was he doing?

Hines: He was raising his voice to stress key points of the sermon.

Patricia: Is that why many people stood up and clapped?

Hines: Exactly!

JoBeth: I still think that was a bit much.

Hines: Okay. That's how you feel. But remember that the purpose of the service was for you to get more cultural insight on the environment of our African American students.

Patricia: You're right.

Nontraditional Church Service Discussion

Hines: Okay. Let's talk about today's service.

Patricia: I noticed that there were White people who attended this church. That was interesting.

JoBeth: And nice.

Hines: Did you feel more comfortable because of that?

JoBeth: Yes—somewhat.

Hines: Okay. That's good. But what were your thoughts of the service?

Patricia: It was very similar to the first service. A lot of singing, clapping, and cheering.

JoBeth: This pastor also seemed to yell to get his point across.

Patricia: Maybe it's how these two pastors preach.

Hines: No. I think that it's more than that. Remember that we talked about Black people and oral expression.

Patricia: Yeah, that's right. You did say that that type of expression matters in Black culture.

JoBeth: Why can't he just be a pastor? Why does this need to be about race?

Hines: JoBeth, that's exactly what this is about. If you want to understand our African American students, you've got to understand their backgrounds. A critical part of understanding them is understanding race.

JoBeth: But it's much more than that to me. They are just kids.

Hines: Kids of African descent, which is different from you and Patricia.

As indicated, both teachers lacked understanding of the relationship between race and culture. As a result, they were naturally unable to make sense of the church services. But JoBeth seemed intent on avoiding the possibility of becoming aware of the relevance of race to the African American experience.

The Juneteenth Experience

On June 19, we were among the 4,000 attendees at the annual Juneteenth Celebration of African American Culture and Freedom that is sponsored by Black community organizations. The theme of the celebration was "Commemorate Freedom—Now and Forever." The rationale for attending this event was for the teachers to see Black culture in action at a community-based event.

The major cultural dimensions of the celebration were communalism, orality, and verve. From a communal standpoint, a strong sense of togetherness existed among the attendees. People hugged and laughed. Other people were engaged in spirited (read: heated) discussions on race, sports, music, and religion.

Another communal example occurred during the singing of "Lift Every Voice and Sing," the Black national anthem. At the beginning of a 40-minute commemoration program, people stood to sing the historic song. They then joined hands and shouted "Together as One, One as Together." Most of the attendees then hugged each other for about 5–10 minutes.

Orality was at play during many parts of the celebration. Examples: After the celebration of the anthem, several speakers used voice and tone to speak passionately about the Black experience. Many of the speakers specifically highlighted the theme of freedom. Powerful speech excerpts regarding freedom included but are not limited to:

- "We've made long strides toward freedom. But we still have a long long way to go."
- "In '62, we said *freedom now*. In 2014, we are still wanting our freedom."
- "Freedom has been a powerful part of the Black experience. We need freedom to make our lives complete."
- "I's free, I's me. I am free, and I am me."
- "Let freedom ring, in the words of Dr. King. Let freedom bring the unity and peace of mind that we as Black people need to succeed."
- "After 250 years of slavery and 140 years of its aftermath, where's our compensation? Where is the equality?"

From a vervistic standpoint, the entire celebration was a seven-block concoction of intense stimulation. In general, the celebration simultaneously consisted of a parade, soul food, arts and crafts, and live music. While "I'm Black and I'm Proud" blared through speakers, vendors shopped African items to attendees. Many attendees eagerly watched a drag race. Other attendees participated in a dance-off to Motown music. Simply put, the Juneteenth Celebration offered multiple forms of celebratory variations.

Response to Juneteenth Experience

Patricia, JoBeth, and I discussed their views of the Juneteenth experience. Patricia indicated that she enjoyed the celebration. In addition, she also gained insight on the rationale of the racial views of African American people. Below is her commentary on race, freedom, and Black people:

The celebration gave me some clear views on why race means a lot to Black people. For them, it's a part of being free. If I am really honest, I see this when I think about African American

kiddos that have been in my classroom. They always seemed
to be keen on justice and fairness. The Juneteenth Celebration
just added so much clarity to me.

JoBeth's views of the Juneteenth Celebration were similar
to her views about the church services. She felt that the event
offered an out-of-school view of African American people and
children. But she still believed that race was not the main factor
in understanding African American students. For example, consider her commentary below on this event:

> I just think that freedom is something everyone has struggled
> for. I mean as Americans, we struggled to free ourselves from
> British rule. And I think that as Americans, we all have privi-
> leges and freedoms.

My response to JoBeth's view was threefold. First, July 4,
1776, marked the beginning of freedom for White people—not
African American people. Second, Black people did not gain
their freedom until 1863. Third, African American slaves in
Texas didn't achieve their freedom until 1865. I also informed
JoBeth that even after the end of slavery, African American
people's freedoms were restricted by White people.

A few days later, I received the following e-mail from JoBeth:

> Dr. Hines,
>   I am writing to say that I will no longer participate in the
> events. I see what you are doing and why you're doing this.
>   I just don't think that this is at all about race.
>   Thanks.
>   Sincerely,
>   JR

After receiving this e-mail, I thought about trying to convince
JoBeth to continue working with me. But I ultimately decided to
continue on with Patricia.

The Festival Experience

Patricia and I attended a Black Community Festival. The event was held on July 4 to provide a Black perspective on Independence Day. This event consisted of many of the previously discussed African American cultural dimensions. But the overarching cultural theme was an integration of harmony and communalism.

Some of the major activities of the festival were as follows:

Black Girl Dream Discussion

A panel of accomplished African American women discussed the interrelatedness between race and gender. They also encouraged African American girls to focus on education and think about future careers.

The Law and Us

Local police department officials talked about their intentions to form stronger relationships with the African American community. Participants were also allowed to ask questions. Many people questioned the police department's approaches to identifying officers to serve on the police force. They also asked the chief of police if she considered the role of race in determining which officers patrolled African American communities.

Heritage Museum

The museum was a large tent that featured various forms of DNA and genealogy. Some participants talked with museum hosts about DNA. Other people conferred with hosts about genealogy. Many people signed up to undergo the process of tracing their heritage to Africa.

Midday Prayer

At noon, all participants paused for prayer. Different clergymen were assigned to different sections of the festival. They then prayed for and with attendees who were located in their section. At 12:10 p.m., all of the participants looked to the sky and yelled, "Praise Him, thank Him, and follow Him!" Overall, the prayer added an immeasurable spiritual and emotional climate to the festival.

Health and Wellness Panel and Pavilion

Several Black doctors and nurses talked with attendees about health. Under the theme of "Healthy Lives, Healthy Body," the panelists talked about health topics related to African American people. Listed below are the main topics reviewed during the pavilion:

African American Men

- Make a Date for the Prostate (Cancer)
- Quit the Nicotine Fit

African American Women

- Breast Awareness Matters
- The ABCs of HIV

African American Men and Women

- We Care, Hair Care
- The Glaucoma Discussion
- Multiple Sclerosis Diagnosis
- Don't Stress over Stroke

The doctors, nurses, and attendees then engaged in conversations about racism. Specifically, attendees received valuable information about the impact of racial bias and prejudice on the health of African American people. At the conclusion of the discussion, many people completed health screenings.

Job Enhancement Field. Carefully selected human resources officials delivered half-hour sessions on careers. They provided participants with tips on preparing resumes. Many attendees gained strategies from mock interviews. The attendees also worked with employment specialists to find career opportunities.

People from other racial groups attended the festival. But I strongly believed that Black participants experienced the festival. The reason is that the Blackness was used to create activities that personally resonated with their lived experiences. Translation: the festival was a replication of reality for Black participants. Consequently, Black participants not only bonded with each other but also connected to the festival's climate and atmosphere.

Response to Festival

Due to a prior commitment, Patricia did not have time to immediately discuss the festival with me. But she did send an e-mail that outlined her views of the event. The correspondence read as follows:

> Dr. Hines,
> I really, really enjoyed the festival. It was another enlightening experience. I got a chance to see again the relevance of culture to Black people. Also, seeing African American students from the school at the festival, as well as other events, made me realize that these children's racial background does matter to them.
> Again, thanks!
> Tricia

A few days before we were to start curriculum work, Patricia sent the following e-mail to me:

> Dr. Hines,
> It's been a week since the festival, and my head is spinning. Being one of the few Whites at the events made me feel extremely uncomfortable. But then I started to think that maybe this is how Blacks and other minorities feel. And that's because maybe we do, after all, live in a White-dominated society. I also know that this White dominance has something to do with me.

What do you think?
Write Back.
PC

I was extremely excited to read Patricia's e-mail. The reason is the events made her uncomfortable to see outside of being White. However, due to my contractual agreement, I wasn't sure of whether or not to respond to her e-mail.

On the one hand, I wanted to engage Patricia in discussion about race and Whiteness. But I did not want to disregard the principal's directive to avoid this discussion. After careful thought and prayer, I gave the following response to Patricia:

> Patricia,
> I am excited that the events prompted you to self-reflect on White culture. I encourage you to continue thinking about your life experiences as a White person. It will go a long way in making you a more culturally aware educator.

A few minutes later, Patricia responded with the following e-mail:

> Dr. Hines,
> There was many times in which I felt guilty or sorry about being White. Please give me some suggestions on what I could do to shake this feeling.
> Thanks.
> PC

My response to Patricia's White guilt was as follows:

> Patricia,
> No. You do not need to feel guilty about being White. The thing to do is analyze—not apologize—yourself as a White person.
> We'll talk in a few.
> Regards,
> MH

Our initial talk progressed into an eight-week discussion about Whiteness. It is beyond the scope of this section to reveal every detail of the discussions. But I will indicate that the focus of the first five weeks was the racial context of Patricia's lived experiences. Specifically, I asked Patricia to explain the meaning of her life as a White person. She immediately admitted that she did not know what it meant to be White. I then directed her to recent e-mails that showed her acknowledgment of Whiteness. The reason is that I wanted her to recognize her ability to see Whiteness in a racialized context.

Through the recognition, Patricia developed an understanding of the need to see herself as a White person. To strengthen this awareness, I encouraged Patricia to not view Whiteness as a rationale for guilt. Instead, Whiteness should be viewed as a starting point to reflect and then rethink aspects of her White identity.

We used the remaining four weeks to discuss White supremacy, White privilege, and White fragility. A four-part protocol was used to anchor each discussion. First, I provided Patricia with a research-based definition of White supremacy, White privilege, and White fragility. Drawing from an unawareness-to-awareness framework, I asked her to think about and look at racial situations pertaining to these concepts.

In the realm of awareness to consciousness, Patricia considered ways to recognize the impact of these concepts on her identity as a White person. The final part of the protocol was consciousness to conscientiousness. Here, Patricia embarked on the journey of determining how to put her consciousness into action. Specifically, she looked at how to make impactful changes in her behavior as a White person.

May 2014–June 2014: Common Ground

Patricia and I used informal dialogue to maintain a focus on race and Whiteness. The focus of the formal discussions was connecting the approaches to teaching mathematics to the cultural experiences of African American students. We devoted six weeks toward integrating the cultural dimensions into the mathematics curriculum. First, we created a learning preference profile of Patricia's African American students. The profile was developed from the previous personality profile and the summer cultural events.

By midweek, Patricia and I focused on developing a mathematics description that matched the learning preferences profile. During the latter part of the week, we carefully matched mathematics standards to the profile and description. That is, I guided Patricia's efforts to identify math standards that would fit certain cultural dimensions. Table 6.8 shows the scope and sequence for developing this curriculum.

Our final step was to carefully consider criteria for determining the relevance of the curriculum to Patricia's African American students. In other words, would some aspects of Patricia's teaching and learning be situated in Black culture? Will the learning environment afford African American students some locus of instructional control? Finally, would the necessary resources of support for African American student success reflect a holistic interpretation of the African American worldview? After a week of deliberating on these questions, we concluded that the curriculum was indeed amenable to African American students.

September–November 2014

At the end of our last curriculum meeting, we agreed to focus on instructional strategies for African American students. Patricia indicated that she would first take some time to prepare for the beginning of school. We would then set up a meeting.

Fast forward to the end of September: Patricia sends an e-mail with a subject line that reads "Ready." When I opened the e-mail, I read the following correspondence:

Dr. Hines,
I would like to have our first instructional meeting on next week. If this works, please see the attached document in preparation for the meeting.

Let me know if you have questions.
Thanks.
Sincerely,
PC

Table 6.9 shows Patricia's development of a learning preference profile of her African American students. During the first meeting, she described her approach to creating this profile. She studied her African American students. Studying consisted of surveying, talking with, and observing the students in and out of the classroom. During her parent phone conferences, she made an extra effort to glean culturally relevant information from African American parents.

We incorporated Patricia's explanation into our alignment of the profile and the curriculum. We then integrated culturally relevant instructional strategies into her mathematics scope and sequence. The crux of integration was ensuring that African American students' learning profile connected to the math standards for each week. To illustrate this alignment, consider the cultural relevance of the following scope and sequence (see table 6.10) and lesson plan.

Lesson

6. RP.A.2 Students will be able to determine if two quantities (numbers) are in proportional relationship (Concept 7MA).

Engagement

- Patricia opens the lesson by saying, "Students, today we will be doing a lesson on equivalent ratios." She continues, "I know that last year, you learned about ratios. But this year we are going to look at this objective from an equivalent point of view."
- Patricia introduces Dr. Mack Hines to the students. She informs them that Dr. Hines will open the lesson.

Table 6.8. Culturally Relevant Curriculum Development

Part I

Week One—Orality		
Profile	*Description*	*Standard(s)*
Patricia's African American students have a strong preference to use verbal expression to become engaged in the learning environment.	Patricia will create a classroom that accommodates the use of verbal expression to teach math to African American students. Math activities will include call and response, whole group discussions, and other forms of oral communication to build African American students' math skills.	• Mental Math and Estimation • Mathematical Reasoning • Justification of Mathematical Arguments and Ideas • Mathematical Problem Solving • Math and Measurement Systems
Week Two—Communalism		
Preference	*Description*	*Standard(s)*
Patricia's African American students are highly interpersonal learners who are attuned to the social aspects of information.	Patricia's classroom environment will be inclusive of group-centered mathematics activities. Patricia will also learn how to apply communal approaches to creating group mathematics discussions and learning communities.	• Mathematical Reasoning • Justification of Mathematical Arguments and Ideas • Mathematical Problem Solving • Math and Measurement Systems • Math Predictions and Probability
Week Three—Movement		
Preference	*Description*	*Standard(s)*
Patricia's African American students are likely to acclimate to learning situations that offer rhythm and movement.	Patricia will use African American students' preferences for rhythm and movement to develop their mathematics skills. A specific goal will be to reconcile the rhythmic similarities between mathematics and African American culture. Patricia will also use this knowledge to build a rhythmic-oriented approach to working through mathematical situations.	• Mental Math and Estimation • Mathematical Representations • Proportionality in Mathematics • Number Sense and Math Operations • Math Predictions and Probability

Part II

Week Four—Verve

Preference	Description	Standard(s)
Patricia's African American students need learning experiences that are filled with varying levels of nonsequential, stimulating activities.	Patricia will commit to creating mathematics experiences that integrate sensory stimulation and task variation. She will also identify and build specific mathematics activities around these themes.	• Mental Math and Estimation • Mathematical Reasoning • Mathematical Representations • Number Sense and Math Operations • Change Rates in Mathematics • Math and Measurement Systems

Week Five—Expressive Individualism

Preference	Description	Standard(s)
Patricia's African American students embrace learning environments that embrace authentic displays of spontaneous self-expression.	Patricia will create math situations that accommodate African American children's need for improvisation. She will also ensure that the mathematics environment allows for adaption to novel mathematics situations.	• Mental Math and Estimation • Mathematical Reasoning • Mathematical Representations • Justification of Mathematical Arguments and Ideas • Mathematical Problem Solving • Math Predictions and Probability

Week Six—Harmony

Preference	Description	Standard(s)
Patricia's African American students rely on the learning environment to make sense of the instruction.	Patricia's instructional approaches will reflect various ways of accommodating the harmonious learning tendencies of African American students. Specifically, she will provide math demonstrations that are congruent to holistic interpretations of mathematics.	• Mental Math and Estimation • Mathematical Reasoning • Mathematical Representations • Proportionality in Mathematics • Justification of Mathematical Arguments and Ideas • Number Sense and Math Operations • Change Rates in Mathematics • Mathematical Problem Solving • Math and Measurement Systems • Math Predictions and Probability

Table 6.9. Patricia's Learning Preferences Profile for Her African American Students

Orality
Class Profile
1. Matthew: Talks to everyone and through lessons. Blurts out answers instead of raising hand.
2. Lanae: Strong tendency to talk with other students before getting settled for work. Has a flair for using dramatics to make points about topics.
3. Keyquan: Communication is often loud, expressive, and very emotional (*Affect maybe?*). Wants to talk about instruction before responding to written requirements for an assignment.
4. Ricky: Connects better to information presented and explained in an oral narrative or storied context. Needs a lot of verbal reassurance from friends and teacher.
5. Karen: Loves to talk about instruction as if in a conversation. Wants to provide immediate oral response to teacher presentations (when I am presenting something, she will often be the first to add her opinion on the topic). Often shuts down if not given the opportunity to explain information and receive verbal feedback.
6. Courtney: Never gives simple explanation—shares ideas and answers as if she is in some type of performance. Thinks out loud to the point of sometimes disturbing other students.

Bottom Line Summary

As previously discussed, my African American students have a strong proclivity for being verbal. This means that I must be sure to build in opportunities for orality to be a part of their daily learning experiences.

Expressive Individualism

Class Profile
1. Lanae: Makes a grand entrance into the class with a certain walk.
2. Ricky: There's a certain way that everything has to be done—very particular about everything from raising hand to contributing to our discussions. Sometimes hard to get him to go along with the group.
3. Karen: A "look at me" personality that permeates her approach to this class. A hard worker who will not hesitate to argue that her ideas deserve considerable attention.

Bottom Line Summary

These three African American students definitely have personalities of their own. I will capitalize on this information by allowing them to be themselves in my classroom.

Movement

Class Profile

1. Matthew: Tends to move a lot while talking or working on assignments.
2. Lanae: When given time for study, will often spend a significant portion of time beating and tapping on desk. Very demonstrative when explaining things to me or other students. More attentive to any assignment that involves any aspect related to rhythm.
3. Karen: Very receptive to activities that allow for rhythm and movement. Constantly fidgeting and touching things.
4. Courtney: Must be able to manipulate key concepts of a lesson.

Bottom Line Summary

The majority of my African American students are prone to movement. I see it on them throughout the week. It definitely shapes their learning styles—that's for sure. I will continue to accommodate these behavioral tendencies.

Verve

Class Profile

1. Matthew: To keep him focused, I sometimes go back and forth between two interrelated concepts. Loves to go back and forth among working on many different aspects of a lesson (working on one aspect for a while, then switching to another aspect, etc.).
2. Keyquan: Prefers to see information presented in a variety of ways—often at the same time.
3. Ricky: Thrives in learning activities that require the recognition of patterns and trends in a variety of ways. Processes information better when I provide a few different types of class activities to reinforce the main ideas of a lesson.
4. Karen: Never phased when a variety of different class activities are going on at the same time.
5. Courtney: Often needs visual and verbal explanations of instruction at the same time. Easily gets bored when participating in routinized activity (activity that doesn't present different ways of understanding concepts).

(continued)

Table 6.9. *(continued)*

Bottom Line Summary

It takes and will take a lot of energy to make sure that verve is used with my African American students.

Communalism

Class Profile

1. Matthew: Tends to want to bond with other students, especially African American students.	4. Ricky: Tends to place more value on friends' (i.e., Black students' feelings) input on subject matter than own perception of subject matter.
2. Lanae: Very gregarious and outgoing—works hard to please and get along with other students, especially other African American boys.	5. Karen: When working in groups, constantly pushes group members to work for betterment of everyone.
3. Keyquan: Loves working in and for the good of the group.	6. Courtney: Because of strong aversion to being by herself, she loves to learn with and from other students.

Bottom Line Summary

My African American students are by far the most relationship-oriented students. In other words, I can maximize their learning by allowing them to experience instruction in relation to other humans.

Harmony

Class Profile

1. Matthew: Relies on class environment to make inferences about the learning.	3. Keyquan: Can be a global thinker at times. Wants to immediately see the connection between anything that I say and do with instruction.
2. Lanae: Circles a lot of key words and phrases in class readings. I have even seen her draw lines from one page to another page and then add the caption "What's the deal?"	4. Ricky: When other students make suggestions, he would quickly yell, "What does that have to do with anything?" Calmed him down to the point of thinking about the connections for himself.

Bottom Line Summary

Everything has to fit for my African American students—plain and simple.

Table 6.10. Scope and Sequence

Unit 3 Proportional Relationships and Quantities Second Six Weeks October 8–November 9		
Concept • Equivalent Ratios and Word Problems • Ratios in Proportion and Word Problems • 7MA	**Concept** • Table and Graph Proportionality and Word Problems • 7MB	**Concept** • Written Equations for Proportional Relationships • Solved Proportions and Word Problems • 7MC
Days for Coverage 4 Days	**Days for Coverage** 2–3 Days	**Days for Coverage** 3–4 Days
Integrated Dimensions Orality Harmony Verve Communalism Expressive Individualism	**Integrated Dimensions** Orality Harmony Verve Communalism Expressive Individualism	**Integrated Dimensions** Orality Harmony Verve Communalism Expressive Individualism

- Dr. Hines says, "Students, to get into the lesson, we're gonna get on the good foot." He demonstrates and then has students participate in the following dance steps:
  1. Movement 1: In a rhythmic fashion, Dr. Hines and students take and verbally count three steps to the right. They then clap and verbally count one time.
  2. Movement 2: In a rhythmic fashion, Dr. Hines and students take and count three steps to the left. Then they clap and verbally count one time.
  3. Movement 3: In a rhythmic fashion, Dr. Hines and students take and verbally count three steps to the right. Then they clap and verbally count one time.
  4. Movement 4: In a rhythmic fashion, Dr. Hines and students take and count three steps to the left. Then they clap and verbally count one time.

Dr. Hines and the students repeat the movements 1–4 to the beat of music. Patricia then provides students with the chart below (see table 6.11).

Table 6.11. Equivalent Ratios Worksheet 1

	Steps	Claps
Movement 1		
Movement 2		
Movement 3		
Movement 4		

Patricia then says, "After I announce out the movement number, you write the number of steps and claps for that movement." Under Patricia's guidance, students record the number of steps and claps for each movement. The section below features this illustration. Table 6.12 features the completed chart.

Table 6.12. Completed Equivalent Ratios Worksheet 1

	Steps	Claps
Movement 1	3	1
Movement 2	3	1
Movement 3	3	1
Movement 4	3	1

Matthew, Karen, and Courtney responded silently to the assignment with the following steps:

1. Mouthed and repeated the steps at their desk.
2. Recorded the number of steps.
3. Mouthed and repeated the number of claps.
4. Recorded the number of claps.

Enlightenment

Patricia then asks "Can anybody tell me how this chart relates to our dance?"

Matthew immediately says, "It describes how we moved."

Patricia then replies, "What do you mean 'how we moved'?"

Matthew says, "Well, it seemed like for every three steps we took, we clapped one time."

Patricia then explains that the step-clap pattern represents a ratio.

Patricia reminds students of the definition of a ratio.

Patricia says, "Let's look to see if the ratios for the steps are equivalent."

She writes the following ratios on the board:

- Movement 1: 3:1 (3 Steps, 1 Clap)
- Movement 2: 3:1 (3 Steps, 1 Clap)
- Movement 3: 3:1 (3 Steps, 1 Clap)
- Movement 4: 3:1 (3 Steps, 1 Clap)

She asks, "Looking at these numbers, what do you think the term *equivalent ratios* means?"

Matthew blurts "equal!" He then says, "I know that equivalent means equal." He continues, "So I would say that it's like every time around, we took the equal number of steps and claps. So it's equal."

After affirming Matthew's responses, Patricia puts the following definition on the overhead projector:

> Equivalent ratios are just like equivalent fractions. If two ratios have the same value, then they are equivalent.

Patricia leads the students through another dance routine. The routine is as follows:

1. Movement 1: In a rhythmic fashion, Patricia and the students take and verbally count three steps to the right. They then clap and verbally count one time.
2. Movement 2: In a rhythmic fashion, Patricia and the students take and count six steps to the left. Then they clap and verbally count two times.
3. Movement 3: In a rhythmic fashion, Patricia and the students take and verbally count three steps to the right. Then they clap and verbally count one time.

4. Movement 4: In a rhythmic fashion, Patricia and the students take and count six steps to the left. Then they clap and verbally count two times.

Patricia and the students repeat movements 1–4 to the beat of music.

Patricia then provides students with the chart below (see table 6.13).

Table 6.13. Equivalent Ratios Worksheet 2

	Steps	Claps
Movement 1		
Movement 2		
Movement 3		
Movement 4		

Patricia then says, "After I announce out the movement number, you write the number of steps and claps for that movement." Under Patricia's guidance, students record the number of steps and claps for each movement. The section below features this illustration. Table 6.14 features the completed chart.

Table 6.14. Completed Equivalent Ratios Worksheet 2

	Steps	Claps
Movement 1	3	1
Movement 2	6	2
Movement 3	3	1
Movement 4	6	2

Matthew, Karen, and Courtney responded silently to the assignment with the following steps:

1. Mouthed and repeated the steps at their desk.
2. Recorded the number of steps.
3. Mouthed and repeated the number of claps.
4. Recorded the number of claps.

Patricia then writes the following ratios on the board:

- Movement 1: 3:1 (3 Steps, 1 Clap)
- Movement 2: 6:2 (6 Steps, 2 Claps)
- Movement 3: 3:1 (3 Steps, 1 Clap)
- Movement 4: 6:2 (6 Steps, 2 Claps)

She asks, "Are the ratios equivalent?"

The class is divided on whether or not the ratios are equivalent.

In response, Patricia says, "The way to work through our opinions is in a multipart step."

Part 1: Patricia directs students to reach each ratio out loud.

Class: The ratio for the first movement and third movement is 3:1. This means that every three steps require one clap. The ratio for the second movement and fourth movement is every six steps require two claps.

Ricky: So basically the more steps we take the more claps we make.

Patricia: Why do you say that, Ricky?

Karen: Well, because it's true. See, let me show you.

(Karen repeats movements 1 and 2 of the dance routine.)

Patricia: Okay, Good, Karen. But my question is this: In proportion to steps and claps for movements 1 and 2, how much did we increase the steps and claps in movements 2 and 4?

Lanae (quickly yelling): Double!

Patricia: Let's see.

Part 2: Patricia writes the ratios as fractions.

$$\frac{3}{1} = \frac{6}{2}$$

Patricia asks, "If you double 3, then what's your number?"

The class responds with the number 6.

Patricia then asks, "If you double 1, then your number is . . ."

The class's response to the questions is 2. Keyquan then says, "Okay, I get it." He continues, "By multiplying the numerator and denominator by the same number, you're good."

Patricia says, "Exactly!" She continues, "But we still don't know if ratios are equivalent."

She then presents the third step—cross-multiplying the fractions.

$3 \times 2 = 6 \qquad 6 \times 1 = 6$

Patricia: Both products are 6, meaning . . .

Matthew: The number of steps and claps in the first movement are equivalent to the steps and claps in the second movement.

Enhancement

Patricia brings closure to the lesson by placing the following chart on the smart board (see table 6.15).

Table 6.15. Equivalent Ratios Summary

		Movement 1		Movement 2	Movement 3		Movement 4
Step	Step		Step	Step	Step	Step	Step
	Step		Step	Step	Step	Step	Step
	Step		Step	Step	Step	Step	Step
Clap	Clap		Clap	Clap	Clap	Clap	Clap
	3:1			6:2	3:1		6:2

She then provides the following commentary:

Students, notice that I have listed the steps, claps, and ratios for each movement. You see that the 3:1 ratio and 6:2 ratio consist of different numbers. But if you add the actual numbers of steps and claps, you see that the relationship for both ratios is the same. The deal is that every three steps deserve one clap. Say it with me. (*In unison.*) Every three steps deserve one clap. This pattern was the same in the first dance routine and second dance routine. In other words, as long as the ratios have the same value, they are equivalent.

* * *

Note Patricia's use of African American culture to address the instructional needs of her African American students. For example, Patricia used a rhythmic dance routine to draw African American students into the lesson. Music added additional syncopation to the dance routine. In addition, orality was emphasized in ways that translated the counting of steps and claps into a performance.

Orality was equally central to African American students' participation in the class discussion on equivalent ratios. As a lead-in to discussion, Patricia announced steps for adding numbers to the ratio chart. As a cultural response, several African American students used whispering as a silent—but verbal—guide to record their answers.

Patricia also used an oral approach to arouse critical thinking among African American students. For example, after writing ratios on the board, Patricia asked, "Are the ratios equivalent?" Drawing from an African American perspective, she then directed students to complete a choral reading of the following movements:

The ratio for the first movement and third movement is 3:1. This means that every three steps require one clap. The ratio for the second movement and fourth movement is every six steps require two claps.

Patricia and several African American students discussed this sequence. These discussions were characterized with expressive individualistic perspectives from the students. The students' responses also showed intentional consideration about equivalent ratios. Such an outcome highlights the significant use of race and culture to create authentic educational experiences for African American children.

Because of her non-Black population, Patricia didn't always gear the majority of a lesson toward African American students.

But she continually considered ways to use the redesigned curriculum to connect math to her African American students. As a result, these students were continually exposed to at least one activity or resource that related to their background experiences.

Another significant outcome of Patricia's cultural responsiveness was increased African American student achievement. Her African American students continued to perform well on formal and informal classroom assessments. These successful performances also carried over to standardized test measures.

Lanae achieved a "Commended Performance" rating on the state test for mathematics. Courtney, Ricky, and Matthew earned "Above Standard" test scores. Courtney and Karen gave "Standard" performances on the test. These scores were higher than the "Standard" and "Below Basic" score averages from African American students of previous years.

Review of Patricia's story as follows:

At the end of last year, I was somewhat hesitant to work with you, Dr. Hines. The reason is that I didn't think that you would be able to help me. I didn't believe that you could truly enlighten me about my Black students. Because, if I am being honest, I thought that I learned a lot about my Black kids through the school's bus tours through poor neighborhoods at the beginning of each year.

Don't get me wrong. I did develop sympathy because some of our Black kiddos live in these environments. But my year with you helped me to see this thing in a whole different light. Our Black children are more than just income. They have a certain insight that I as a White woman had no idea existed. When I discovered this, I felt a lot of guilt, which I still do at times. But I thank you for helping me see that I can't stay in sympathy and guilt.

What I needed to do is stay in a state of deep thought about how I can really reach our African American students. I can't guarantee that I'll get this right all of the time. But I damn sure will do my best to see these kids in a way that helps them to succeed with me.

Transcending test scores, this narrative can be best summarized as "A Tale of Two Teachers." Initially, neither Patricia nor JoBeth saw the need to learn about cultural responsiveness to African American students. The reason is that both teachers believed that race was irrelevant to teacher effectiveness. A salient effect of this belief was their color-blind approaches to teaching African American students.

But unlike JoBeth, Patricia began to consider the need for understanding the role of race and culture in teaching Black children. As previously indicated, she just needed a context for moving forward with pursuing this goal. The professional development program was filled with context—namely, the cultural events.

As such, let's revisit both teachers' responses to the cultural events. JoBeth was at the events. That is, she could be seen inside the church services and Juneteenth Celebration. But these attendances did nothing to increase the cultural awareness of JoBeth. That's why she withdrew from professional development experience.

This reason also reflects White superiority, White privilege, and White fragility. The fragility could be seen in JoBeth's irritation with being asked to consider a non-White perspective about African American students. The imbedded superiority within this expression conveyed the following message—nothing of substance could be gained from the culture of African American students. In many ways, JoBeth's responses reiterated the historical view of Blacks as having nothing of value to White culture. This is a privileged standpoint that can only be assumed by White people.

Unsurprisingly, I made no effort to reclaim JoBeth back into the events or professional development experience. Truth be told, I just didn't really believe that she wanted to learn from me or about African American students. In retrospect, I wished I would have given more effort toward working with JoBeth. I could have at least helped her understand the difference between an activity and experience. This would have ensured that she received the knowledge shared with Patricia.

Patricia immersed herself in the cultural events. She asked a lot of informative questions about each event. Answers were used to develop a deeper racial and cultural context for reconsidering her African American students.

On the surface, these actions shed light on what it means for White teachers to acquire culturally responsive perspectives about African American children. Below the surface, Patricia is an excellent example of how the process of decentering Whiteness should look with White people. As you now know, I was forbidden to talk about race with Patricia. But I violated this part of the contract. The reason is that Patricia truly wanted insight on the relevance of her race to our work with African American students.

We spent considerable time on discussing Whiteness. I do not know enough about Patricia to determine if these discussions permeated her personal life. From a professional standpoint, the discussions benefited her in two ways. First, Patricia learned that her White-framed view of African American students was just that—a view. She transcended this view by humbly determining the best ways to teach Matthew, Lanae, Keyquan, Ricky, Karen, and Courtney.

In the context, humility was Patricia's authentic expression of "I don't know what I don't know" regarding African American students. Her follow-up to this admission was to "get into the know" of these students. The resulting comprehension was seen in Patricia's incorporation of Black culture into her engagement of African American students.

The Practical Application

Directions: Use this section to analyze your use of culturally responsive instruction to teach African American students.

Step 1: Background Investigation

1. How many African American students are in your classroom?

2. What are the most prominent African-centered character-istics of your African American students?
   A. African American Students as a Group
   B. African American Students as Individuals within the African American Group

Step 2: Curriculum Modifications

1. Based on your background investigation, how have you modified the curriculum to match the cultural back-grounds of African American students?

Step 3: Instructional Delivery

1. Identify a lesson that will be delivered to your African American students. Based on curriculum modifications, what are the culturally responsive instructional strategies that will be used to deliver this lesson to your African American students?

Step 4: Post-implementation Reflection

A. Effectiveness (the strategy achieved the desired academic response[s] from African American student[s])
   1. What is your evidence of effectiveness?
   2. To what extent did each of the factors contribute to the effectiveness of the lesson with African American students?
      A. Investigation of Cultural Background
      B. Curriculum Modifications
      C. Delivery of the Lesson
      D. Other:_____
   3. How can you use your findings from this experience to increase your teaching effectiveness in similar situa-tions with African American students?
B. Ineffectiveness (the strategy did not achieve the desired academic response from African American students.)
   1. What is your evidence of ineffectiveness?

2. To what extent did each of the factors contribute to the ineffectiveness of the lesson with African American students?
   A. Investigation of Cultural Background
   B. Curriculum Modifications
   C. Delivery of the Lesson
   D. Other:_____
3. How can you use your findings from this experience to modify your approaches in ways that add cultural responsiveness to instructional strategies for African American students?

Conclusion

Teaching and learning is vital to the success of African American children. As such, these experiences must consist of White teachers who are informed of the cultural background experiences that emanate from Black culture. As indicated in my narratives, this approach is a combination of time and willingness to see the assets within Black lived experiences. Through this process, White teachers can better understand that Black children are the main sources to consult for delivering instruction that truly accommodates their interests and needs.

Overall, this chapter concludes the trilogy (relate, discipline, teach) for what cultural responsiveness should look like for White teachers of African American students. Each chapter consisted of a set of uniquely developed principles, approaches, samples, and strategies. The principles highlighted the importance of understanding the racial context for relating, disciplining, and teaching African American students. The approaches demonstrated specific ways of engaging African American students in the context of their culture.

Samples were used to narrate the cultural portrait of brokering White teachers' connections to African American students. The strategies section provided White teachers with a guide for reflection. Here these teachers consider the best approaches to applying the content of this chapter toward their own African

American students. The underlying premise here is that cultural responsiveness is a passport to effectiveness for White teachers of African American students.

The rationale for the passport analogy is twofold. First, due to Whiteness, White teachers lack an authentic cultural awareness of African American students. In addition, they often fail to see the need to understand the culturally conditioned behaviors of African American students. As a result, cultural responsiveness to African Americans is still a foreign concept for these teachers.

Like a passport, cultural responsiveness provides White teachers with the segue into the worlds of Black children. Initially, the world of Blackness would be a naturally uncomfortable feel for these teachers. But with an open mind and heart, they could overcome the discomfort to discover the richness of Black students' culture.

A significant part of this learning curve is growth in understanding race. In other words, without consistent and authentic engagement on race, Whites reject the understandings conducive to becoming racially literate people. But with this engagement comes the probability of Whites understanding the racial significance of others.

With this passport of knowledge, White teachers learn to value the lived experiences of African American students. Such growth affords White teachers proper insight and familiarity with the needs of these students. They can then become authentically prepared and committed to facilitating Black student achievement.

Conclusion

The Will to Change

There were many factors that influenced my decision to write this book. One of the main driving forces was "Can White teachers teach African American students?" This book began by answering "yes" to this question. Then it provided a four-step approach for moving this *yes* from affirmation to realization of success for White teachers. A recap of the steps are as follows:

Step 1: Learn the Role of Whiteness and Blackness in the Racialized Development of America

Michael Jackson once asked us to consider if it matters if we are Black or White. On the record—no. But off the record—yes. Hell, yes. Yes, it matters if you are Black or White in this country. The reason is that America is a system of Whiteness that was built by and for White people. Parallel to this construction is the White-framed oppression of Black people. Because of this systemic racism, unequal power relationships continue to exist between White people and Black people.

Step 2: Recognize the Impact of America's Racial History on Your Role as White Teachers of Black Students

By living in a White-framed society, White teachers operate out of a frame that endorses supremacy, privilege, and fragility. These factors do impact White teachers' approaches to teaching African American students.

Step 3: Grapple with Whiteness on a Personal and Professional Level

Now is not the time for teachers who happen to be White or Whites who happen to be teachers. This is the time for White teachers to identify as racial beings. With this identification comes the challenge of working through Whiteness. Such work is sorely needed to equip White teachers with the humility and awareness for understanding perspectives and representations offered by Black children.

Step 4: Use Black Culture as a Culturally Responsive Guide to Success with African American Students

At the center of relating to, instructing, and redirecting Black children is Black culture. Drawing from this central point will increase the likelihood of positive relational, instructional, and disciplinary interactions between White teachers and African American students.

Another way of looking at these steps is with a lockstep lens. To truly teach Black children, White teachers must understand Black culture. An understanding of Black culture is maximized with White teachers' examination of themselves as White people. Personal and professional analyses of Whiteness must be connected to America's deeply racialized history.

Having made this clarion call for change, I now pose the following question: Will White teachers change? That is, will White teachers embrace the suggested changes in this book? Will White teachers be humble enough to look at the strengths and weaknesses of their current approaches to Black children? Will White teachers open themselves to be vulnerable to new ways of thinking about their roles as White teachers of Black children?

The significance of this questioning lies in the reality of change. Change is a process—not an event. The process is developed through moments that warrant responses to situations with specific movements.

At this very moment, Black children are preparing to start the first year of their educational experiences in schools and classrooms. Their success in these venues will be influenced by the movements of White teachers. What this means is that, other than Black families, White teachers will continue to have significant influence in the lives of Black children.

Such influence will not materialize through White teachers needing to do something *with* Black children. With this power comes the responsibility to do something *for* Black children. The something is the creation of unlimited opportunities for Black students to achieve. Therefore, carpe diem now and forever to *White Teachers, Black Students in the Spirit of Yes to African American Student Achievement*!

References

Akintunde, O. (1999). White racism, White supremacy, White privilege, and the social construction of race. *Multicultural Education, 7*(2), 1.

Aldridge, D. (2008). *The educational thought of W.E.B. Du Bois: An intellectual history.* New York, NY: Teachers College Press.

Allen, J., Als, H., Lewis, J., & Litwick, L. (2000). *Without sanctuary: Lynching photography in America.* Santa Fe, NM: Twin Palms.

Angelou, M. (1978). *And still I rise: A book of poems.* New York, NY: Random House.

Asante, M. (1987a). *The afrocentric idea.* Philadelphia, PA: Temple University Press.

Asante, M. (1987b). *Afrocentricity.* Trenton, NJ: Africa World Press.

Avery, R., & Rendall, M. (2002). Lifetime inheritances of three generations of Whites and Blacks. *American Journal of Sociology, 107*(5), 1300–1346.

Bell, D. (1993). *Faces at the bottom of the well: The permanence of racism.* New York, NY: Basic Books.

Bennett, L. (2000). *Forced into glory: Abraham Lincoln's White dream.* Chicago, IL: Johnson Publishing Company.

Bertrand, M., & Mullainathan, S. (2004). Are Emily and Greg more employable than Lakisha and Jamal? A field experiment on labor market discrimination. *American Economic Review, 94*(4), 991–1013.

Blackmon, D. (2005). *Slavery by another name: The re-enslavement of Black Americans from the Civil War to World War II.* New York, NY: Anchor Books.

Bodrova, E., & Leong, D. J. (2007). *Tools of the mind: The Vygotskian approach for early childhood education.* Englewood Cliffs, NJ: Prentice Hall.

Bonilla-Silva, E. (2001). *White supremacy and racism in the post Civil-Rights era.* Boulder, CO: Lynne Rienner.

Bonilla-Silva, E. (2009). *Racism without racists: Color-blind racism and the persistence of racial inequality in the United States.* Lanham, MD: Rowman & Littlefield.

Boykin, A. (1983). The academic performance of Afro-American children. In J. Spence (Ed.), *Achievement and achievement motives* (pp. 324–371). San Francisco, CA: W. H. Freeman.

Boykin, A. (1986). The triple quandary and the schooling of Afro-American children. In U. Neisser (Ed.), *The school achievement of minority children* (pp. 57–92). Hillsdale, NJ: Erlbaum.

Boykin, A. (1995). Culture matters in the psychosocial experiences of African Americans: Some conceptual, process and practical considerations. Paper presented at the annual meeting of the American Psychological Association, New York, NY.

Boykin, A., & Bailey, C. (2000). *The role of cultural factors in school relevant cognitive functioning: Synthesis of findings on cultural contexts, cultural orientations and individual differences.* Washington, DC and Baltimore, MD: Howard University and Johns Hopkins University, Center for Research on the Education of Students Placed at Risk (CRESPAR).

Branch, T. (2013). *The King years: Historic moments in the civil rights movement.* New York, NY: Simon & Schuster.

Brown, T., Linver, M., & Evans, M. (2010). The role of gender in the racial and ethnic socialization of African American adolescents. *Youth and Society, 41,* 357–381.

Bruening, M. (2014, April 14). The single mother, child poverty myth. *Demos.* Retrieved January 27, 2016 from http://www.demos.org/blog/4/14/14/single-mother-child-poverty-myth

Bullard, S. (1994). *Free at last: A history of the civil rights movement and those who died in the struggle.* Oxford, UK: Oxford University Press.

Camera, L. (2015, December 11). African-American students lagging far behind. *U.S. News and World Report.* Retrieved January 24, 2016, from http://www.usnews.com/news/articles/2015/12/11/african-american-students-lagging-far-behind

Coles, R. (2010). *The best kept secret: Single Black fathers.* Lanham, MD: Rowman & Littlefield.

Coles, R., & Green, C. (2009). *The myth of the missing Black father.* New York, NY: Columbia University Press.

Cook, L. (2015, January 28). U.S. education: Still separate and unequal. *U.S. News and World Report.* Retrieved January 24, 2016, from http://www.usnews.com/news/blogs/data-mine/2015/01/28/us-education-still-separate-and-unequal

Cousins, L., & Mickelson, R. (2011). Making success in education: What Black parents believe about participation in their children's education. *Current Issues in Education, 14*(3), 1–17.

Cunningham, D. (2012). *Klansville, U.S.A.: The rise and fall of the civil rights–era Klu Klux Klan.* Oxford, UK: Oxford University Press.

Degruy, J. (2005). *Post-traumatic slavery syndrome: America's legacy of enduring injury and healing.* Portland, OR: Uptone Press.

Delgado, R. (1996). *The Rodrigo chronicles: Conversations about America and race.* New York, NY: New York University Press.

Delpit, L. (1988). The silenced dialogue: Power and pedagogy in educating other people's children. *Harvard Educational Review, 58*(3), 280–298.

Delpit, L. (2006). *Other people's children: Cultural conflict in the classroom.* New York, NY: New Press.

DePaoli, J., Fox, J., Ingram, E., Maushard, M., Bridgeland, J., & Balfanz, R. (2015). *Building a grad nation.* Retrieved January 24, 2016, from http://www.gradnation.org/report/2015-building-grad-nation-report

DiAngelo, R. (2010). Why can't we all just be individuals? Countering the discourse of individualism in anti-racist education. *Interactions: UCLA Journal of Education and Information Studies, 6*(1), 1–24.

DiAngelo, R. (2011). White fragility. *International Journal of Critical Pedagogy, 3*(3), 1–15.

DiAngelo, R. (2012a). Nothing to add: A challenge to White silence in racial discussions. *White Privilege Journal, 2*(1), 1–17.

DiAngelo, R. (2012b). *What does it mean to be White? Developing White racial literacy.* New York, NY: Peter Lang.

DiAngelo, R. (2015, April 9). White fragility: Why it's so hard to talk to White people about racism. *The Good Men Project.* Retrieved February 8, 2017, from https://goodmenproject.com/featured-content/white-fragility-why-its-so-hard-to-talk-to-white-people-about-racism-twlm/

DiAngelo, R., & Sensoy, Ö. (2014). Getting slammed: White depictions of race discussions as arenas of violence. *Race, Ethnicity and Education, 17*(1), 103–128.

Dixson, A., & Rousseau, C. (2005). And we are still not saved: Critical race theory in education ten years later. *Race, Ethnicity and Education, 8*(1), 7–27.

Dobbie, W., & Fryer, R. G. (2009). *Are high-quality schools enough to close the achievement gap? Evidence from a social experiment in Harlem* (NBER Working Paper No. 15473). Cambridge, MA: National Bureau of Economic Research.

Dray, P. (2003). *At the hands of persons unknown: The lynching of Black America.* New York, NY: Modern Library.

Du Bois, W. E. B. (1903). *The souls of Black folk.* Chicago, IL: A. C. McClurg.

Dyer, R. (1997). *White.* New York, NY: Routledge.

Egalite, A., Kisida, B., & Winters, M. (2015). Representation in the classroom: The effect of own-race teachers on student achievement. *Economics of Education Review 45*(2), 44–52.

Erikson, K. (1966). *Wayward puritans.* Hoboken, NJ: John Wiley and Sons.

Feagin, J. (2013). *The White racial frame: Centuries of racial framing and counter-framing.* New York, NY: Routledge.

Fenning, P., & Rose, J. (2007). Overrepresentation of African American students in exclusionary discipline: The role of school policy. *Urban Education, 42*, 536–559.

Ferguson, A. (2001). *Bad boys: Public schools in the making of Black masculinity.* Ann Arbor, MI: University of Michigan Press.

Fields, B. (2004). Breaking the cycle of office referrals and suspensions: Defensive management. *Educational Psychology in Practice, 20*(2), 103–114.

Foster, A., & Hawk, W. (2013). *Spending patterns of families receiving means-tested government assistance: Beyond the Numbers.* Washington, DC: Bureau of Labor Statistics.

Foster, M. (1998). *Black teachers on teaching.* New York, NY: New Press.

Frankenberg, R. (1993). *White women, race matters: The social construction of Whiteness.* Minneapolis, MN: University of Minnesota Press.

Frankenberg, R. (1997). Introduction: Local Whitenesses, localizing Whiteness. In R. Frankenberg (Ed.), *Displacing Whiteness: Essays in social and cultural criticism* (pp. 1–33). Durham, NC: Duke University Press.

Frankenberg, R. (2001). Mirage of an unmarked Whiteness. In B. Rasmussen, E. Klinerberg, I. Nexica, & M. Wray (Eds.), *The making and unmaking of Whiteness* (pp. 72–96). Durham, NC: Duke University Press.

Franklin, J., & Higginbotham, E. (2010). *From slavery to freedom: A history of African Americans.* New York, NY: McGraw-Hill.

Freedman, S. (1995). *Roger Taney: The Dred Scott legacy (Justices of the Supreme Court)*. Berkeley Heights, NJ: Enslow.

Gay, G. (2000). *Culturally responsive teaching*. New York, NY: Teachers College Press.

Gershenson, S. (2015). The alarming effect of racial mismatch on teacher expectations. Washington, DC: Brookings Institute. Retrieved January 24, 2016 from http://www.brookings.edu/blogs/brown-center -chalkboard/posts/2015/08/18-teacher-expectations-gershenson

Gillborn, D. (2005). Education policy as an act of White supremacy: Whiteness, critical race theory and education reform. *Journal of Education Policy, 20*, 485–505.

Gillborn, D. (2006). Rethinking White supremacy: Who counts in "WhiteWorld." *Ethnicities, 6*, 318–340.

Giroux, H. (1997). Rewriting the discourse of racial identity: Towards a pedagogy and politics of Whiteness. *Harvard Educational Review, 67*, 285–320.

Goff, P., Jackson, M., Allison, B., Di Leone, L., Culotta, C., & DiTomasso, N. (2014). The essence of innocence: Consequences of dehumanizing Black children. *Journal of Personality and Social Psychology, 106*(4), 526–545.

Gordon, E. & Armour-Thomas, E. (1991). Culture and cognitive development. In L. Okagaki & R. J. Sternberg (Eds.), *Directors of development: Influences on the development of children's thinking* (pp. 83–99). Mahwah, NJ: Erlbaum.

Grooms, A. (2002). *Bombingham*. New York, NY: Free Press.

Grusec, J., & Hasting, P. (2014). *Handbook of socialization: Theory and research*. New York, NY: Guilford Press.

Hale, J. (2001). *Learning while Black: Creating educational excellence for African American children*. Baltimore, MD: Johns Hopkins University Press.

Hale-Benson, J. (1986). *Black children: Their roots, culture, and learning styles*. Baltimore, MD: Johns Hopkins University Press.

Haskins, J., & Benson, K. (1998). *African beginnings*. New York, NY: Lothrop, Lee & Sheppard.

Helms, J. (1990). *Black and White racial identity attitudes: Theory, research, and practice*. Westport, CT: Greenwood Press.

Helms, J. (1992). *A race is a nice thing to have: A guide to being a White person or understanding the White persons in your life*. Topeka, KS: Content Communications.

Hoffer, W. (2012). *Plessy v. Ferguson: Race and inequality in Jim Crow America* (Landmark Law Cases and American Society). Lawrence, KS: University Press of Kansas.

Holbrook, C., Fessler, D., & Navarrete, C. (2016). Looming large in others' eyes: Racial stereotypes illuminate dual adaptations for representing threat versus prestige as physical size. *Evolution and Human Behavior, 37*(1), 67–78.

Holzman, M. (2013). *The Black poverty cycle and how to end it.* Briarscliff, NY: Chelmsford Press.

Howard, G. (2006). *We can't teach what we don't know: White teachers, multiracial schools* (2nd ed.). New York, NY: Teachers College Press.

Irvine, J. (2002). *In search of wholeness: African American teachers and their culturally specific classroom practices.* London, UK: Palgrave Macmillan.

Irving, D. (2014). *Waking up White, and finding myself in the story of race.* Boston, MA: Elephant Room Press.

Jackson, J. (2007). *Strengthening the African American educational pipeline: Informing research, policy, and practice.* Albany, NY: State University of New York Press.

Jackson, P. (1996). Those who control the education of the children, control the future of that race. Retrieved January 24, 2016, from http://www.blackstarproject.org/

Jensen, R. (2005). *The heart of Whiteness: Confronting race, racism and White privilege.* San Francisco, CA: City Light Bookstore.

Johnson, A. (2005). *Power, privilege, and difference.* New York, NY: McGraw-Hill.

Jones, J., & Mosher, M. (2013). *Fathers' involvement with their children: United States, 2006–2010.* Atlanta, GA: Centers for Disease Control and Prevention.

Jones, M. (2015, November 20). The second racial wealth gap. *Washington Monthly.* Retrieved January 25, 2016, from http://www.washingtonmonthly.com/magazine/novemberdecember_2015/features/

Kailin, J. (1999). How White teachers perceive the problem of racism in their schools: A case study in "liberal" Lakeview. *Teachers College Record, 100*(4), 724–750.

Katznelson, I. (2006). *When affirmative action was White: An untold history of racial inequality in twentieth-century America.* New York, NY: Norton.

Kendall, F. (2006). *Understanding White privilege.* New York, NY: Routledge.

Kennedy, S. (1990). *Jim Crow guide: The way it was.* Boca Raton, FL: Florida Atlantic University Press.

Kersten, A. (2006). *A. Philip Randolph: A life in the vanguard.* Lanham, MD: Rowman & Littlefield.

Kochman, T. (1981). *Black and white styles in conflict*. Chicago, IL: University of Chicago Press

Kunjufu, J. (2002). *Black students, middle class teachers*. Chicago, IL: African American Images.

Kunjufu, J. (2005). *Keeping Black boys out of special education*. Sauk Village, IL: African American Images.

Kunjufu, J. (2007). *An African centered response to Ruby Payne's poverty theory*. Sauk Village, IL: African American Images.

Ladson-Billings, G. (1994). *The dreamkeepers: Successful teaching for African-American students*. San Francisco, CA: Jossey-Bass.

Ladson-Billings, G. (1998). Just what is critical race theory and what is it doing in a nice field like education? *International Journal of Qualitative Studies in Education, 11*, 7–24.

Ladson-Billings, G. (2001). *Crossing over to Canaan*. San Francisco, CA: Jossey-Bass.

Ladson-Billings, G. (2006). It's not the culture of poverty, it's the poverty of culture: The problem with teacher education. *Anthropology and Education Quarterly, 37*(2), 104–109.

Ladson-Billings, G., & Tate, W. (1995). Toward a critical race theory of education. *Teachers College Record, 97*, 47–68.

Landsman, J., & Lewis, C. (2006). *White teachers, diverse classrooms: A guide to building inclusive schools, promoting high expectations, and eliminating racism*. Herndon, VA: Stylus.

Levine-Rasky, C. (2000). Framing Whiteness: Working through the tensions in introducing Whiteness to educators. *Race, Ethnicity and Education, 3*(3), 271–292.

Lewis, D. (2001). *W. E. B. Du Bois, 1919–1963: The fight for equality and the American century*. New York, NY: Holt Paperbacks.

Lively, D. (1992). *The constitution and race*. New York, NY: Prager.

Lorde, A (1983). The master's tools will never dismantle the master's house. In C. Moraga & G. Anazaldua (Eds.), *This bridge called my back: Writings by radical women of color* (pp. 94–101). New York, NY: Kitchen Table Press.

Losen, D., Hodson, C., Ee, J., & Martinez, T. (2013). *Disturbing inequities: Exploring the relationship between racial disparities in special education identification and discipline*. Los Angeles, CA: Center for Civil Rights Remedies at the Civil Rights Project.

Love, D. (2017, February 10). Recently uncovered FBI report reveals long history of White supremacists infiltrating law enforcement. *Atlantic Black Star*, pp. 1–2. Retrieved February 16, 2017, from http://atlantablackstar.com/2017/02/10/recently-uncovered-fbi-report

-reveals-long-history-white-supremacists-infiltrating-law-enforce
ment/

Mapping Police Violence (2015). Unarmed Black killings. Retrieved
January 25, 2016, from http://mappingpoliceviolence.org/

Marx, S., & Pray, L. (2011). Living and learning in Mexico: Developing
empathy for English language learners through study abroad. *Race,
Ethnicity and Education, 14*, 507–535.

Massey, D. (2001). Residential segregation and neighborhood condi-
tions in U.S. metropolitan areas. In N. Smelser, W. Wilson, & F.
Mitchell (Eds.), *America becoming: Racial trends and their consequences*
(pp. 391–445). Washington, DC: National Academy Press.

McIntosh, P. (2000). White privilege and male privilege: A personal account of coming to see correspondences through work in women's
studies. In A. Minas (Ed.), *Gender basics: Feminist perspectives on
women and men* (pp. 30–38). Belmont, CA: Wadsworth.

McIntyre, A. (1997). *Making meaning of Whiteness: Exploring racial identity with White teachers.* Albany, NY: State University of New York
Press.

McWhorter, D. (2001). *Carry me home: Birmingham, Alabama: The climac-
tic battle of the civil rights revolution.* New York, NY: Simon & Schuster.

Mettler, S., & Sides, J. (2012, September 24). We are the 96 percent. *The
New York Times*, p. 1. Retrieved January 28, 2016, from http://cam
paignstops.blogs.nytimes.com/2012/09/24/we-are-the-96-percent/

Monroe, C. (2005a). Why are bad boys always Black? Causes of disproportionality in school discipline and recommendations for change.
The Clearing House, September/October, 45–50.

Monroe, C. (2005b). Understanding the discipline gap through a cultural lens: Implications for the education of African American students. *Intercultural Education, 16*(4), 317–330.

Monroe, C. (2009). Teachers closing the discipline gap in an urban
middle school. *Urban Education, 44*(3), 322–347.

Monroe, C., & Obidah, J. (2004). The impact of cultural synchronization
on a teacher's perceptions of disruption: A case study of an African
American middle-school classroom. *Journal of Teacher Education,
55*(3), 256–268.

Mooney E., & Thornton, C. (1999). Mathematics attribution differences
by ethnicity and socioeconomic status. *Journal of Education for Students Placed at Risk, 4*, 321–332.

Moore, A. (2014, September 22). Eight facts debunking poverty myths
and racial stereotypes. *Atlantic Blackstar*. Retrieved February 8, 2016,
from http://atlantablackstar.com/2014/09/22/8-facts-debunking
-poverty-myths-racial-stereotypes/

Muhammad, K. (2011). *The condemnation of Blackness: Race, crime, and making of modern urban America.* Cambridge, MA: Harvard University Press.

Neal, L., McCray, A., Webb-Johnson, G., & Bridgest, S. (2003). The effects of African American movement styles on teachers' perceptions and reactions. *Journal of Special Education, 37,* 49–57.

Neville, H., Worthington, R., & Spanierman, L. (2001). Race, power, and multicultural counseling psychology: Understanding White privilege and color-blind racial attitudes. In J. G. Ponterotto, J. M. Casas, L. A. Suzuki, and C. M. Alexander (Eds.), *Handbook of Multicultural Counseling* (pp. 257–288). Thousand Oaks, CA: Sage.

Ng, J., & Rury, J. (2006). Poverty and education: A critical analysis of the Ruby Payne phenomenon. *Teachers College Record.* Retrieved from www.tcrecord.org. ID Number: 12596.

Nobles, W. (1972). African philosophy: Foundations for Black psychology. In R. Jones (Ed.), *Black psychology.* New York, NY: Harper & Row.

Nobles, W. (1974). Africanity: Its role in Black families. *Black Scholar, 15,* 10–17.

Nobles, W. (1980). Extended self: Re-thinking the so-called Negro self concept. In R. Jones (Eds.), *Black psychology* (2nd ed.). New York, NY: Harper & Row.

Nobles, W. (1985). *Africanity and the Black family: The development of a theoretical model.* Princeton, NJ: Institute for Advanced Study.

Noddings, N. (1992). The challenge to care in schools: An alternative approach to education. New York, NY: Teachers College Press.

Noguera, P. (2003). Schools, prisons, and social implications of punishment: Rethinking disciplinary practices. *Theory into Practice, 42*(4), 341–350.

Obidah, J., & Teel, K. (2001). *Because of the kids: Facing racial and cultural differences in schools.* New York, NY: Teachers College Press.

Orfield, G. (1969). *The reconstruction of southern education: The schools and the 1964 Civil Rights Act.* New York, NY: Wiley-Interscience.

Owen, J., Wettach, J., & Hoffman, K. (2015). *Instead of suspension: Alternative strategies for effective school discipline.* Durham, NC: Duke Center for Child and Family Policy and Duke Law School.

Pager, D., & Shepherd, H. (2009). The sociology of discrimination: Racial discrimination in employment, housing, credit, and consumer markets. *Annual Review of Sociology, 34,* 181–209.

Patterson, K., Grenny, J., McMillan, R., & Switzler, A. (2012). *Crucial conversations: Tools for talking when stakes are high.* New York, NY: McGraw-Hill Education.

Perry, T., Steele, C., & Hilliard, I. (2004). *Young, gifted, and Black: Promoting high achievement among African-American students.* Boston, MA: Beacon Press.

Pfeffer, P. (1996). *A. Philip Randolph, pioneer of the civil rights movement.* Baton Rouge, LA: Louisiana State University Press.

Picca, L., & Feagin, J. (2007). *Two-faced racism: Whites in the backstage and frontstage.* New York, NY: Routledge.

Pilkington, E. (2008, January 23). Obama has given people a little more hope. *The Guardian.* Retrieved from https://www.theguardian.com/world/2008/jan/23/usa.uselections2008

Raiford, L., & Romano, R. (2006). *Civil rights movement in American memory.* Athens, GA: University of Georgia Press.

Reaves, M. (2008). *Somebody scream! Rap music's rise to prominence in the aftershock of Black power.* New York, NY: Farrar, Straus & Giroux.

Reese, F. (2014, September 22). Who's getting caught in the "school to prison" pipeline? And why? *MintPress News.* Retrieved February 18, 2016, from http://www.mintpressnews.com/whos-getting-caught-school-prison-pipeline/196812/

Robertson, D. (2000). *Denmark Vesey: The buried story of America's largest slave rebellion and the man who led it.* New York, NY: Vintage Books.

Roediger, D. (2003). *The wages of Whiteness: Race and the making of the American working class.* Brooklyn, NY: Verso.

Rosenbaum, R. (2013). *The relationship between SNAP and work among low-income households.* Washington, DC: Center on Budget and Policy Priorities.

Rothenberg, P. (2013). *Race, class, and gender in the United States: An integrated study.* New York, NY: Worth.

Rowe, W., Bennett, S. K., & Atkinson, D. R. (1994). White racial identity models: A critique and alternative proposal. *Counseling Psychologist, 22*(1), 129–146.

Sandow, G. (1990, April 27). "*Fear of a Black Planet* review." *Entertainment Weekly.* Retrieved February 21, 2017, from https://en.wikipedia.org/wiki/Fear_of_a_Black_Planet

Sizemore, B. (1981). *The ruptured diamond: The politics of the decentralization of the District of Columbia public schools.* Lanham, MD: University Press of America.

Skiba, R., Horner, R., Chung, C., Rausch, M., May, S., & Tobin, T. (2011). Race is not neutral: A national investigation of African American and Latino disproportionality in school discipline. *School Psychology Review, 40,* 85–107.

Skiba, R., Michael, R., Nardo, A., & Peterson, R. (2002). The color of discipline: Sources of racial and gender disproportionality in school punishment. *Urban Review, 34*(4), 317–342.

Skiba, R., & Williams, N. (2014). *Are Black kids worse? Myths and facts about racial differences in behavior.* Bloomington, IN: Equity Project at Indiana University.

Slaughter-Defoe, D., & Carlson, K. (1996). Young African American and Latino children in high-poverty urban schools: How they perceive school climate. *Journal of Negro Education, 65*(1), 60–70.

Sleeter, C. (2001). Preparing teachers for culturally diverse schools: Research and the overwhelming presence of Whiteness. *Journal of Teacher Education, 52*, 94.

Sleeter, C. (2013). *Power, teaching, and teacher education: Confronting injustice with critical research and action.* New York, NY: Peter Lang.

Smith, E., & Harper, S. (2015). *Disproportionate impact of K–12 school suspension and expulsion on Black students in southern states.* Philadelphia, PA: University of Pennsylvania, Center for the Study of Race and Equity in Education.

Smitherman, G. (1977). *Talking and testifying.* New York, NY: Harper & Row.

Starobin, R. (1970). *Denmark Vesey: The slave conspiracy of 1822.* Englewood Cliffs, NJ: Prentice Hall.

Statistics Brain Research Institute (2015). Welfare statistics. Retrieved March 1, 2016 from http://www.statisticbrain.com/welfare-statistics/

Sue, D. (2003). *Overcoming our racism: The journey to liberation.* San Francisco, CA: Jossey-Bass.

Tatum, B. (2003). *Why are all the Black kids sitting together in the cafeteria? And other conversations about race.* New York, NY: Basic Books.

Taylor, C. (2006). *A. Philip Randolph: The religious journey of an African American labor leader.* New York, NY: New York University Press.

Thompson, C. (1998). *African civilizations: The Asante Kingdom.* New York, NY: Franklin Watts.

Trail, T., & Karney, B. (2012). What's (not) wrong with low-income couples? *Journal of Marriage and Family, 74*, 413–427.

U.S. Department of Education Office for Civil Rights (2014). Data snapshot: School discipline. Retrieved January 24, 2016, from http://ocrdata.ed.gov/Downloads/CRDC-School-Discipline-Snapshot.pdf

Valencia, R. (2010). *Dismantling contemporary deficit thinking: Educational thought and practice.* New York, NY: Routledge.

Vasquez, J. A. (1988). Context of learning for minority students. *Educational Forum, 56,* 6–11.

Vavrus, F., & Cole, K. (2002). I didn't do nothin: The discursive construction of school suspension. *Urban Review, 34*(2), 87–111.

Villegas, A., & Lucas, T. (2002). Preparing culturally responsive teachers: Rethinking the curriculum. *Journal of Teacher Education, 53*(1), 20–32.

Vygotsky, L. (1978). *Mind in society: The development of higher mental processes.* Cambridge, MA: Harvard University Press.

Ware, F. (2002). Black teachers' perceptions of their professional roles and practices. In J. J. Irvine (Ed.), *In search of wholeness: African American teachers and their culturally specific classroom practices* (pp. 33–46). New York, NY: Palgrave.

Ware, F. (2006). Warm demander pedagogy: Culturally responsive pedagogy that supports a culture of achievement for African American children. *Urban Education 41*(4), 427–456.

Webb-Johnson, G. (2002). Are schools ready for Joshua? Dimensions of African-American culture among students identified as having behavioral/emotional disorders. *Qualitative Studies in Education, 15*(6), 653–671.

Weinstein, C., Curran, M., & Tomlinson-Clarke, S. (2003). Culturally responsive classroom management: Awareness into action. *Theory into Practice, 42*(4), 269–275.

Weinstein, C., Tomlinson-Clarke S., & Curran, M. (2004). Toward a conception of culturally responsive classroom management. *Journal of Teacher Education, 55*(1), 25–38.

Wellman, D. (1977). *Portraits of White racism.* New York, NY: Cambridge University Press.

Wijeyesinghe, C., & Jackson, B. W. (2012). *New perspectives on racial identity development: Integrating emerging frameworks.* New York, NY: New York University Press.

Williams, S. (2007, October 14). In S.C., beauty salons are also political soapboxes. *The Washington Post.*

Wingfield, A. (2009). *Doing business with beauty: Black women, hair salons, and the racial enclave economy (perspectives on a multiracial America).* Lanham, MD: Rowman & Littlefield.

Wise, T. (2002). Membership has its privileges: Thoughts on acknowledging and challenging Whiteness. In P. Rothenberg (Ed.), *White privilege: Essential readings on the other side of racism* (pp. 133–136). New York, NY: Worth.

Wise, T. (2005). *Affirmative action: Racial preference in Black and White.* Berkeley, CA: Soft Skull Press.

Wise, T. (2010a). *Colorblind: The eise of post-racial politics and the retreat from racial equity.* San Francisco, CA: City Lights.

Wise, T. (2010b). *White like me: Reflections on race from a privileged son.* San Francisco, CA: Soft Skull/Counterpoint Press.

Wood, A. (2011). Lynching and spectacle: Witnessing racial violence in America, 1890–1940. Chapel Hill, NC: University of North Carolina Press.

Woodson, C. (1933). *The mis-education of the Negro.* Trenton, NJ: Africa World Press.

Yosso, T. (2005). Whose culture has capital? A critical race theory discussion of community cultural wealth. *Race, Ethnicity and Education, 8*(1), 69–91.

About the Author

Dr. Mack T. Hines III is one of the nation's most sought-after authors, educators, scholars, and speakers. The South Carolina native is widely known and regarded for his dynamic, down-to-earth approaches and strategies in the areas of race, culture, and diversity and the facilitation of African American student success in classrooms. Dr. Hines continually uses these topics to engage educators on the importance of using race, culture, and student background to strengthen children's ability to achieve.

Dr. Hines centers his work on self-conducted investigations on issues that influence the academic, relational, and behavioral development of African American children and teachers' abilities to achieve racial and cultural diversity in classrooms. Dr. Hines then trains teachers and principals on how to analyze and use the findings from his work to produce measurable gains in achievement and diversity for their schools.

As a result, educators have found great success in using Dr. Hines's work to create policy-driven change in schools. Consequently, Dr. Hines is frequently called on to provide school systems with customized, organized, and personalized approaches to achieving African American student success and racial and cultural diversity in schools. His expertise has been used in school districts across the country.

Dr. Hines has been the subject of many interviews and specials. He has also been invited to present his research in over 200 conferences and symposiums across the country. Above all, Dr. Mack T. Hines III attributes these successes to God and his personal belief in that *all* children learn, when learning is centered on using who children are, as the guide to inspire them to reach their destinies and dreams. On a personal note, Dr. Hines is married to the former Kathryn J. Davis of Garland, Texas. They have two beautiful boys, Mack T. Hines IV (Tye) and Grayson Harrison Hines.

www.ingramcontent.com/pod-product-compliance
Lightning Source LLC
Chambersburg PA
CBHW021811270326
41932CB00007B/137